Being and Order

Catholic Thought from Lublin

Andrew N. Woznicki
General Editor

Vol. 1

PETER LANG
New York • Bern • Frankfurt am Main • Paris

Andrew N. Woznicki

Being and Order

The Metaphysics of Thomas Aquinas in Historical Perspective

PETER LANG
New York • Bern • Frankfurt am Main • Paris

Library of Congress Cataloging-in-Publication Data

Woznicki, Andrew N.
  Being and order : the metaphysics of Thomas Aquinas
in historical perspective / Andrew N. Woznicki.
      p.   cm. — (Catholic thought from Lublin: vol. 1)
  Includes index.
  1. Thomas, Aquinas, Saint, 1225?-1274—Contributions
in metaphysics. I. Title. II. Series
  B765. T54W65 1990   117—dc19   89-2843
  ISBN 0-8204-0919-7   CIP
  ISSN 1051-693X

© Peter Lang Publishing, Inc., New York 1990

All rights reserved.
Reprint or reproduction, even partially, in all forms such as microfilm,
xerography, microfiche, microcard, offset strictly prohibited.

Printed in the United States of America.

To my Parents.
A.W.

FOREWORD

Not only *habent sua fata libelli*, but every idea which an author expresses in a given work, has its own life-history. And since ideas are phenomena of our minds, their spiritual odyssey is a veritable reflection of our own human destiny. (Our nature is to be *zoon logistikon*).

The purpose of this book is to give a rational account (*logos*) of the odyssey of two most basic ideas of Western civilization, as seen through the eyes of St.Thomas Aquinas. These two most fundamental and quintessential concepts of all time are indisputably those of BEING and ORDER.

Further, these two seminal notions are interrelated so inextricably that it is absolutely impossible to understand one without the other. (*To on/to einai* is, in fact, *diathesis/taxis* and vice versa.)

In literary form, Joseph Conrad expresses this interrelationship in the following way:

"We want in so many different ways to be," he began again. "This magnificent butterfly finds a little heap of dirt and sits still on it; but man he will never on his heap of mud keep still.[sic] He wants to be so, and again he want to be so..." He moved his hand up, then down..."He wants to be a saint, and he wants to be a devil - and every time he shuts his eyes he seems himself as a very fine fellow - so fine as he can never be ... In a dream ..."

The author's interest in the problematics of order and being dates back to his days as a youth during World War II. In those cataclysmic days, human existence had truly become "a dirty joke" (Jean Paul Sartre). The Nazi war cry of *Ordnung musst sein* was constantly dinned into the young man's ears. The author experienced, at that time, the menacing feeling, which Martin Heidegger expresses so fatalistically in his *Holzwege:*

Man in his being menaced by the conviction, that the technical development will dominate the order of the world; and this domination reduces all *ordo* .... The world is losing the possibility of salvation. Not only sanctity, that was the road leading to God, is lost, but even the access to sanctity, i.e., the very notion of sanctity, must be laid aside.

* * * *

Years ago, as a graduate student in the University of Toronto, the writer of this book chose as his doctoral dissertation, "The Metaphysical Foundations of the Order of Being in St.Thomas Aquinas."

At the public defense of his doctoral thesis, he was asked by the examiners, why he had selected this particular topic. The candidate's reply was that, since he had actually lived and suffered under various ideo-socio-political systems in Europe, he felt a compulsion to search for an answer to Heidegger's charge, that the crisis of the contemporary world is due both to a neglect of being and a traumatic uprooting of man from the earth.

And because the author of this word does not share Heidegger's pessimistic and fatalistic outlook that "only a god can save us from this contemporary situation," he attempts to re-examine here the diathetical structure of reality, i.e., to find being in order and order in being.

* * * *

The author wishes to express his deepest gratitude to Peter Lang Publishers for making this work available to American readers. At a time when even many university presses are printing fewer titles in philosophy in preference to the "soft sciences," Peter Lang deserves the plaudits of all serious scholars for this undertaking. In this connection, the author wishes to reiterate the first law of philosophical experience so aptly phrased by Etienne Gilson, in his *William James Lectures* at Harvard University, namely, "Metaphysics always buries its undertakers."

Foreword

The original inspiration for the present book occurred during the authors graduate-study days. Hence, his primary debt of gratitude is owed to his professors and directors of theses/dissertations, specifically, Professors Stefan Swiezawski and Albert Krapiec at the University of Lublin, and Professor Joseph Owens at the University of Toronto and the Pontifical Institute of Mediaeval Studies.

During the ensuing years, the author was afforded the opportunity of discussing and deepening his understanding of the various aspects of *Being and Order*, at numerous national and international congresses, conferences, and symposia. The author wishes to single out two of his colleagues, Professor Paul Grimsley Kuntz and Professor Marion Leathers Kuntz. As Co-chairpersons for many years, of the International Congresses of Mediaeval Studies in Kalamazoo, they contributed immensely to the author's insights contained in this volume.

In a special way I am indebted to professors: Dr. Francis Lescoe and Dr. Marie Lescoe. While enthusiastically propagating the newest version of Polish Thomism known as Lublinism, and in making it known to the English-speaking world by establishing the International Center for Lublin (KUL) Translations with Mariel Publications as its publishing house, both Lescoes were of constant assistance to me during the last decade of finalizing my present book. Their devoted care in consultation and readiness in supplying me with their generous comments for my work is warmly appreciated.

Finally, the writer wishes also to thank all who have helped him in the preparation of the manuscript for publication. To Czeslaw Jan Grycz, who made his expertise and artistry so generously available. I would also like to thank Mrs. Wladyslawa Grycz for her constant assistance in making valuable remarks in the English text of my manuscript. Last but not least, my gratitude goes to Mrs. Wanda Grycz-Hernandez, for her technical instructions while I was preparing this book for printing.

TABLE OF CONTENTS

INTRODUCTION   1
  I: The Historical Development of the Notion of Order   1
  II: "Marvelous Connection of Things"   4

PART A: UNITY AND PLURALITY OF BEING   7
INTRODUCTION   9

I. THE NOTION OF ORDER   11
  A. The Definition of Order   12
  B. The Essential Characteristics of Order   14
    1. Ratio prioris et Posterioris   14
    2. Distinctio   17
    3. Ratio Ordinis   19
  C. The Principal Divisions of Order   20

II. ORDER OF NATURAL THINGS   23
  A. Order in Its Integrity and Composition   23
  B. Order and Nature   26
  C. Order of Nature and Its Constitutive Components   28
    1. Order as the Measure of Real Beings   28
    2. Order as the Number of Real Beings   32
    3. Order as the Weight of Real Beings   33

III. BEING IN ITS SINGULARITY AND UNIVERSALITY   37
  A. Participation as the Ontological Foundation of the Order of Being   38
  B. Predication of Being and the Ontic Structure of the Order of Natural Things   42
  C. Essential and Existential Order of Being   46
    1. Participation and Predication of Being   49
    2. The Order of Being as a Disposition of Actuality and Potentiality   51

PART B: THE TRANSCENDENTAL ORDER OF BEING 55
INTRODUCTION 57

I. INTELLIGIBLE ORDER OF INVESTIGATION 59
   A. *Wisdom as Speculative Virtue of Human Intellect* 60
   B. *Wisdom as Knowledge of Divine Things* 63
   C. *Deictic Character of Metaphysical Wisdom* 66
      1. Inductive Reasoning 67
      2. Deductive Demonstration 72

II. RATIONAL ORDER OF CREATED THINGS 79
   A. *Order and Relation* 80
   B. *Order and Analogy* 84
   C. *Analogy of Being* 87
      1. Being and Analogy 88
      2. Metaphysical Analogy of Being as Being 91
      3. Principal Analogate as the Ultimate Source of Being 93

III. THE EXISTENTIAL ORDER OF BEING 97
   A. *The Order of Diversity and Community* 97
   B. *The Order of Community and Transcendentality* 103
   C. *Transcendental Order of Predication* 108
      1. The Order of Priority and Posteriority 109
      2. The Order of Distinction 113
      3. The Principle of the Order of Transcendentals 115

IV. METAPHYSICAL ORDER OF BEING AND TRUTH 119
   A. *The Connotations and Meaning of Being* 119
   B. *The Priority of Being* 121
   C. *The Authenticity of Truth* 125
      1. The Order of Intelligibility of Being as Taken from an Actual Existent 126
         a. *Ordo cognitionis* 127
         b. *Ordo intellectuum* 129
      2. The Order of Comprehensibility of Being Taken from a Factual Essent 131
         a. What is the Ontological Difference between Being and Beings 132
         b. What Kind of Being Belongs to **Dasein** 134

c. How Beings and Being are Uncovered by **Dasein**   136

PART C: THE IMMANENT ORDER OF BEING   139
INTRODUCTION   141

I. THE ORDER OF BEING AS HARMONY AND HIERARCHY   143
    A. *The Primacy of* Esse   143
    B. *The Real or Formal Distinction*   147
    C. Omne Ens Ordinatum Est   150

II. USIADISTIC ORDER OF BEINGS   153
    A. *Usiadistic Theory of Being*   154
    B. *Being as Becoming*   156
    C. *Doctrine on Predication of Being*   160
        1. Historical Note of Overcoming Usiadistic Predication of Being   161
        2. The Predicamental Predication of Being   162
            a. The Logical Order of Predication   162
            b. The Metaphysical Order of Predication   165

III. PREDICATIONAL ORDER OF NATURAL THINGS   173
    A. *Ontological Order of Natural Things*   174
        1. Nature and Order   174
        2. New Conception of Substance   174
        3. Twofold Kind of Principal Attributes   176
    B. *Metaphysical Order of Natural Things*   178
        1. *Ratio* of the Metaphysical Order of Being   179
            a. The Order of Priority and Posteriority   180
            b. The Order of Distinction   182
            c. The Principle of Order of Being   185
        2. The Substantial Order of Being   186
            a. The Order of Composite Substances   187
            b. The Order of Simple Substances   189
                (1) The order of united substances   191
                (2) The order of separate substances   193
        3. The Accidental Order of Being   195
            a. Order in Quantity   195
            b. Order in Quality   200

IV. TELEOLOGICAL ORDER OF BEING AND BECOMING 209
   A. Nature and Becoming 210
   B. Finality and Activity of Nature 213
   C. Creativity and Perfectibility of Nature 219

CONCLUSIONS 231
REFERENCES 237
ABBREVIATIONS 297
INDEX 299

INTRODUCTION

INTRODUCTION

The title of the proposed study indicates that order is an attribute of being. This relationship can be expressed in two ways: order is being, and being is order.[1] In a word, *ens et ordo convertuntur*.[2]

That being constitutes an order is for St. Thomas an evident fact. By sense observation we do find an unchaotic plurality of beings which constitute the universe. Wherever there exists such a plurality of beings there would be an order.[3]

In reality there is a plurality of things which are to be found at different levels of being. At the top of all beings is God, and at the bottom is prime matter. Between God and prime matter there are several degrees of perfection which can be reduced either to intellectual or material being. In the order of intellectual being there is a composition of essence and existence, of substance and accidents, and of potency and act. In the order of material beings there is, moreover, a composition of prime matter and substantial form.

In establishing the mutual relation between 'being' and 'order' one must realize how St. Thomas uses the terms. In general, the order of being consists in a disposition of unity and plurality. But, since unity and plurality follow upon being, the order of being has to be considered according to the modes by which being can be expressed in reality.

To better understand the mutual relationship between 'being' and 'order', however, one must realize the historical development of the concept of order and how St. Thomas uses the term 'order' in his metaphysics of being *qua* being.

I: *The Historical Development of the Notion of Order*

In the history of Western Philosophy the notion of order is one of the basic ideas commonly accepted in the explanation of the structure of reality.[4] The notion of order, however, has never been understood independently of the many various philosophical doctrines of being. Now, on the basis of the various metaphysical doctrines of being we would have many different ways of understanding the notion of order. In general, the notion of order can be analyzed in two ways, namely:

1. as some integrated unity, i.e., as a harmony;
2. as some arranged plurality, i.e., as a hierarchy.

Since this twofold meaning of order can also be found in the philosophical works of St. Thomas, let us consider briefly the historical background of the Thomistic concept of order considered as a harmony and hierarchy.

The Pythagoreans were among the first to hold that the universe is ordered, and as such they called it *kosmos*[5]. Because of the mathematical presupposition which the Pythagoreans recognized as supreme principles of all beings, the order of the universe should be explained in terms of numbers[6]. The ideas that "all things are numbers" was the philosophical kernel of Pythagoreanism[7]. Aristotle writes: "Contemporaneously with these philosophers and before them, the so-called Pythagoreans, who were the first to take up mathematics, not only advanced this study, but also having been brought up in it they thought its principles were the principles of all things."[8]

The order of the universe the Pythagoreans saw as a harmony of opposites, in which one element imposed itself on another. The essence of such conceived harmony is a symmetrical unification of the contrary elements in beings[9]. Since numbers are the elements of everything, the harmony of the universe would consist in symmetry and numerical proportion. As a matter of fact, the harmony of the universe rests upon a concordance with the numerical proportion of the stars[10]. Accordingly, the whole universe forms a "musical scale and number,"[11] and in consequence the universe is spherical in shape and finite in size.[12]

The Pythagorean theory of the universe as a harmony of opposites had great influence in the development of the problem of order, especially in astronomy and ethics.

The starting point of the ethical order is, according to Plato, the notion of virtue. Virtue is to the soul what health is to the body. Health consists of the order and harmony of the body. Analogically, virtue consists of the order and harmony of the soul. Therefore, the whole ethical order depends upon the order that exists in the soul of the individual man.[13]

The Stoics held that the essence of order depends on the proportion and symmetry of the parts to the whole.[14] Applying this definition to the ethical order, the Stoics said that the harmony and the proportion of human acts consists of the concordance of man and nature. The human soul, therefore, is the cause of the ethical order, because it is able to introduce harmony into all human acts. In other words, the ethical order is a composition of the soul itself.

Basing himself on the Stoics' principles, Cicero gave the following definition of the order: "composition of things which are agreeable and suitable with place."[15] A similar definition can be found in St. Augustine: "order is an arrangement of like and unlike things whereby each of them is disposed in its proper place."[16] The further development of the idea of order is connected with the Neoplatonic notion of hierarchy. For Proclus the whole of reality consists in a hierarchy of being which is expressible in the following principle: "Everything which by its existence bestows a character on others, itself primitively possesses that character which it communicates to the recipient."[17] In view of this principle, all beings constitute a specific order of emanation. In the order of emanation all beings gradually emanate from a first monad, and establish higher and lower degrees of perfections[18]. But as emanated, being is related both to the absolute perfection of the highest Goodness[19] and the degree of perfection of its own order (*taxis*[20]). In a word, being is realized in different grades of perfection and constitutes an order of higher and lower beings.

The order of higher and lower beings Plotinus explains as an order of diminishing perfections: the lower form of being emanates from the higher form of being. Plotinus enumerates the following three hypostases: spirit — soul — matter, and says that all beings are related to each other according to the power which comes from the order of intelligibility[21]. Plotinus transfers the sensible order to the intelligible, because the visible world is only an image of the intelligible one.[22] The whole of reality Plotinus considers as an intelligible cosmos: "we consider it, accordingly, an intelligible cosmos, since there are also the individual intellectual powers and intelligences included in it — for it is not one alone, but one and many."[23] In that way the order of being would mean a plurality out of unity whereby there is a continuous process of emanation[24] expressible in the following principle: *bonum est diffusivum sui* (goodness is diffusive of itself).[25]

The Neoplatonic notion of order as a hierarchy of being was adapted by the medieval thinkers through the writing of Pseudo-Dionysius Areopagita[26]. Pseudo-Dionysius distinguishes in the very notion of hierarchy three elements: order, knowledge, and action[27]. Adapting the Neoplatonic notion of being as a hierarchy of different grades of perfection Pseudo-Dionysius combines the notion of emanation with that of creation[28]. In view of this, every created thing constitutes in the hierarchy of being a specific grade, a proportion, as instituted by God. Being considered as a hierarchical grade Pseudo-Dionysius calls order (*taxis*).[29]

St. Thomas in developing his own train of thought uses both expressions: *harmonia* and *hierarchia*. Accepting these terms from his predecessors, however, Aquinas gives new meaning to them. We would now like to outline the Thomistic notion of order as expressed by the terms of 'harmony' and 'hierarchy'.

II: "Marvelous Connection of Things"

St. Thomas, commenting on the Pythagorean theory of harmony, applies it to music and astronomy. Harmony in a strict sense, according to Aquinas, means a concord of sounds.[30] This concord depends on their velocity and the motion, and is, as it were, in function of the definite numerical proportion which exists among the sharps and flats[31]. Moreover, numerical proportion can be considered also in regard to the movement of the stars: "the sound of the stars which move around is harmonious."[32]

St. Thomas extends the Pythagorean theory of harmony, and transfers it to all kinds of beings that are compound, i.e., constituted of the natural union of two or more parts, principles or elements[33]. However, St. Thomas's theory of the order of being is independent of the Pythagorean theory of numbers. The error of the Pythagoreans consists, according to Aquinas, in that, that "they do not distinguish the unity that is the principle of the number, from the unity that is identified

Introduction

with being and means the substance of the thing."[34] Moreover, they do not distinguish between things being numbers, having numbers and merely resembling them.

Generally speaking, harmony can be defined as a constitution and formation of things in their twofold composition: "Harmony has two senses; for it can be taken to signify the composition itself or the mode of composition."[35] Harmony considered as a composition itself would mean the pure structure of the composite being. But harmony considered as a mode of composition would mean the arrangement and proportion of the components of the composite being.

In the universe harmony depends upon the proportion of matter and form, which are united in one act of being[36]. But this proportion is greatly differentiated in the mode of composition of different beings. Since the act of form transcends the potentiality of matter, there is in the universe the following range of forms:

(1) the forms of the four elements,
(2) the forms of mixed bodies,
(3) the forms of plants,
(4) the forms of animals, and
(5) the forms of intellectual beings.[37]

This proportional descent of forms constitutes a particular harmony which St. Thomas describes as follows: "A living thing, likewise, is nobler than any non-living body, and the life of a living-body is nobler than it, since it is this life that gives to the living body its nobility above other bodies."[38]

In the universe, however, there is not only an order of individual beings, but also an order of species and genus. This order means a proportional descent from the highest things to the lowest,[39] and is based upon the principle that the lowest in the higher genus touches the highest of the lower species.[40] St. Thomas, calling our attention to observation, says that a careful consideration of the nature of things leads us to the conclusion that in the universe there is a "marvelous connection of things."[41]

This marvelous connection of things implies the distinction of parts: "Where there is no distinction, there is no order."[42] Distinction of parts is necessary, because the universe achieves the good and the best by mutual order of its parts, which is impossible without their distinction from one another.[43]

From the distinction and diversity of things the gradation of being follows. The gradation of being St. Thomas calls *hierarchia*: "the reason (*ratio*) of hierarchy requires that there be a diversity of orders."[44] Aquinas, commenting on the definition of hierarchy given by Pseudo-Dionysius says: "In the definition of hierarchy there is placed order, in which the degree of power is expressed, and knowledge, as something which directs, and action, as leading it to the end, and similitude of God as the end which is sought."[45]

The hierarchical order of being, however, establishes a specific gradation of things according to the various modes of the nature of things, because "nature is the cause of ordering."[46] But the order of being considered in its hierarchical gradation consists, according to Aquinas, in a disposition of unity and plurality of things. The question which might arise is, what is the foundation on which being is understood as hierarchical order of unity and plurality? St. Thomas, having recourse to Boethius, argues: "When we say that being and that which is, are diverse, we distinguish the act of existing from that to which that act coincides."[47] In view of this doctrine the hierarchical order of being can be analyzed as some disposition in which the essential and existential characteristics of being are related to each other mutually and reciprocally. Consequently, the order of being in its hierarchical gradation would consist in a disposition of unity and plurality of things but as expressed by a proportion that obtains between essence and existence.[48]

PART A

UNITY AND PLURALITY OF BEING

INTRODUCTION

The concept of order is one of the basic notions in St. Thomas' doctrine of being. To discover the order of reality and to reflect this order in the human mind is, according to the Angelic Doctor, the ultimate end of philosophical wisdom: "The ultimate perfection of soul, which she can attain according to the philosophers, lies in describing in her the whole order of the universe and its causes. In this consists also the final end of man, which according to us [theologians] will be realized in the beatific vision of God."[1] But in the natural order of philosophical wisdom, the highest and the most perfect science is that which is concerned with the understanding of being, i.e., metaphysics.

For St. Thomas the very nature of things displays a specific order according to the modes of being. The reason for this is the fact that the natural things are mutually related to each other, thus constituting an unchaotic whole. Therefore, to grasp properly the concept of order of reality, being must be analyzed in its unity and plurality of things, in the composition of their essential and existential characteristics. But, before examining the unity and plurality of being, one must examine the very notion of order as such.

I: THE NOTION OF ORDER

The very notion of 'order' Aristotle defines as disposition of a thing having parts: "Disposition describes things properly arranged" (*diathesis legetai tou echontos mere taxis*).[1] Order so considered is a disposition of things according to some principle, because every order is a plan: "Order is the whole structure of a meaning" (*taxis de pasa logos*).[2] Order then consists in a disposition of a thing having parts in three ways, namely, according to place, power, and species.[3] In a word, an order consists in a disposition which is predicated in relation to various parts of a thing both in its being and operation.

Following Aristotle, St. Thomas defines disposition in terms of order: "The name of disposition signifies an order."[4] Aquinas, however, does not reduce the notion of disposition to the order of parts only, but also to the order of finality. In view of this St. Thomas says: "disposition can be said about both the reason [*ratio*] of the order of things in respect to the end, and the reason [*ratio*] of the order of parts in respect to the whole."[5]

For both Aristotle[6] and St. Thomas[7] the order and being are found in reality as related to each other. As a matter of fact, in the ontological structure of being there is an intrinsic coherence between the nature of things and order. In other words, each being is intrinsically ordered according to the mode of the nature of things. Consequently the nature of things is the cause of the order of being.[8]

St. Thomas has written no general treatise on order, and, therefore, he did not give any general definition of it. Aquinas did not give a full definition of the concept of order, because order as an analogical concept is not definable. But, sometimes in discussing a particular problem, St. Thomas indicates in passing some specific elements that constitute the essential conditions of order, and he gives certain descriptions as he develops his own arguments.

A: The Definition of Order

All philosophical doctrines recognize that the essence of order consists in relation. In regard to this there is no controversy, especially in respect to the order that exists in human knowledge. As a matter of fact, human cognition from its very nature seeks order. Following Aristotle, St. Thomas repeats: "the office of a wise man is to make an order."[9]

But, in describing the order in terms of relation, St. Thomas is specific about how to understand the very nature of relation itself. First of all, relation can not be classed among the primary and secondary substances, because no substance can be relative. [10] But, not being a substance, relation is a modification of the substance to whose being it adds another kind of being. In this sense, relation becomes an accident, that is, a being which inheres in another. But in its function as an "inherence in another" relation goes beyond the thing itself, and refers it to something else. In other words, the essence of relation consists in referring any kind of being to something which is outside itself.[11]

Secondly, among the categories relation is the last and the weakest kind of being, because it presupposes not only substance but also certain accidents. However, relation being the weakest category has particular properties. Aristotle enumerates three instances of the properties of relative things:

> Things are "relative": first, as double to half, and triple to a third, and in general that which contains something else many times to that which is contained many times in something else, and that which exceeds to that which is exceeded; second, as that which can heat to that which can be heated, and that which can cut to that which can be cut, and in general the active to the passive; third, as the measurable to the measure, and the knowable to knowledge, and the perceptible to perception.[12]

Thirdly, since the essence of anything that is relative is relative to something, relation presupposes a correlation. Otherwise, the relative thing would be related to something else casually and accidently. Moreover, if one of two relative things would not be determined by the other to which it is related, there will not be any connection and interdependence between them, and as such the relation itself would be irrelevant there. In the very nature of relation then there must be correlatives which according to Aristotle are thought to come into existence simultaneously.[13]

St. Thomas describes the relative things by such expressions as: *respectus*,[14] *habitudo*,[15] *proportio*,[16] *comparatio*,[17] *dependentia*,[18] *adequatio*,[19] *dispositio*,[20] *inclinatio*,[21] *assimilatio*,[22] *communicatio*,[23] *commensuratio*,[24] etc. These expressions reveal that things related to each other constitute some causality which Aquinas describes by such words as: *fundari*,[25] *causari*,[26] *sequi*,[27] *consequi*,[28] *ordinari secundum*,[29] *nasci*,[30] *innasci*,[31] *acquiri*,[32] etc. Now among such relative things which are causally linked to each other, there is a special order.

In the ontological structure of the categories which are the foundation of relative things there exists a twofold order of relation, namely, the order of static and dynamic relations. To the order of static relations belong all relative things which have quality as a foundation, and to the order of dynamic relations all those based on action and passion. The general principle of the order of relation St. Thomas expresses as follows: "This which is the most simple and most perfect, it is the measure of all other beings."[33]

Order, considered as relation can be described as some unity and plurality of being. Order, when considered as some unity, constitutes an arrangement which takes place among the perfections of one and the same thing. Order when considered as some plurality constitutes an arrangement which takes place among the perfections of different things. In a word, order considered as some unity consists in relations which are referring perfections within one and the same thing, and order conceived as some plurality consists in relations which refers the perfections of one being to another.

The order considered as some unity consists in the arrangement of perfections which are included in the very structure of a particular being. This mode of arrangement St. Thomas describes usually by the following terms: *ordo in, sub ordine contineri, in ordine esse*, etc. These expressions indicate the absolute character by which a particular being is independent of another both in its *modus essendi* and *modus praedicandi*. In view of this, St. Thomas can classify all modes of being into particular species of order, for example, *ordo universi, ordo coelesti, ordo in divinis, ordo idearum*, etc.

B: The Essential Characteristics of Order

St. Thomas in his *Commentary on the Sentences*, discussing the theological problem of the nature of the Trinity — *"utrum in personis divinis sit ordo"* — gives the following definition of order:

> Order in its reason [*ratio*] contains three elements, namely, the principle of priority and posteriority; in view of this, all things could be described as an order of something which is prior to something else according to place, and time, and other similar ways. It includes also distinction because there cannot be an order of something which does not have distinct things. But this more presupposes the name of the order than can signify it as such. Finally, it includes also a principle of order through which it can be united in a species. Therefore, one order can happen according to place, another to dignity, origin, and so on.[34]

In view of this text, the concept of order contains the three following conditions:
1. *ratio prioris et posterioris;*
2. *distinctio;*
3. *ratio ordinis.*

Let us analyze more precisely these three ontological conditions of any order.

1. *Ratio Prioris et Posterioris*

The first essential constituent of the concept of order is *ratio prioris et posterioris*. St. Thomas argues: "priority and posteriority are described according to some principle. Order includes in itself some mode of priority and posteriority Therefore, wherever there is some principle, there is also some order."[35] In view of this text, the very nature of order consists in a mutual reference of two things related to each other according to a particular principle by which all individual beings are mutually subordinated in conformity with the proper sequence of succession. In this way the relation of priority and posteriority becomes an essential part of any order and a principle of composition of each being. The interdependence of order and relation of priority and posteriority St.Thomas expresses very simply: "in some order, namely, priority and posteriority."[36]

The Notion of Order

The definition of order in terms of priority and posteriority leads to the conclusion that in the very nature of any order we have to distinguish two elements, namely, a mutual relation of two things, and a reference to particular principle. The concept of order contains a mutual relation of one thing to another, because priority and posteriority in any series are relations. But the concept of order includes also a reference to some specific principle, because priority and posteriority being relations suppose the existence of some principle according to which one thing is prior or subsequent to another. Having in mind this double meaning of priority and posteriority Aquinas gives the following definition of order "priority and posteriority are described in any order by comparison to principle of its order."[37]

Wherever there is then a mutual reference of one thing to another there should be also a particular principle[38] by which all individual beings are related to each other according to a specific sequence. To understand, then, the proper meaning of order as a particular sequence we have to analyze St. Thomas's doctrine of principle.

The basic meaning of principle St. Thomas derives from the concept of priority and defines it as an order or sequence.[39] However, according to this definition, principle does not signify merely the relationship of things but the origin of priority.[40] In general, the term 'principle' means that from or in which a thing in any way whatsoever begins.[41]

Principle, being an origin from or in which a thing begins, has to be distinguished from a cause. Every cause is a principle, but not conversely. In other words, principle implies a sequence of things, and cause implies some influence on the being of the thing caused.[42] The general conditions of being a principle in any order are the following:

1. Principles are not from other things;
2. Principles are not from each other;
3. All other things are from them.[43]

Principle, then, being an origin from or in which a thing begins, implies a certain order in progression.[44] However, the order in progression is found in different ways, and as such things are arranged according to different principles. Commenting on Aristotle's *Metaphysics*, Aquinas considers the various meanings of the term 'principle' in three ways, that is, in reference to what is the first in the order of motion, generation, and cognition.

The meaning of principle considered in reference to the order of motion designates what is first in a thing over which motion passes.[45] Principle so conceived can have two senses:
1. That from which someone first moves something, that is, any part of a continuous quantity from which local motion begins;
2. That from which a thing best comes into being, that is, the point from which each thing begins to be moved most easily.[46]

The term 'principle' considered in reference to the order of generation designates what is first in a thing which is in the process of coming to be. However, this order of generation is either inherent or non-inherent, that is, intrinsic or extrinsic.[47] In the order of intrinsic generation the principle of coming to be of a thing means that part of a thing which is first generated, and from which the generation of the thing begins, for example, in the cause of the house the first thing that comes into being is the foundation.[48] But in the order of extrinsic generation the principle of coming to be of a thing means that from which a thing's process of generation begins but which is outside the thing, for example, in the case of generation of natural things, of human acts and artifacts.[49]

Finally, the term 'principle' considered in the order of cognition designates that from which a thing first comes to be known. This order of cognition also contains two kinds of principle, namely, intrinsic and extrinsic. The intrinsic principle of knowing is related to the order of apprehension and designates what is first in an act of understanding; for example, axioms or assumptions are principles of demonstration. But the extrinsic principle of knowing is related to the order of being, and designates what is first known by our intellect; for example, local motion is first known by us because that kind of motion is most evident to the senses.[50] All of the above-mentioned senses of principle we can reduce, therefore, to two kinds of order of priority and posteriority, namely, intrinsic and extrinsic.

In establishing the proper meaning of principle the question of the relationship between the principle and priority arises. Is there any difference between them? What kind of interdependence can we find there? In order to answer these questions, we have to know how we are using terms. In general, the principle in each class of things is what is first in that class, and the term prior means what is nearest to some determinate principle. But this interrelationship of principle and priority can be considered from several points of view.[51]

The order of priority and posteriority, then, consists in the reference of a particular being to its principle. But since there are several principles according to which all things are arranged, the order of priority and posteriority should be considered in its various references to principles; for example, the point is a principle in reference to place, the reasoning in regard to intellect, and the cause in respect to being as such.[52] In general, since a principle is what is first either in being or in becoming or in knowledge, the order of things can be considered in three ways, namely, in quantity, in knowing, and in being itself.

2. Distinctio

The second essential element of the concept of order is distinctness which consists in the multiplicity of different constituent parts of being separated from and contrasted with each other in any kind of arrangement. Distinctness is an essential condition of any order, because order is possible only where things are distinguishable: "order without distinction cannot exist."[53] Otherwise, if there would not be a determinate separation among things related to each other, there would not be any reference and subordination either, and any kind of collection of things would be a chaos. In this sense St. Thomas says: "Wherever there is plurality without order there must be a confusion."[54] Consequently, distinctness is a presupposition of any kind of order which as some particular relation of priority and posteriority makes the arrangement among all things possible. The interdependence of distinction and order St. Thomas expresses very simply: "Where there is an order there must be distinction."[55]

The term *distinctio* in its literal meaning is used by St. Thomas as the opposite of identity or unity, and as such it involves a negation.[56] But distinction conceived as a negation of identity can be considered in two ways, namely, as something which is undivided in itself and separated from others.[57]

However, distinction as a negation of identity does not signify only the diversity but also some likeness between things related to each other. Otherwise, if the members of any arrangement did not correspond to each other they could not be brought into mutual relation, and as such they could not constitute a definite order. St. Thomas enumerates three

conditions under which the likeness between distinct things is possible, namely:
1. *convenientia*, that is, a concordance which consists in possession of some characteristic which is common to all, although not in the same degree;[58]
2. *cooperatio* that is, a concurrence which consists in mutual dependence between the members of a particular order both in being and existence;[59]
3. *finis*, that is, a cause which consists in adjustment of things into a proper direction by realization of the purpose of their nature.[60]

How are things distinguished from one another? What is the real foundation of distinction among things? St. Thomas considers two instances in which things possibly can be said to be distinct from one another, namely:
1. Things are distinct from one another if their being would be specified through certain added differences so that diverse things were diverse according to their species;
2. Things are distinct from one another if their being would be specified through certain differences in natures that are diverse in species.

Since no addition can be made to a being in the manner in which a difference is added to a genus,[61] things are said to be different because they have diverse natures, to which being accrues in a diverse way.[62]

Nature, then, is the real and proper foundation of the distinction in any form of things. But, since nature means both matter and form things are said to be distinct from each other according to material and formal distinction.[63] The formal distinction occurs if there are diverse and opposite forms, and the material distinction if there is any kind of numerical division.[64] The formal distinction occurs among beings which are diversified according to genus and species, and the material distinction among beings which are distributed according to numbers. As a matter of fact, in the very nature of distinct things, there is a mutual interdependence between the formal and material distinction[65]. In general, this interdependence can be expressed as follows: since the form of things and the definitions that signify them are like numbers, the addition or subtraction of one difference changes the species.[66]

Distinction having its foundation in the nature of things is recognized by St. Thomas as the principle of the plurality of beings.[67] But, since there are two kinds of distinction, the plurality of things can be considered both in regard to the formal and the material distinction. The formal distinction is a principle of plurality of beings in the diversity of their perfections, and as such it constitutes a specific order of genus and species according to their proper forms; for example, the organic beings are more perfect than the inorganic, animals than plants, man than animals.[68] But the material distinction is the principle of plurality of beings in their numerical distribution, and as such it constitutes a particular order of individual beings according to their specific differences.

For the plurality of beings, however, all things are not ordered to each other in the same way. Again, things are related to each other according to different principles. Considering the order of things in view of their common good, St. Thomas distinguishes two kinds of beings: those which never fail in their proper natural activity, and those which sometimes do fail in their proper natural activity. But, since the two groups contribute in their own way to the whole, there are two requirements in the order of things, namely, distinction between the things ordered, and the contribution of the distinct things to the whole.[69]

3: *Ratio Ordinis*

The third essential element of order St. Thomas defines as *ratio ordinis*. The term *ratio* St. Thomas uses here to designate the nature and the fundament of any particular order. But the question is: what is the proper foundation of any order? To answer this question we have first to ask what the difference is between the meaning of *ratio* as it is used by Aquinas in connection with the first element of order, namely, *ratio prioris et posterioris*, and that of *ratio ordinis*. In answering this question we have to keep in mind that *ratio prioris et posterioris* is in *res ordinata* the same as *ratio ordinis*. Hence, in searching for the difference between these two meanings of *ratio* we can consider these two notions only according to the mode of signification.[70]

The notion *ratio* has many different meanings, and is used by St. Thomas as a synonym with *intellectus* and *intelligentia*,[71] *ratiocinatio* and *discursus*,[72] *conceptio* and *definitio*,[73] *modus* and *processus*,[74] *probatio* and *terminus*,[75] *significatio* and *oratio*,[76] *intentio* and *relatio*,[77] etc. In explaining the concept of order in terms of *ratio*

Aquinas uses this term in two ways, namely, as a generic and as a specific term. Thus, in the case of the element of priority and posteriority, the notion *ratio* is used as a generic term which designates a *relatio*, that is, a reference between two or more things related to each other according to a determinate sequence of succession. But, in the case of the element of foundation of particular order, the notion *ratio* is used as a specific term which designates an *origo*, that is, a source from which things related to each other primarily proceed. To sum up, in the definition of order in terms of *ratio*, the relation of priority and posteriority means *ratio generis* and the origin constitutes the *differentia specifica*.[78]

The proper meaning of *origo* consists in being a source from which things related to each other proceed (*ad originem autem pertinet, a quo alius et qui ab alio*)[79]. But *origo* considered as a source is a principle of procession of one from another without causal dependence on that other. Briefly, *origo* is the foundation of any arrangement of things related to each other.

Origin considered as a source of any procession of things is in fact identified with the nature of things related to each other.[80] For this origin is the principle of different types of orders and the various modes of one thing proceeding from another.[81]

In the mode of procession there are two things, namely, a thing from which something proceeds, and a thing which proceeds from something else. In other words, there are two relations, one in the originator, the other in the originated;[82] the former is an active origin, and the latter is a passive one.[83]

The very nature of origin, then, consists in being a principle of relation founded either on quantity or on passion and action.[84] However, in the nature of any procession there is a difference between the origin and relation according to the mode of signification.[85]

C: The Principal Divisions of Order

From the previous considerations it is evident that there are as many orders as principles of things.[86] In general, all principles

St. Thomas reduces to the following two kinds, namely: (1) principle of knowing--"*unde res primo innotescit,*" and (2) principle of being--"*a quo aliquid procedit quocumque modo.*"[87] In view of this distinction, we may distinguish between logical and real order; the former requires mental distinction and the latter demands real distinction.

The logical order is constituted from and found among logical relations in regard to both first and second intentions. The logical relations of first intentions arise from subordination of the concepts of things, for example, the logical relations of genus and species. But the logical relations of the second intentions arise from subordination of the concepts themselves. In subordination the concepts of second intentions Aquinas enumerates four kinds of logical relation, namely:

1. *relatio in carentia alterius termini;*
2. *relatio de entis ad non entis;*
3. *relatio relationis;*
4. *relatio in diversa ordine.*[88]

To sum up, we may say that the logical order consists in a composition of logical relations either discovered by the intellect or included in the intellect. In other words, the logical order which is discovered by the intellect is founded among such logical relations which depend on the subject of knowing, and the logical order which is included in the intellect is founded among those which are derived from a specific mode of human understanding.

The real order proceeds from a composition of various real relations and as such it can be divided inasmuch as there are different principles of priority and posteriority. This kind of order St. Thomas calls *ordo realis, ordo naturae.*

* * * * *

The concept of order is one of the basic notions in St. Thomas's philosophical doctrine. To discover the order of reality and to reflect this order in the human mind is, according to the Angelic Doctor, the ultimate end of man's knowledge.

But establishing the very notion of order is only the first step which enables Aquinas to apply it in analyzing the very structure of being of things and being as such. In the following two sections we attempt to outline St. Thomas's approach to the question of unity and plurality of reality in both cosmological and metaphysical ways.

II: ORDER OF NATURAL THINGS

The search for order in nature is a necessary condition of every science. Einstein expresses this conviction by saying that "without the belief in the inner harmony of our world there would be no science."[1] The same conviction was expressed by A.N. Whitehead:

> "There can be no living science unless there is a widespread instinctive conviction in the existence of an *Order of Things*, and, in particular, of an order of nature."[2]

That nature constitutes an order is for St. Thomas an evident fact. By sense observation we do find an unchaotic plurality of things which constitute the universe. Wherever such a plurality of things existed, there would be an order.[3]

The question arises: what is the principle of plurality of the created world? In searching for this principle we have to recall the Aristotelian theory of hylomorphism as it was understood by St. Thomas Aquinas and the reason for his radical rejection of the current panhylomorphistic attitudes of his times.

A: Order in Its Integrity and Composition

In the history of philosophy the Aristotelian theory of hylomorphism has been interpreted in many different ways. The interpretation given by St. Thomas is one of the greatest achievements in his philosophical career and greatly influenced the proper understanding of the Aristotelian theory of hylomorphism, especially in the area of philosophical anthropology. In general, St. Thomas recognized two misinterpretations which endanger the proper understanding of Aristotelian hylomorphism, namely:

1. A misinterpretation which usually is caused by inappropriate understanding of prime matter as some potentiality;

2. A misinterpretation which is caused by improper understanding of substantial form as some actuality.

The former leads to the doctrine of duplicity of matter, and the latter to the theory of multiplicity of substantial forms in particular created beings. A typical example of these misinterpretations of the Aristotelian theory of act and potency which occurred in the Middle Ages was that of panhylomorphism.

The originator of panhylomorphism in the Middle Ages was the Jewish philosopher Avencebrol, the author of *Fons vitae*.[4] Avencebrol, following the Neoplatonic tradition, taught that all created beings are composed of prime matter and substantial form. In this universal composition of all beings of matter and form Avencebrol saw the main principle of distinction between contingent being and God. Several medieval thinkers followed Avencebrol's panhylomorphistic theory; among others: Alexander of Hales[5], St. Bonaventure,[6] Roger Bacon,[7] and others.[8] The universal composition of all created beings from matter and form they called *binarium famosissimum*, which they used to explain the whole order of creation. However, in order to avoid the difficulty of the revealed truth about the existence of pure spiritual substances, they accepted the theory that there are two kinds of matter: the gross corporeal matter of all material beings, and the spiritual matter of angels and human souls.[9]

St. Thomas rejected the notion of spiritual matter as contradictory, and calls the panhylomorphistic theory of Avencebrol "a frivolous and impossible solution."[10] The primary error committed by Avencebrol and his Christian followers consisted in identifying the potentiality which occurs in material beings with the potentiality which appears in spiritual beings. Instead of the duplicity in matter, we have to accept the duplicity in potentiality. The potentiality of matter exists because of the changeable character of the substance in material beings. The potentiality which occurs in spiritual beings does not have any local movement, because of the different kind of contingency in their existence.[11] In a word, the potentiality which occurs in material beings is a kind of potentiality because of local movement, and the potentiality which appears in spiritual beings is a kind of potentiality because of the contingency of their act of existing.[12]

The panhylomorphism of Avencebrol also included a theory of the multiplicity of forms according to which particular being is made up of matter and a number of forms by which being is established in its genus and species. Each being has many forms arranged according to their degree of generality. This order of being Avencebrol explains in terms of addition of one form to another. Less general form is added to more general, but the more general forms are inferior to the more particular ones that are added to them. In other words, the higher the form the more it contains the inferiors.

Many scholastics adapted the theory of multiplicity of forms as the best explanation of the metaphysical structure of created beings. St. Thomas, on the other hand, was one of the first who opposed the doctrine of plurality of forms and recognized it as a misinterpretation of the Aristotelian theory of act and potency. St. Thomas, in distinguishing between substantial and accidental forms, states that in every being, apart from many accidental forms, there can be but one substantial form.[13] The higher the form the more simple and the more perfect is its being. Consequently, beings are arranged according to the unity and diversity of their substantial and accidental forms. The metaphysical structure of being so considered is understood by St. Thomas not in terms of the addition of one form to another, but as a composition of a unity out of plurality.

This composition of a unity out of plurality, however, requires that there be among the created things a specific order of nature. Referring to his doctrine on divine providence, St. Thomas quotes the *Book of Wisdom*, and says that God ordering all things in measure, number, and weight displays a specific rational plan: "We may understand by measure: the amount or mode or grade of any perfection of a thing; by number: the plurality and diversity of species resulting from the different degrees of perfection; and by weight: the different inclinations to proper end and operations, and also the agents, patients, and accidents which result from the distinction of species."[14] This order and rational plan of divine providence

> is occupied by divine goodness as the ultimate end, which is the first principle in matters of action. Next comes the numerical plurality of things, for the constitution of which there must be different degrees in forms and matters, and in agents and patients, and in actions and accidents. Therefore, just as the first rational principle of divine providence is simply the divine goodness, so the first rational principle in creatures is their numerical plurality, to the establishment and conservation of which all other things seem to be

ordered. Thus, on this basis it seems to have been reasonably stated by Boethius, at the beginning of his *Arithmetic*, that "all things whatsoever that have been established, at the original coming into being of things, seem to have been formed in dependence on the rational character of numbers."[15]

Before going into the details of the rational plan of natural things, one must realize how Aquinas is using the terms of 'order' and 'nature', and how he applies the meanings of those terms to the question of unity and plurality of beings.

B: Order and Nature

In establishing the mutual relation between 'order' and 'nature' one must realize how St. Thomas uses the terms. In general, the order of nature consists in a disposition of unity and plurality. But, since unity and plurality follow upon being, the order of nature has to be considered according to the modes by which being can be expressed in reality.

Each being is intrinsically ordered according to the mode of the nature of things:

> Now it is clear that no natural thing nor anything which naturally agrees with things can exist without order. For nature is the cause of order. For we see that nature in its own operations proceeds in an orderly way from one to another. Therefore, that which has no order and which is not according to nature cannot be taken as a principle.[16]

The order of nature can be analyzed with respect to the essential threefold element of any order, namely, priority and posteriority, distinction, and principle (*ratio ordinis*)[17]. The order of nature in regard to priority and posteriority manifests the **unity** of things in their composition. The order of nature examined in view of distinction reveals the **plurality** of things in their oneness. Finally, the order of nature treated with reference to the principle of arrangement (*ratio ordinis*) shows the mutual **dependence** of things on each other.

Order of Natural Things

The order of nature, then, can be considered in many aspects, but mainly in its unity, plurality, and dependency. The question which might arise is: what is the foundation on which nature is understood as a disposition of unity and plurality. But, since disposition requires some composition, the order of unity and plurality in nature must be analyzed according to the very structure of being.

The structure of the composite being, because of the plurality of its components, requires:
1. A constitution of act and potency;
2. A relation of the parts and whole;
3. A principle of its unit.

The basic composition of every composite being is the constitution of act and potency.[18] The parts of a composite being cannot be brought together and cannot create a unity, unless there is something in act and something in potency. The parts of a composite being are united together as a being in potency with respect to the union, because they are united in act after being potentially unitable.[19]

The structure of the composition of act and potency indicates that there is a special relation between the parts and the whole of the composite being. The relation considered from the parts of the composite being shows us that the components are prior to the composition itself, because neither act nor potency are prior to the being as such.[20] But the relation considered from the unity of the composite being indicates that the whole is more perfect than the parts, and the less composite being is more noble than the more composite. The whole is more perfect than the parts,[21] because the good belongs to the whole rather than to its parts. The less composite being is more noble than the more composite, because dignity depends upon the simplicity of being and not upon complexity.[22]

In view of the fact that nothing could be prior to itself, the composition is posterior to its components, and as such requires some principle of unity. The composition needs some principle for two reasons: (1) because of the actual unity of composite being, and (2) because of the potential dissolubility of composite being. Since every composition is made up of a plurality, there is a need for the composite being to have some principle of uniting all components into some union.[23] Since every composition is potentially dissoluble, there is also a need for the composite being to have some principle which would prevent the dissolution.[24]

C: Order of Nature and Its Constitutive Components

The order of natural things St. Thomas analyzes in regard to its three entitative aspects, namely, essence, species, and relation. Due to its essence, a real thing is some substance which becomes its measure; due to its species, a particular thing constitutes some form through which it can be numbered; and due to its relation, one thing can be ordered to other things. Thus, the whole reality constitutes such an order of being in which all natural things can be arranged according to measure, number, and weight:

> Any creature whatsoever subsists in its own being, possesses form through which it is determined in regards to its species, and is ordained to something else ... and that to which each and every thing is ordained can be reduced to these three things--number, weight, and measure, as the *Book of Wisdom* proposes to us [Sap., 11, 21], for measure refers to a substance of a thing, the substance having been limited by its own principles; number refers to species; and weight to order.[25]

1: Order as the Measure of Real Beings

St. Thomas considerably enlarged the theory of measure which he found in Aristotle, by including in it all the various aspects and different orders of being.[26] Measure is defined by St. Thomas in terms of quantity: "measure is properly defined in terms of quantity."[27] Number, however, can be a measure of beings in different ways: as a *modus*, as *prioritas et posterioritas*, and finally as *gradus*.[28]

In describing the term *modus*, St. Thomas follows St. Augustine's definition: "measure determines each and everything."[29] St. Thomas replaces the term *'praefigere'* with *'determinatio'*, or *'commensuratio'*, applying it to form.[30] Measure, then, as *modus*, denotes the order of the element of the way particular things exist.[31]

The ontic element of measure in things deliberated as *modus* can be further analyzed in the following threefold way:
1. In respect to the nature of a particular thing;
2. In respect to the characteristics of the principles of a being;
3. In respect to the numerical proprieties of a natural thing.[32]

St. Thomas discusses a concrete being also in terms of the element of *prius et posterius*.[33] These elements denote the measure of things in their succession, that is, that which is earlier and that which is later. In the order of succession, that which is earlier in development and in time is less perfect than that which is later, since in any singular thing potentialities precede the actuality in time, and imperfection precedes that which is already perfect. In the order of succession, on the other hand, that which is earlier *simpliciter* and according to nature is always more perfect than that which follows, since in a given thing the act precedes potentiality, and perfection antecedes imperfection.[34]

The *prius et posterius* element of measure in the order of natural things appears in various ways. St. Thomas enumerates the *prius et posterius* element of measure in the order of things in respect to size, motion, and time. Generally speaking, the *prius et posterius* order of succession in respect to size follows that of motion; the *prius et posterius* order of motion follows that of time.[35]

The third element of being in the order of measure is *gradus*. *Gradus* is defined by St. Thomas as the order of diversity of things according to their superiority and inferiority:[36] "Gradation is defined according to the order of superiority and inferiority." In the universe there are various levels of perfection, which create a particular gradation of things.[37] In the order of gradation, things on a lower level of perfection depend in their mode of being and performance on things on a higher level of perfection[38]. The order of gradation among natural things can be either:
1. based on one only level of perfection, and thus be part of the gradation of all beings; or
2. based on different levels of perfection and contain various *ratio* of relations existing between different levels of perfection of things.[39]

Gradus then is the measure of things as related to their different levels of perfection and denotes a specific kind of order of perfection, either in respect to natural thing's dignity or position.[40]

The diversity of things, then, is based upon the fact that one thing is more perfect than others, and is accomplished by means of gradations. Hence the highest members of a lower genus seem quite close to the next higher genus, and vice versa. From this St. Thomas concludes: "It is apparent that the diversity of things requires that not all be equal, but that there be an order and gradation among things."[41]

Diversity of things requires a special order and grades of goodness among them,[42] and as such they are related primarily to species, because they contribute far more to the perfection of the whole of created beings than individuals. In this regard Aquinas says:

> The good of the species is greater than the good of the individual, just as the formal exceeds that which is material. Hence, a multiplicity of species adds more to the goodness of the universe than a multiplicity of individuals in one species. It therefore pertains to the perfection of the universe that there be not only many individuals, but that there be also diverse species of things, and, consequently, diverse grades in things.[43]

This multitude of species results in the order of perfection, but in such a way that they embrace both necessary and contingent beings,[44] generable and corruptible,[45] defectible and indefectible,[46] noble and base.[47] Aquinas goes so far as to say that if there would not be any contingent being, the creation itself would not be perfect.[48]

The order of created things based upon the diversity of things includes the gradation of their beings. But, since each order has a principle, we have to inquire after it in regard to the gradation of perfection that exists among created beings. According to St. Thomas, the principle of gradation of perfection of all things is their form, because things are differentiated by possession of different forms by which they receive their species. In other words, the order of created beings is derived from the diversity of forms.[49]

Diversity of forms, as a principle of gradation of all perfections, is established in many orders, among others the following: the order of operation and generation, matter and form, agents and patients, properties and accidents[50]. Since the order of agents and patients is a result of the diversified relationship to matter, and the order of properties and accidents is a consequence of different substantial principles, among created beings we can distinguish the following two kinds of orders, namely:

Order of Natural Things

1. the order of operation and generation;
2. the order of matter and form.

Diversity of forms produces diverse operations among created beings, because the form is a principle of operation. St. Thomas says: "For, since everything acts insofar as it is actual (because things that are potential are found by that very fact to be devoid of action), and since every being is actual through form, it is necessary for the operation of a thing to follow its form. Therefore, if there are different forms, they must have different operations."[51]

Since matter is not always commensurate with form and since the higher the form the more it surpasses matter in its being,[52] we would have a specific order of operation of things. This order of operation St. Thomas explains more precisely by distinguishing three kinds of operation, namely:

1. *operatio moventis*, that is, operation which pertains to a thing as the mover of another;
2. *operatio moti*, that is, operation of a thing which is moved by another;
3. *operatio perfectionis agentis*, that is, operation of a thing which perfects itself.[53]

Upon this threefold division of operation, St. Thomas distinguishes two kinds of motion: passive and active motion, and establishes a specific order of generation[54]. This order of generation results in a specific gradation of composite substances both inorganic and organic.[55] In the order of generation there is the following succession: at the start of generation there is the embryo living with plant life, later with animal life, and finally with human life.[56] The human soul is the ultimate end of the whole order of generation and matter tends towards it as towards an ultimate form. So the composite substances with inorganic nature exist for the sake of the composite substances with organic nature which reach this fulfillment in human nature.[57]

St. Thomas, explaining why man is the ultimate end of the whole order of generation, has recourse to the principle that the more posterior and more perfect an act is, the more fundamental is the inclination of matter directed towards it. Hence, in regard to the last and most perfect act matter can attain, the inclination of matter whereby it desires form must be inclined towards the ultimate end of generation. But the most perfect form of composite substances is the human soul because of its intellectuality. Therefore, man is the noblest form in the order of generable and corruptible things to whom is directed the whole process of generation.[58]

2: Order as the Number of Real Beings

St. Thomas describes the order of natural things in terms of number which is nothing but another aspect of the previous element, i.e., measure: "number is a certain measure."[59] He ranks number among the order of quantity[60] and following Aristotle gives the following definition of it: "a number is the plurality measured by unity."[61] Among the essential elements of number considered as another aspect of measure, St. Thomas distinguishes the three following ones: *distinctio, species,* and *pulchritudo*.[62]

Real beings considered in the order of number are different from each other, since where there is no difference, number cannot exist: "where there is no distinction, there is no number."[63] Distinction of being is the foundation of number[64] and brings about the fact that one thing is not another one.[65] The distinction or distinctness of a thing in the order of number is based on the multitude and variety of created things and can be the principle of differentiation of things according to their level of perfection of a given species.[66]

The united plurality of things and the arrangement of various parts of natural things into one distinct whole reality without confusion, led St. Thomas to conclude that the numerical order of the world constitutes proportion and beauty of all created beings in their totality. As a matter of fact, the beauty of natural things originates in the very proportion of the universe, constituting thus a plenitude of real beings integrated to/with each other according to the numerical distinction that takes place among different species and various genera.

The beauty of the natural order of things as its essential elements of numerical coordination has, according to St. Thomas, two meanings:

> In its first meaning it denotes a specific relation of one quantity to another one, and in this case 'double', 'triple', or 'equal' relates to the kind of proportion. In the second meaning, we refer to proportion as a relation of one member to another one. In this sense a proportion between a creature and God can exist, since creature is related to God in the same way as effect to its cause, or potentiality to activity.[67]

The beauty of things creates also an order, an order based on clarity of form and on a specific symmetry.[68]

3: Order as the Weight of Real Beings

St. Thomas defines *pondus* as order which exists in the natural process of tending of one being towards other ones. We have here, then, an order of a dynamic character. In created things, the natural tendency of various beings towards each other is based on form, and can therefore be of various types. This variety of interaction between different natural beings demands a certain unity and specific goal. This unity and goal is understood here as *pondus* or *ordo*.[69] In the essential structure of *weight* as a certain order, St. Thomas distinguishes the following three basic elements: *inclinatio, relatio,* and *finis*.[70]

In the process of tendency between natural beings we can discern certain natural inclinations.[71] In defining natural inclination St. Thomas uses such terms as: *inclinare, tendere, appetere, appetitus naturalis, dilectio naturalis, directio...*

The very essence of natural inclination consists in the communication of forms, because inclination is derived from it; for example, the fire has a natural inclination to communicate its form to other things.[72] The inclination as a communication of the form is a common disposition of every being, and as such depends upon its nature. Since all created things of the universe are divided into organic and inorganic beings, the natural inclination is found in the following gradation:
1. The organic being with intellectual nature has an inclination according to its voluntary desire;
2. The organic being with sensitive nature has an inclination according to the sensitive desire;
3. The inorganic being without any cognitive nature has an inclination according to the natural desire.[73]

The natural inclination as a communication of form is a spontaneous source of natural activity, because the form is a principle of any operations. But, since the thing by form is in act, and since every agent acts insofar as it is in act, the mode of operations consequent upon a form must be in accordance with the mode of that form.

St. Thomas, distinguishing in the agent two modes of operations, namely, the operation in which a form does not proceed from the agent and that in which such a form proceeds, describes all created beings as mutually subordinated to each other.[74]

In order to understand the mutual subordination of created beings, St. Thomas distinguishes two kinds of natural inclination: internal and external. Aquinas, explaining this distinction, says:

> Hence we see that, in natural bodies, the inclination which pertains to the being [*esse*] of a thing, is not through something which has been added over and above essence; but it is through matter, which seeks being [*esse*] before it possesses it; and through form, which holds a thing in being [*esse*] after it comes into being. But an inclination to something external to the being itself is through something added over and above the essence. Just as the inclination to a place is through weight and lightness, and the inclination to make something like unto itself is through active qualities.[75]

In the very structure of natural inclination there are two elements: (1) appetency, and (2) appetible object. Appetency is an active inclination towards something[76] which the thing does not possess, but which is by it desired and wanted.[77] Appetency so conceived implies some deficiency which the being would like to fulfill.[78] But this fulfillment is just the meaning of that which is appetible, that is, the end of natural inclination.[79] The relationship between appetency and appetible object St. Thomas explains in terms of love, and says: "The first change of the appetite, brought about by that which is appetible, is called love, which is nothing other than complacence of the appetite, and from this complacence there follows a motion towards the object of the appetite, which is the desired; and ultimately there is repose, which is joy."[80]

Since the essence of that which is appetible consists of that which is good for the agent, the end of every natural inclination consists of realization of that which is desired. In this sense St. Thomas defines the causality of the end: "the causality of the end consists in this, that other things are desired for its sake."[81] But, since "every agent acts according to that which is in act," how can an end be a cause, if that which is appetible is not yet in act, but only an object of desire? Aquinas, answering this difficulty, says: "The appetible moves the appetite and the appetite tends to really result from the appetible, so that the end of motion will be where the beginning was."[82]

Comparing the causal influence of the efficient cause of the agent, and the final cause of the end, St. Thomas opts for the final cause to

Order of Natural Things

which he gives the highest rank among all causes: "The end holds first place over other types of cause, and to it all other causes owe the fact that they are cause in act; for the agent acts only for the sake of the end."[83]

* * * * *

Having established the twofold ends, St. Thomas states that all created beings are subordinated to one ultimate end, namely, God. But God, as the ultimate end and source of the order of the universe, established all created beings according to a rational plan. This rational plan of the order of the universe is accomplished in measure, number, and weight, and as such can be conceived in two ways, namely:
1. As an integrated whole, that is, as a harmonious constitution of each individual being;
2. As an arranged plurality, that is, as a hierarchical descent from the highest to the lowest things.

In the universe then, there is a plurality of things which are instituted on different levels of being. At the top of all beings is God, and at the bottom is prime matter. Between God and prime matter there are several degrees of perfection which can be reduced to either intellectual or material beings. In the order of the intellectual beings there is a composition of essence and existence, of substance and accidents, and of act and potency. In the order of material beings there is, moreover, a composition of prime matter and substantial form. In a word, the order of the universe is a unity of diversity, instituted by God in a harmony and hierarchy of all created beings.

III: BEING IN ITS SINGULARITY AND UNIVERSALITY

The pre-Socratic thinkers tried to resolve the problem of singularity and universality of being by reducing either the plurality of things to the unity of being (Parmenides) or the unity of being to the plurality of things (Heraclitus). So formulated, this problem led the ancient Greek philosophers to the unsolved question of being and becoming. On the one hand, if the diversity of things has an underlying unity in being, then the becoming and movement of things must be illusion. On the other hand, if the diversity of things does not have any unity in being, then all natural things are deprived of any identity of their being, and as such they will remain unexplained, for the world of sensible phenomena is the world of constant flux (Cratylus). As a matter of fact both positions merge and become the same as Plato stated:

> For you, in your writings, declare that the all is one; and he on the other hand says, there is no many. You affirm unity, he denies plurality. And so you both deceive the world into believing that you are asserting different things when really you are saying much the same. This is a strain of art beyond the reach of most of us.[1]

As a result of so formulating the question of the singularity and universality of being, the pre-Socratic philosophers were unable to reach a true and certain knowledge of natural things, and all that they could expect was to explain reality only on a conceptual level through some metaphysical intuition.

In order to locate properly this problem, one should analyze the question of singularity and universality of being as proposed by St. Thomas Aquinas but to do so against the background of the age-old dispute regarding the multiplicity and particularity of forms in things.

A: Participation as the Ontological Foundation of the Order of Being

In order to breach the dichotomy between being and becoming, Plato starts his philosophical investigation of the singularity and universality of being not from the sensible substances of natural things as perceived by our sense perception but from the epistemological premise that if the human mind is able to know *ta onta* by thinking (*noesis*), then not the natural things as such but their conceptual representations can serve as the basis in establishing a true and certain knowledge. In other words, not the concrete sensible phenomena (*aistheta*) but the rational account of our mind (*logos*) can guarantee a true knowledge (*episteme*).[2]

The question arises: where is the ground of true knowledge? Is the ontological foundation of the really real being of things (*ontos onta*) found in knowing the singularity or the universality of being? In other words: is the original *aitia* of being grounded in singular concrete sensible things (*aistheta*) or in the universal forms (*eide*)?

As it is well known, Plato's view on true knowledge is that it can be based only on the universal forms, and that the singular forms of particular sensible phenomena exist only on the account of *eide*. Consequently a true knowledge is eidetic in nature, and it corresponds to knowing the singular forms of sensible things by our reason (*nous*).[3] In this way, Plato can oppose *episteme/eide* against *doxa/aistheta*,[4] which opposition he illustrates with the Divided Line Diagram[5] and the Allegory of the Cave.[6]

However, in order to have a true knowledge of the pure being of singular things, we have to discover their universal forms in our mind by dialectical reasoning. For Plato, dialectical reasoning is "the coping-stone of the sciences"[7] and consists in a synoptic ascent from the singularity to the universality of being until the ultimate Form(s) is reached.[8] And since for Plato a true knowledge is based only on knowing universal forms, there must exist an opposition between the visible world of things and the invisible world of pure forms:

> We have at last arrived at the hymn of dialectic. This is that strain of cognition which is of the spiritual only. Sight was described by us to behold the living things and stars, and last of all

the sun himself. Not so with dialectic when a person starts on the discovery of the spiritual by the help of understanding only, and without any assistance of sense, and perseveres until by mere thinking he arrives at the knowledge of the absolute good, he at last finds himself at the end of the intellectual world, as in the case of sight at the end of the visible world.[9]

Dialectical reasoning which allows our intellect to ascend to *eide* is, according to Plato, ontological in nature and progressive in character. The dialectical progress from the lowest to highest entity(ies) consists in a twofold process, namely, collection (*synagoge*) of the universal from particular characteristics of being and division (*diairesis*) of specific forms which can constitute a genus.[10] But, since *diairesis* is dealing with *eidos* which is the 'really real' (*ontos on*) of all things, then the very nature of dialectics as such must have an ontological status and be able to unfold the suprasensible reality. However, since dialectics as the intellectual account of our mind (*logos*) is only the capacity of man's *psyche* to go "directly to the first principle"[11] through which man can perceive *eide*, the *eide* itself must transcend the sensible world of things and to have some objective content of its own.

Being of different natures, things are known differently by the senses and by the intellect; in the former things are known as "created, always in motion, becoming in place and again vanishing out of place," and in the latter as "uncreated and indestructible, never receiving anything into itself, nor itself going out to any other, but invisible and imperceptible by any sense, and of which the contemplation is granted to intelligence only."[12] In view of the differences between sensible and nonsensible knowledge, Plato gives the priority to *episteme* over/against *doxa* and argues that the singularity of being in concrete things exists only on account of their universal forms which are "to be regarded as most real and certain."[13] As a matter of fact, the sensibles (*aistheta*) are only images (*eikon*) and imitation(*mimesis*) of the true reality of the *eide*.

Plato's view then is that it is not the sensible but rather the supersensible which forms the objective content which transcends the natural order of things, and as such exist *a parte rei*. Distinguishing between *doxa*, which is the knowledge of sensible things, and *episteme*, which is the knowledge of nonsensible things, Plato argues: "If mind and true opinion are two distinct classes, then I say that there certainly are these self-existing ideas unperceived by sense, and apprehended only by the mind."[14] To the question of why there must be two kinds of knowledge, Plato answers that the things known by us are of two distinct classes and are absolutely different in nature, namely, the ones which are known in their singularity and the others in their universality of being:

> The one is implanted in us by instruction, the other by persuasion, the one is always accompanied by true reason, the other without reason; the one cannot be overcome by persuasion, but the other can; and lastly, every man may be said to share in true opinion, but mind is the attribute of the gods and very few men.[15]

However, if singular things are only imitations of universal ones, then what is the relationship between *aistheta* and *eide*? This question Plato tries to resolve by his doctrine of participation (*methexis*). Plato asks himself:

> I would like to know whether there are certain ideas of which all other things partake; similars, for example, become similar, because they partake of similarity; and great things partake of greatness; and just and beautiful, because they partake of justice and beauty.[16]

The reason for participation of *aistheta* in *eide* is the fact that the former do not have their forms on their own account but on account of the latter. As a matter of fact, *aistheton* is only a copy (*eikon*) of some eternal model (*paradeigma*) which represents the most original and universal form, namely, *eide*. Participation, then, understood as the origin of the forms of *aistheta* by/in *eide*, is "an active or passive energy, which arises out of a certain power of elements meeting with one another."[17] Participation, therefore, is the cause (*aitia*) of *aistheta* by *eide* which establishes a specific order of generation of the forms in singular things. Referring to his theory of the divided line, Plato says: "The sun is not only the author of visibility in all visible things, but of generation and nourishment and growth, though he himself is not generation."[18]

In the order of generation of forms in singular things, however, *eide* is neither the efficient nor formal cause of *aistheta*'s being, because participation so understood would imply an ontic "distinction between ideas in themselves and the things which partake of them."[19] Moreover, *eide* cannot be the efficient or formal cause of *aistheta*, because in such a case participation would lead to the separation (*diairesis*) of their being, and consequently there would be no unity in being but only a plurality of beings. In other words, if participation would imply *diairesis* of being in reality, then in the order of generation of forms *aistheta* would not be subordinated to *eide*, and both would be divided ontically. As a matter of fact, the really real being (*ontos onta*) can be found only in *eide*, because the generated being of *aistheta* is only a reflection or even a shadow of the really real being.[20] Consequently, participation consists in subordination of *aistheta* to *eide*, establishing "two ruling powers, and that one of them is set over the intellectual world, the other over the visible."[21]

Being the cause of subordination of *aistheta* to *eide*, participation is the very origin of the forms in singular things, but only in the order of exemplar causality. As an exemplar causality participation is a principle of communion (*koinonia*) between the sensible and nonsensible forms,[22] a communion in which *eide* is an originative power from which the singular forms are emanated to *aistheta*. However, the process of emanation of forms in *aistheta* is not conceived in the order of being, but only in the order of becoming. The reason why *eide* do not emanate being of forms in singular things is the nature of *aistheta* as something which is generated and always in motion. Being in motion, *aistheta* is absolutely alien to *eide*, and for Plato "motion cannot participate in being at all."[23] Consequently, we cannot really attribute being to generated being, and *aistheta* have only formal unity with *eide* as an imitation (*mimesis*) of its being. Participation conceived as *mimesis* of universal forms in singular things led Plato to attribute an ontic transcendent character to *eide*, granting *aistheta* the status of being only a copy of the universal forms: "I cannot help thinking that if there be anything beautiful other than absolute beauty, it is beautiful only insofar as it partakes of absolute beauty, and I should say the same of everything."[24]

B: Predication of Being and the Ontic Structure of the Order of Natural Things

Discussing Plato's doctrine of participation understood as the imitation of universal forms by singular things, Aristotle charges his master with making only a verbal difference between *methexis* and *mimesis* without offering any satisfactory explanation of "what the participation or imitation of the forms could be,"[25] and by the same token leaving the whole problem of the unity and plurality of being unresolved. Without an explanation of the nature of *eide*, Plato's doctrine of participation becomes unreasonable: "For they make many things out of the matter, and the form generates only once, but what we observe is that one table is made from one matter, while the man who applies the form, though he is one, makes many tables."[26] Moreover, not giving any proof for a separate existence of *eide*, Plato's participation cannot explain the relationship between nonsensible and sensible things, and confusing the logical and ontological order of universal forms:

> For if the forms exist and 'animal' is present in 'man' and 'horse', it is either one and the same in number, or different. In formula it is clearly one; for he who states the formula will go through the same formula in either case. If then there is a 'man-in-himself' who is a 'this' and exists apart, the parts also of which he consists, for example, 'animal' and 'two-footed', must indicate 'thises', and be capable of separate existence, and substances; therefore 'animal' and 'man' as well must be of this sort.[27]

Without an explanation of how *eide* can possibly exist, Plato's participation becomes not only useless but a contradictory hypothesis. If Platonic ideas exist, and as entities have separate existences, they have to have the same nature as the sensible things, and they should be singular, and as such they ought to have the particular forms. But in this situation the idea could not have the common form which is the essence of its own nature. In fact, Platonic ideas can be neither singular nor universal. They are not singular, because the ideas as entities should be indefinable. Plato's participation of universal forms by singular things is groundless because *eide* can be neither cause nor a principle. In conclusion Aristotle writes:

Being in Its Singularity and Universality

The universal also is thought by some to be in the fullest sense a cause, and a principle; therefore let us attack the discussion of this point also. For it seems impossible that any universal term should be the name of a substance. For, firstly, the substance of each thing is that which is peculiar to it, which does not belong to anything else; but the universal is common, since that is called universal, which is such as to belong to more than one thing. Of which individual then will this be the substance? Either of all or of none; but it cannot be the substance of all. And if it is to be the substance of one, this one will be the other also; for things whose substance is one and whose essence is one are themselves also one.[28]

The question of singularity and universality of being Aristotle resolves in view of his doctrine on substance. For Aristotle "substance means that which is not predicable of a subject, but the universal is predicable of some subject."[29] In view of this distinction Aristotle reasons:

> [T]he universal, while it cannot be substance in the way in which the essence is so, can be present in this; for instance, 'animal' can be present in 'man' and 'horse'. Then clearly it is a formula of the essence. And it makes no difference even if it is not a formula of everything that is in the substance; for nonetheless the universal will be the substance of something, as 'man' is the substance of the individual man in whom it is present, so that the same result will follow once more; for the universal, for instance, 'animal', will be the substance of that in which it is present as something peculiar to it. And further it is impossible and absurd that the 'this', that is, the substance if it consists of parts, should not consist of substances nor of what is a 'this', but of quality; for that which is not substance, that is, the quality, will then be prior to substance and to the 'this'. Which is impossible; for neither in formula nor in time nor in coming to be can the modifications be prior to substance; for then they will also be separable from it. Further, Socrates will contain a substance present in a substance, so that this will be the substance of two things. And in general it follows, if man and such things are substance, that none of the elements in their formulae is the substance of anything, nor does it exist apart from the species or in anything else; I mean, for instance, that no 'animal' exists apart from the particular kinds of animal, nor does any other of the elements present in formulae exist apart. If, then, we view the matter from these standpoints, it is plain that no universal attribute is a

substance, and this is plain also from the fact that no common predicate indicates a 'this', but rather a 'such'.[30]

The whole problem of singularity and universality Aristotle resolves by his doctrine on the predication of being. Only the singular (*tode ti*) exists and only the concrete individual thing can be called substance (*ousia*).[31] Aristotle opposes the universal (*katholou*) to *tode ti*,[32] and defines universal as "that which by its nature is capable of being predicated of several subjects";[33] for example, 'man' is a universal, and Socrates is a singular. Consequently, *tode ti*, being a real thing and a true substance, cannot be defined as such, but *katholou*, which Aristotle quite often identifies with genus,[34] is that through which things are defined and which constitutes a true object of science.[35]

The question of singularity and universality then can be resolved only if it is analyzed in regard to being as viewed in its entitative characteristics. Being according to Aristotle can be expressed in many ways. Generally speaking, Aristotle distinguishes four kinds of predication of being: (1) being as accidents, (2) being as true, (3) being as in ten categories, and (4) being as act and potency.[36] This fourfold predication describes being as entity:

> [T]here are many senses in which a thing is said to be, but all refer to one starting point; some things are said to be because they are substances, others because they are affections of substance, others because they are a process towards substance, or destructions or privations or qualities or substance, or productive or generative of substance, or of things which are relative to substance, or negations of one of these things or of substance itself.[37]

Describing being in its entitative characteristics, Aristotle enumerates various instances of entities which he reduces to four main aspects: essence, universal, genus, and substratum.[38] The concept 'what-is-being' (that is, essence) for Aristotle means 'shape or form'[39]. The universal and the genus are expressions of these kinds of entities which we reach by a process of reasoning.[40] The universal is contrasted with the singular, and the genus with the species. The substrate at the end means in the logical order the ultimate subject of predication, and in the physical order the underlying matter of change.

Applying various instances of entities as they are found in reality, Aristotle analyzes two questions: the difference between singularity and universality of being, and their relationship to sensible things.[41] These two questions the Stagirite analyzes in both the cognitive and real order.

In the cognitive order we have to distinguish between actual and potential knowledge; in the former we know the singular either by mind or by senses,[42] and in the latter we have a universal knowledge of the singular being. But, what is the reason for this twofold mode of knowledge of the singular and universal? Aristotle's answer:

> For knowledge, like the verb 'to know', means two things, of which one is potential and the other actual. The potency being as matter, universal and indefinite, deals with the universal and indefinite; but the actuality, being definite, deals with a definite object--being a 'this', it deals with a 'this'.[43]

Moreover, we know the sensible thing because we know its form, and who knows the form knows what its being is. Therefore, **form is prior** to the singular and universal. Consequently, the **singular** and the universal are to be explained in terms of forms, and not vice versa.

The form is the act and the cause of being in each sensible entity which is singular. In the cognitive order the same form, as an act of the passive mind, is without its physical matter, and as such can be conceived as universal, and can be applied to all the singular beings; the form in the last sense is a species.

In the physical order the differences between singular and universal depends upon the structure of the sensible being. The sensible being can be understood as singular and as universal.[44] As a singular it is an entity, but as a universal it is not an entity.[45] The singular is a 'this', because of the form in the sensible being. The universal cannot be a 'this', because no universal can be an entity.

The term 'this' Aristotle uses for both the form as separated from matter and the form as an act of a whole composite.[46] A 'this' can be conceived as a singular, when the form is not separated from its matter.

When the form is conceived as an act of a sensible composite, the 'thisness' of this form is entity and singular. When the form is conceived as separate from the matter the 'thisness' of the form cannot be singular, because such a form is universal. In other words: because of the element of the 'this', the form is individual and identified with the singular being as its act.

However, this twofold aspect of conceiving form as both separate from and unified with matter led Aristotle to attribute to genera and species some kind of being, and consequently to overcome completely the Platonic realistic dualism. On the one hand, universals cannot exist *a parte rei*, and in reality there are concrete individual existents. But, on the other hand, singular things are composed of matter and form; their elements have various ontic structures according to different genera and species. Consequently, the question of the singularity and universality of being contains some ontic inconsistency, and the "tragedy" of Aristotle consists of the dilemma arising from his empirical and idealistic attitude.

C: *Essential and Existential Order of Being*

In the view of St. Thomas, neither Plato nor Aristotle could satisfactorily resolve the problem of singularity and universality of being, because they approached this question only from the essential aspect of being. Essence alone cannot explain the real being, because in itself essence does not have any kind of being. Essence always remains in the realm of possible being,[47] and itself cannot transcend to the domain of actuality. But, having no being whatsoever, essence has no intelligibility and as such it cannot be grasped by the intellect.[48] Consequently, essence cannot guarantee the cognoscibility of being as such, and does not give a sufficient ground for metaphysical knowledge of reality.[49]

For St. Thomas, essence could explain the very structure of being, but only as related to *esse*. This view is in agreement with the Aristotelianconcept of essence as 'what-is' and as a principle according to which a thing can be understood and placed in a category. Essence so considered cannot be detached from existence because they both enter into the very nature of being *qua* being. But, since *ratio entis* is taken from *actus essendi*, it follows that essence when expressing the very nature of being is conceived in its relation to the act of being.[50]

In this relation, however, existence can be taken in two ways, namely, as signified and as exercised. When we think of existence in

Being in Its Singularity and Universality

the first way, we can form a concept of it, that is, as if it were an essence. The metaphysics of Thomas Aquinas is not concerned with the concept of existence, but with existence as exercised by a subject.[51] St. Thomas derives this distinction from the structure of science. No science can stop at the concept, but must proceed to the reality expressed by it: "We only form propositions or expressions [*enuntiabilia*] to obtain through them cognition of things; as it is the case in knowledge, and so also in faith."[52]

In what way is being attained by our intellect when it is expressed in terms of the relation of essence to existence? Because the act of existing cannot be conceived by the human intellect in a direct way, the being's act of existing might be grasped as joined to something which exercises this act of existing. This is evident from the way in which the notion of being is attained by our intellect. Although being is the first concept which the intellect forms, its existential aspect is not always distinguishable from the concrete apprehension of sensible qualities,[53] and so the quidditative aspect of the sensed object predominates and as such it stands in the focus of the intellect.[54] In other words, in the entitative order existence is that which is first grasped by our intellect, but in the cognitive order essence is that through which the very nature of being is expressed. To sum up we might say that the ontological and epistemological orders of being are the converses of each other.

But *esse*, as the primary object of our intellect, attained both in its quidditative and existential characteristics, is expressible according to a twofold mode of being. However, this twofold mode of being requires two different intellectual operations: "Since in a thing we find both the quiddity of that thing and its being (*esse*), the twofold operation of the intellect corresponds to these two elements."[55]

This twofold operation of the intellect in grasping the following twofold aspect of being St. Thomas describes as follows:

> Since there is a twofold operation of the intellect: one which is called the intellectual imagination which the Philosopher [III De Anima, text. 21] describes as indivisible intelligence consisting in apprehension of simple quiddity or formation; the other operation is called faith, which consists in the composition or division of a proposition; the former operation regards the quiddity of a thing, and the latter regards the being of the same thing.[56]

In view of this twofold aspect of being, St. Thomas describes *esse* as something which can be possessed potentially or actually by a subject. *Esse* so considered is an act which can be grasped in the second operation of the intellect and expressed by the copula of a judgment, which is the verb 'to be'.[57] But, since *esse* grasped in a judgment is then represented by the human intellect after the fashion of an essence, the being's act of existing is thought of as something which is expressed by and contained in the quidditative substratum of being. *Esse* so considered does not signify essence itself but that by which essence has something positive in reality. Consequently, although existence is conceived as though it were essence, existence itself is expressed and not merely the concept of existence. In a word, when we think of existence as if it were an essence, the concept of existence formed in the manner of essence does not display essence itself but that which has for its essence not to be an essence--to use Gilson's expression.[58]

In the notion of being, then, the act of existing must be emphasized and not the quiddity. Although existence as an act cannot be known to us in a direct way, it still remains as the only proper aspect through which our intellect can grasp the very nature of being by considering the manifold modes of existing (*modi essendi*)[59] insofar as they express something which is common to all being. In this sense being is predicate of every thing that is, and the starting point from which metaphysics proceeds to its conclusions by way of *propter quid* reasoning, and to which all other concepts are reducible.[60]

For St. Thomas *esse* is something which always belongs to being[61]. In this sense we can say that being consists in an *ordo ad esse*. But in its *ordo ad esse* being is considered as something which duplicates itself and which forms an immediate inference between being understood existentially and being understood essentially.[62] Being, so conceived, is attained by our intellect in a judgment in which we can distinguish between being as subject and being as predicate, in the following way:

1. When being in the subject is taken in its essential characteristics and being in the predicate in its existential characteristics;
2. When being in the subject is taken in its existential characteristics and being in the predicate in its essential characteristics.[63]

But the question arises: What is the principle of this twofold characteristic of being? How is one being different from another? To answer these questions we have to analyze the principle of distinction according to which being is considered in its unity and plurality.

Being considered in its *ordo ad esse* presupposes a real composition.[64] The reason is that any order includes two things: that which is ordered, and that to which something is ordered. According to St. Thomas, the order *ad esse* is expressed by the composition of essence and existence, because in the very nature of being essence is that which the being is in itself and existence is that by which being subsists in the nature of things.[65] In a word, being as *ordo ad esse* consists in a composition of essence and existence.

Now the composition of essence and existence can be considered in two ways:
1. As they are related to each other;
2. As they are opposed to each other.

In the former way being, conceived in its unity, expresses an order *ad esse* as a composition in which essence and existence are related to each other, and by which one and the same being is constituted.[66] Being, considered in its plurality, expresses an order *ad esse* as a composition in which essence and existence are opposed to each other, and by which many different kinds of being are established.[67]

Unity and plurality of being, however, in expressing the order *ad esse* as a composition of essence and existence, requires a real distinction between them.[68] The reason for this seems to lie in the fact that *esse* cannot be diverse in itself, but only by something extrinsic to itself; for example, a stone's act of existing is other than that of a man.[69] Being is an order *ad esse* as a composition of essence and existence, because in every created thing essence is distinct from existence.[70] Although the doctrine of the real distinction of essence and existence can be shown in many different ways,[71] the very foundation of this distinction we can analyze either in view of the essential or existential characteristics of being.[72]

1. Participation and Predication of Being

The question which might arise in regard to the composition of essence and existence is: How does one explain this twofold characteristic of being? What is the principle of distinguishing two modes of being? To answer these questions we must recall St. Thomas's doctrine of predication.

In the third article of the second *Quodlibet*, St. Thomas distinguishes two ways of predication of being, namely, *per essentiam* and *per participationem*.[73] Being can be predicated *per essentiam* only of God, because only in God is there an absolute order *ad esse* according to which His essence is identical with His existence.[74] All other beings subsist in reality as expressing different degrees of participation in *esse*.[75] In view of this distinction, St.Thomas argues:

> Therefore, according to this it should be said that being is predicated essentially only of God, in whom divine being (*esse*) is 'to-be' subsistence and absolute; [*esse*] is predicated of any other creature whatsoever through participation; for no creature is his own being [*esse*], but it is that which has being.[76]

Participation St. Thomas defines as 'having something partially'[77]. But 'having something partially' means 'receiving something as a part', that is, as something which belongs to something else.[78] Participation so considered consists in a composition of two things,[79] namely, that which participates and that which is participated; and this way is defined according to the following principle: whatever is participated is related to the participator as its act.[80] But, since the participated act of existing is limited by the capacity of the participator, being consists in an order *ad esse* in many different ways.[81]

In resolving the various ways of participation in being, we have to consider the condition under which participation of being takes place. Having recourse to the primacy of *esse* in being,[82] St. Thomas says that the variety of participation depends on the disposition of actuality and potentiality in singular beings, because essence is related to existence as potency to act: "Everything which participates in something can be compared to that in which it participates, as potency to act; for through that which is participated in it becomes a participant in such act."[83] The various kinds of participation of being then St. Thomas analyzes according to different kinds of composition of potentiality and actuality but in the order *ad esse*.[84] In this order participated *esse* is received by and contracted into a limited nature.[85] In view of this we might say that being is an order *ad esse*, because in its composition of essence and existence there is a real distinction by which one being is different from another.

2. The Order of Being as a Disposition of Actuality and Potentiality

The order of essence and existence is congruent to the order of actuality and potentiality because the composition of act and potency is the most universal composition of all being: "Being is divided by act and potency."[86] In this sense St. Thomas says also that act and potency are the first differentiae of being: "Potency and act are the first differentiae of being."[87] As the first principles, however, act and potency cannot be defined in a direct way but only in view of a proportion of two things to each other.[88]

In the order of being potency is related to an act: "potency, insofar as it is potency, is ordered to act."[89] The reason for the reference of potency to an act St. Thomas explains in view of the fact that the notion of potency is derived from actuality: "The *ratio* of potency is taken from the act"[90] In this sense actuality is in the composite a principle of intelligibility: "from act potency is known."[91] In other words, potency presupposes an act but not vice versa. Hence potency is grasped by the intellect but insofar as it is found in some actual being. Having recourse to Aristotle,[92] St. Thomas argues: "Something is known not insofar as it is in potency, but only insofar as it is in act, as is clear in IX Metaph.: hence neither is potency known except through act."[93] In a word, potency is known through act which is in itself not definable: *potentia innotescit et definitur per actum, actus autem non potest definiri* (potency becomes known and is defined through act, but act cannot be defined).

In the order of being there is also a specific reference of actuality to potentiality: "act has its own proper relation to potency."[94] This order requires that act should be proper to and congruent with potency: "the proper act corresponds to the proper potency."[95] In defining this order St. Thomas says that an act is related to potency as something which fulfills and completes the existing substance.[96] But, since one and the same act can be related to many different potencies, there must be in being many different manners of completion by which potentiality could be fulfilled. These various ways of completing potentiality by act St. Thomas bases on different objects.[97]

The order of being, then, consists in a disposition of actuality and potentiality in which act and potency are related to each other. In this mutual relation of actuality and potentiality there is a specific order of priority and posteriority: "Any given things participate in one given thing according to priority and posteriority as potency and act."[98] Following Aristotle,[99] the Angelic Doctor considers the order of priority and posteriority which obtains between act and potency in three ways, namely, in intelligibility, in time and in perfection.[100]

First of all, the order of priority and posteriority can be established in regard to the intelligibility of act and potency in being. For Aristotle to be prior in intelligibility means that by which another is necessarily defined. In this sense the Stagirite says that the elements of a definition are prior to the thing defined; for example, in the definition of 'man' as 'rational animal' the terms 'animal' and 'rational' are logically prior to 'man'.[101]. The reason for this is that which is known first is the basis for understanding the others. But, since actuality enters into the definition of potentiality, act must be in intelligibility prior to potency; for act is the perfection of potency :*actus est perfectio potentia* (act is the perfection of potency).[102]

Secondly, the order of actuality and potentiality can be analyzed according to priority and posteriority in time. The order of priority and posteriority however, considered in respect to time can be understood in two ways, namely:
1. When actuality and potentiality are considered as something in which one element is changing and another changed;
2. When actuality and potentiality are considered as something in which one element is actualized by another.

In the former case, potency is conceived as prior to act, because in one and the same thing which is at one time in potency and at another in act, the change proceeds from potentiality to actuality, that is, potency temporarily precedes act.[103] In the latter case, however, act is conceived as prior to potency, because potentiality is not actualized except by being actually existing.[104] But, since in reality potentiality depends on actuality, act is naturally prior to potency.[105]

Finally, the order of priority and posteriority which takes place between act and potency can be established in regard to the perfection of a thing. But, since the perfection of a thing means both its form and end, the order of actuality and potentiality can be considered in respect to their priority and posteriority in either way.[106] In this order act is always conceived as prior to potency, because the perfections of a thing belong primarily to the act, and secondarily to potency. Act precedes potency in respect to the form, because the perfections of the form are derived from the act and not from potency; for what is more perfect in being must be prior to that which is less perfect.[107] Act precedes potency also in regard to the end,[108] because act is the end of potency, and not vice versa; for that which is the end of a thing must be prior to that which tends to it.[109]

The order of being, then, consists in a disposition of actuality and potentiality: *actus et potentia ad illum essentialiter ordinata sunt in eodem supremo genere* (act and potency are essentially ordered within the same highest genus). This order can be considered in two ways: when act and potency in being are related to each other, or when act and potency in being are opposed to each other. Act and potency are related to each other, because they are the first differentiae of being by which a thing is constituted: *ex potentia et actu fit unum simpliciter* (from potency and act, a unity simply arises). Act and potency are opposed to each other, because they are found in reality in many different ways according to various types of composition of being: *actus et potentia ad illum essentialiter ordinata sunt primo immediate oppositi* (act and potency are essentially ordered primarily to their immediate opposites).

Having established a twofold meaning of the notion of 'being', the question arises: what is the principle of composition of actuality and potentiality in natural things? For St. Thomas the principle of composition in natural things is found in the material, formal, efficient, and final causes. The material and formal causes are the intrinsic principles of composition, and as such they indicate the basic elements of natural things, that is, matter and form. The efficient and final causes are the extrinsic principles of composition, and as such they show the origin of natural things, that is, the beginning and purpose of things.

In view of this relationship between the intrinsic and the extrinsic order of causes a specific order of natural things follows. The intrinsic order of reality occurs within all particular concrete beings and takes place by manifold modes of composition according to the nature possessed by a particular thing; for example, this concrete stone is not a simple being, but composed in many ways. The extrinsic order of reality happens between particular things and can be obtained according to the different modes of dependency in view of which one being is related to another; for example, this stone is multiple related to all other things.

*****

In this chapter we have tried to analyze the problem of singularity and universality of being as proposed by St. Thomas, but against the background of the ancient dispute about multiplicity and particularity of forms in things. Analyzing the problematics of multiplicity of forms of things in the order of exemplar causality, Plato arrived at the conclusion that the fact of multiplicity of forms requires a unifying preexisting principle which he calls *eide*; particular sensible forms of things exist by participation (*methexis*) in the universal *eide*. Aristotle, however, analyzes the whole question of multiplicity of forms in things in the order of efficient causality, and concludes that everything which really is a being, truth or good, must also be really its own cause; for example, the hottest things must be the very source of any heat in all other hot things.

St. Thomas, trying to reconcile both Plato's and Aristotle's interpretations of universality and singularity of being, analyzes the question of multiplicity of forms in things in the order of existence (*esse*). Distinguishing two ways of predication of being, namely, *per essentiam* and *per participationem*, the Angelic Doctor discerns among the beings a twofold mode of their *esse*, namely, being which exists by having some particular mode of existing, and being which is identified with existence as such.

PART B

TRANSCENDENTAL ORDER OF BEING

INTRODUCTION

In establishing the mutual relation between 'being' and 'order' one must realize how St.Thomas uses the terms. Being St.Thomas describes as what is innermost in each and every thing, and what is the deepest in them all, because it is the most formal in respect of all that is in a thing. In this sense Aquinas considers being as something which includes in itself all perfections of everything that is. Being, so considered, St.Thomas calls *esse*.

The aim of this part is to analyze the notion of order as it is found in the very structure of being. In being there is an order and this order is expressed in the very nature of things in many different ways. The sign of this is that being is predicated analogically of everything that is. Being as an analogical term can be considered either in relation to a particular thing or in its own notion. In the former case, being signifies a principle of diversity, and, in the latter, being means a principle of community. As a principle of diversity being varies according to different modes of being, but as a principle of community it remains analogically the same in every being. In other words, being is found in a disposition of some unity and plurality.

I: INTELLIGIBLE ORDER OF INVESTIGATION

In the twenty fourth chapter of the second book of his *Summa contra gentiles*, (SCG) St. Thomas describes the office of the wise man, and later explains:

> For things can be ordered only by knowing their relation and proportion to one another, and to something higher, which is their end; for the order of certain things to one another is for the sake of their order to an end. But only a being endowed with intellect is capable of knowing the mutual relations and proportions of things and to judge of certain things by the highest cause is the prerogative of wisdom. All ordering, therefore, is necessarily effected by means of the wisdom of a being endowed with intelligence.[1]

To grasp properly the use of the concept of order in the Thomistic doctrine of being we must realize how St. Thomas explains the Aristotelian concept of metaphysics. The very nature of metaphysics St. Thomas analyzes in terms of a ruling science:

> As the Philosopher teaches in the *Politics*, when various beings are ordered to one end, one of them must be regulating or ruling and the others regulated or ruled. This, for instance, is obvious in the union of the body and the soul, for the soul naturally commands and the body obeys. The same holds true with regard to the powers of the soul, for the irascible and concupiscible are ruled in the natural order by reason.[2]

But since all science is ordered to the perfection of man, the purpose of metaphysics as the highest science of human intellect consists in wisdom: "Now, since all sciences and arts are ordered to one end, it is necessary that one of them be the ruler of the others, and this rightly is entitled to the name of wisdom."[3] In view of this text let us consider more precisely St. Thomas's notion of order as the formal object of wisdom which is also the proper foundation of the *itinerarium* of the soul to God in a twofold way: *via ascensionis et descensionis*.

A: Wisdom as Speculative Virtue of Human Intellect

In the very nature of wisdom there is science and understanding. St. Thomas says: "Wisdom contains within itself knowledge and understanding; it is a specific knowledge and the foremost among the different areas of knowledge."[4] In order to explain the meaning of wisdom as science and understanding Aquinas has recourse to the Aristotelian theory of intellectual virtues.[5]

Aristotle divides all virtues into intellectual and moral. The intellectual virtues are based upon the activity of the intellect itself, and the moral virtues consist in the right relation of the irrational appetite to the rational part of the soul, that is, in the activity of the whole composite. The human intellect is divided into speculative intellect, with the virtues of understanding, science, and wisdom; and the practical intellect, with the virtues of prudence and art. The highest place among the virtues of speculative intellect belongs to wisdom and, among the virtues of practical intellect, to prudence.

St. Thomas, adopting the Aristotelian theory of virtues, bases the division of intellectual and moral virtues upon the difference between knowledge and appetite. St. Thomas says:

> There is this difference between knowledge and appetite; that knowledge takes place according as the known is in some way in the knower, whereas appetite does not take place in this way, but rather conversely, according as the appetite is related to the appetible thing, which the one pursuing seeks or in which he rests. And on this account good and evil, which have reference to appetite, are in things, whereas the true and the false, which have reference to knowledge, are in the mind.[6]

As a matter of fact, virtue, depending on the perfections of the activities of human faculties, perfects the human soul, because virtue as such belongs in the order of goodness.[7] But, since there are two kinds of virtues, the moral virtues perfect the appetitive faculties, and the intellectual virtues perfect the intellectual ones.[8]

The intellectual virtues of wisdom, science, and understanding perfect the intellectual faculty of man by consideration of the truth, because truth is the good in operations of the intellect itself. St. Thomas says:

Intellectual virtue is a certain perfection of the intellect in knowing. But according to intellectual virtue no intellect expresses what is false, but always what is true; for to speak the true is the good of the act of the intellect, and it belongs to virtue to make an act good.[9]

But truth could be considered in two ways: as something which is known by itself, and as something which is known through something else. If truth is conceived as something known by itself, then it belongs to principle, and as such it is conceived by the intellect immediately. In this sense a virtue which perfects the intellect by consideration of the truth as something that is known by itself, is called *intellectus* which is *habitus principiorum*.

However, truth that is known not by itself, but through something else is not conceived by the intellect immediately, but by some investigation.[10] This investigation of truth could be twofold: a searching into ultimate reasons in some genus, and an inquiry into the totality of human knowledge. The investigation as a searching into ultimate reasons in some specific genus perfects the human intellect by a virtue of *science*. And investigation as a sense of inquiry into reasons of all human knowledge, is called *wisdom*, which perfects the human intellect by judging and ordering all things by resolving them to ultimate causes.[11] In other words, the speculative virtue of understanding deals with basic principles. The speculative virtue of science deals with the knowledge of particular spheres of being. And the speculative virtue of wisdom deals with ultimate causes and reasons, and as such it is the virtue of the highest metaphysical knowledge.[12]

However, there is among speculative virtues of wisdom, science, and understanding a specific order of knowledge. St. Thomas distinguishes two kinds of knowledge: the knowledge of principles, and the knowledge of conclusions.[13] The knowledge of principles is proper to the virtue of understanding, because *intellectus* is *habitus principiorum*.[14] The knowledge of conclusions pertains to the virtue of science, because *scientia* is *habitus conclusionum*.[15] Now, a very important question arises here. If answered correctly, it can help to clear up much of St. Thomas's concept of wisdom as science. We can ask: how is wisdom related to other speculative virtues of human intellect, namely, understanding and science? Is there only a question of gradation of human knowledge? Do the speculative virtues of science and understanding have a mutual relationship to wisdom? In order to answer these questions let us consider, first of all, the relationship between wisdom and science, and, secondly, the relationship between wisdom and understanding.

General speaking, wisdom is science insofar as it is concerned with conclusions. But, since the science is also a knowledge of conclusions, there is a question in what sense wisdom and science are about the same thing, namely, about conclusions? In order to answer this question St. Thomas has recourse to the meaning and the role of certitude and certain judgment in human knowledge, and says: "The certainty of knowledge is found in different manners in various natures, according to the singular condition of each particular nature."[16]

The human intellect may reach a certain judgment about something by discursive reasoning. Reasoning is discursive when someone proceeds from the consideration of one thing to another, as when in syllogistic reasoning we proceed from principles to conclusions. But, when someone examines how a conclusion follows from principles, and considers both together, he is not on this account reasoning or discoursing, but he is judging.[17] The certitude of judgment would depend upon the kind of principles. If our intellect examines how a conclusion follows from proximate causes, then it would reach the certitude of scientific knowledge. But, if our intellect examines the derivation of conclusions from ultimate causes, then we would have a certitude of wisdom.

Wisdom, therefore, is a science in which someone knows the ultimate cause by which he can certainly judge about everything. In the most proper sense wisdom means knowledge of the ultimate cause *simpliciter*, that is, God.[18] In this sense wisdom is the highest and the most noble science of human knowledge.

However, it remains to consider the relationship between the speculative virtue of understanding and wisdom. It was stated above that the speculative virtue of understanding is concerned with the knowledge of principles. The question now is: what is the relationship between wisdom and principles?

In general, human knowledge is concerned with the principles of its subject, because the intelligibility of its subject depends upon them. But in the process of apprehending these principles there is a specific order of perfections, depending on their different kind of certitude. The speculative virtue of understanding regards the most universal principles which are known to all immediately. The speculative virtue of science is concerned with some definite principles specific to particular spheres of beings which are under the consideration of single sciences. Finally, the speculative virtue of wisdom is related to the most common principles of all beings by way of predication and ultimate causality.[19] St. Thomas, considering the characteristics of the principles of wisdom, writes:

> Wisdom, in the simple sense, is most certain among all the sciences, precisely inasmuch as it touches upon the first principles of things, principles which are in themselves most knowable, although some of them, namely the immaterial ones, are less knowable for us. But universal principles are still more knowable to us, as, for example, those which pertain to being in as much as it is being, and the knowledge of these principles pertains to wisdom.[20]

B: Wisdom as Knowledge of Divine Things

Knowledge means, according to St. Thomas, both an act of apprehension and judgment. But in the process of apprehension there is a special gradation. In regard to the intellectual faculty of apprehension there is a gradation of intellects, namely, the human, angelic, and divine intellect. This gradation of intellects is as follows: the angelic intellect surpasses the human intellect much more than the intellect of the greatest philosopher surpasses the intellect of the most uncultivated simple person, and the divine intellect surpasses the angelic intellect much more than the angelic surpasses the human.[21]

All knowledge takes place through the assimilation of the knower and the known thing. For the gradation of intellects, however, there is a specific order of assimilation. The assimilation in human knowledge takes place through the action of sensible things on man's knowing powers, because the origin of human knowledge is taken from sensible things.[22] The assimilation in angelic knowledge takes place through the action of the intelligible forms on the angel's knowing powers, because the origin of angelic knowledge is taken from intelligible species that they receive immediately from God.[23] Finally, the assimilation in divine knowledge takes place through the action of the forms of the divine intellect on the things known, because God knows everything in Himself.[24]

In the order of assimilation of the knower and the known thing, there is a natural tendency to possess the highest good even though it could be only attained in a very imperfect way.[25] In the case of the human intellect, the natural tendency to possess the highest good is by way of the natural desire to know whatever is.[26] This natural desire to know whatever is, is directed toward understanding of the most perfect intelligible object, that is, God.[27] But, since the human intellect begins its knowledge with sensible things, the attainment of the most perfect knowledge about divine things can only be fulfilled gradually by investigation. St. Thomas says:

> In order to know the things that reason can investigate concerning God, a knowledge of many things must already be possessed. For almost all of philosophy is directed towards the knowledge of God, and that is why metaphysics, which deals with divine things, is the last part of philosophy to be learned. This means that we are able to arrive at the inquiry concerning the aforementioned truth only on the basis of a great deal of labor spent in study. Now, those who wish to undergo such a labor for the mere love of knowledge are few, even though God has inserted into the minds of men a natural appetite for knowledge.[28]

The human knowledge of divine things is among other intellectual substances the most imperfect. But even the most imperfect knowledge about the most noble reality can bring the greatest perfection of the soul.[29] St. Thomas, stating that the highest grade of human knowledge consists in knowing God, says that there is given to man a certain way through which he can rise to the knowledge of God;[30] otherwise the natural desire to know the ultimate end of human understanding would be in vain, and as such the human intellect would be created to no purpose.[31] But, since the human intellect starts its knowledge with sensible things, it cannot reach the knowledge of divine substance through itself, because God as such is above all other things. It remains, therefore, to examine how the human intellect attains the knowledge of God. In other words, what is the principle of investigation of divine things?

The principle of investigation of divine things St. Thomas explains as follows: *est autem eadem via ascensus et descensus.*[32] In accord with this principle, there are in man three ways of attaining a knowledge of divine things. In the first way, man by the natural light of reason ascends to a knowledge of God through creatures. In the second way, divine truth exceeding the human intellect, descends on man in the manner of faith, as something spoken in words to be believed. Finally, in the third way the human mind is elevated to gaze perfectly upon the things revealed.[33]

In the natural order, the human intellect can reach the knowledge of God by considering the perfections of created beings. Since the perfections of things descend in a certain order from the highest summit of things, namely, God, man may progress in knowledge of God by beginning with lower things and gradually ascending.[34] There is a twofold account of the descent of perfections from God: (1) from the first origin of things; (2) from the things themselves. In regard to the origin of things there is such an order that the universe of creatures should embrace the highest of things and the lowest. But, in regard to the things themselves, there is in the universe such a diversity of created beings in which appear also the diversity of ways to know God. In other words, according to the diversity of things, there appears the diversity of the ways, as though these ways began in one principle and terminated in various ends.[35]

The knowledge of God which is achieved by natural reason St. Thomas calls first philosophy. But this knowledge of God is the lowest and the most imperfect, because of the weakness of the human intellect.[36] Therefore, St. Thomas concludes, there should be above the philosophical knowledge of God a higher and more perfect knowledge than that of the natural order of human intellect.[37]

Above the philosophical knowledge of God stands the theological knowledge of revealed truths. In the theological knowledge of God there are two kinds of revealed truths: (1) the truths revealed to man in the path of faith; and (2) the truths revealed to man as his goal which is salvation. In the first case, divine truths are so revealed to man as not to be understood, but only to be believed when heard, for the human intellect in this state in which it is connected with sensible things cannot be elevated entirely to gaze upon things which exceed every proportion of sense. But, in the state of beatific vision, when the human intellect will be free from the connection with sensibles, it would be elevated to gaze upon the things which are revealed.[38]

Keeping in mind this threefold knowledge of God, we can distinguish three kinds of wisdom, namely, the philosophical, theological, and beatific wisdom. Philosophical wisdom is restricted to the area of natural reason, theological wisdom is based upon faith, and beatific wisdom is dependent on the supernatural experiences of grace given in the state of beatific vision.[39] In philosophical wisdom the human reason ascends to a knowledge of God through creatures, but in the theological wisdom the divine truth of God descends to us by a divine revelation. Since the beatific wisdom given in the state of beatific vision is supernatural *simpliciter*, and exceeds every natural power,[40] we would have in the natural state of man twofold knowledge of God, namely, philosophical and theological.

C: Deictic Character of Metaphysical Wisdom

For the contemporary follower of St. Thomas there arises a serious methodological question: how Aquinas's doctrine on the predication of God in its twofold way of *via ascensionis et descensionis* can be justified both logically and ontologically. Realizing that St. Thomas was mainly a theologian, our question is even more difficult to answer and becomes a very important one because his usage of philosophical reasoning is subordinated to theology. Today, however, both disciplines are not only considered as autonomous with regard to each other, but quite often are disregarded as lacking scientific justification. Moreover, as Professor Stefan Swiezawski pointed out in his study on fifteenth century philosophy, we have since that time witnessed the fact that "transcendental reflections on being. . . give way to the categorical analyses of limited areas of reality and to the questions relating to these particular areas."[41] Consequently, there is a real need to reevaluate the way of demonstration by the medieval masters, especially in the realm of the philosophy of being and God.

Wisdom defined by St. Thomas as both science and understanding presupposes that reality is intelligible ontologically as well as logically. In the ontological order reality is comprehended in its concreteness as a set of individually existing beings, each being having a unique and irrepeatible act of existing. In the logical order, however, the same reality is apprehended by the human mind under some universal conceptions we have of things in their ideality, presenting thus some unity of beingwhich the intellect predicates of various kinds of actually existing things according to their particular species and genus. This twofold order of intelligibility can be established and based upon two ways of reasoning, namely, inductive and deductive; in the former by heuresis of our sensitive representations and in the latter by syllogistic demonstration. Aristotle states: "For we accept all things either through syllogism or induction."[42] Consequently, in order to grasp more deeply the conception of wisdom as science and understanding, we have to scrutinize the metaphysical foundation of its methodology by analysis to determine how induction and deduction can be applied in the philosophy of being and God.[43]

1. Inductive Reasoning

One of the leading Polish logicians, Tadeusz Czezowski, divides all types of inductions into two main forms, namely, that of the Ionians and that of Socrates.[44] Generally speaking, the Ionic induction consists in a transition from the content of things observed to their extension, and the Socratic one a transition from the content of particular things observed to their general connotation; the former can be found in David Hume, and the latter among others in Plato, Aristotle, St. Thomas, Francis Bacon, John Stuart Mill, etc.[45] For instance, Aristotle, following Socrates, stressed in the inductive reasoning its heuristic and transphenomenal character,[46] and says: "Induction is a passage from individuals to universals" which "is more readily learnt by the use of the senses, and is applicable generally to the mass of men."[47] Stressing the role of senses in inductive reasoning the Stagirite could also overcome Plato's theory of innate ideas: "It never happens that a man starts with a foreknowledge of the particular, but along with the process of being led to see the general principle he receives a knowledge of the particulars, by an act (as it were) of recognition. For we know things directly; for example, that the angles are equal to two right angles, if we know that the figure is a triangle."[48]

The realistic approach of Aristotle to the question of inductive reasoning persuades St. Thomas to use in his philosophy the Aristotelian *epagoge* rather than Plato's *synagoge* which requires *diairesis* and *eide*.[49] Commenting on the Stagirite description of induction as "the leading on from particulars to the universals (*katholou*) and from the known to the unknown,"[50] Aquinas repeats almost *litteratim* Aristotle: "In induction a universal is inferred from those singulars which are manifested to the senses."[51] Induction understood as a heuresis of sensible representations and observations, enables St. Thomas to solve realistically the three most basic problems in philosophy, namely, the origin of intellectual concepts, the nature of universals, and the character of so-called self-evident premises of scientific knowledge.[52]

The very structure of human knowledge is conditioned by two factors, namely, sense perception, through which man experiences reality in its concreteness, and intellectual conceptualization, through which the same reality is conceived by our mind in its universality. In order to provide the objectivity of human knowledge on one hand, and to save the integrity of sense perception and intellectual cognition on the other hand, one has to give priority to sense perception, and to explain "how we pass from the individual and concrete state of the existing reality to the generalness of our knowledge of it [to the existence of concepts]."[53] It is the conviction of Krapiec that heuristic induction is able to give the only proper solution to the obvious fact of the discrepancy which appears between the concreteness of sense perception and intellectual conceptualization. The metaphysician from Lublin reasons:

> Induction, essentially identical with abstraction, is the only explanation, non-contradicted by facts, of the genesis of universal concepts [also of universals in a broader sense: laws and transcendentals] in the field of science. No logical process can ever produce concepts, but these, once formed, are submitted to the laws of logical thinking. Logic does not offer any explanation as to how universals arise, for it analyzes the laws of reasoning, an operation which presupposes thought. Considered in relation to logic, heuristic induction is then a condition of logical activity. And for that reason, too, induction, conceived of as a fallible or an infallible mode of reasoning, does not touch on the problem of the acquisition of concepts.[54]

But if in the order of intelligibility the priority in human knowledge belongs to the sensibles, and if heuristic induction explains satisfactorily the transition from sense apprehension to the intellectual comprehension, then the question arises: how is the universal content of the mental conception found in a given concrete thing? Generally speaking, there can be in this respect two main propositions, namely, that of Plato and that of Aristotle.

Plato maintains that although a concrete sensible phenomenon (*aistheton*) corresponds to its *eide*, nevertheless the latter is the cause (*aitia*) of the former.[55] But, if *eide* is the cause of *aistheton*, then it is only a copy of the eternal *eidos*. Moreover, if *aistheton* is only a copy of *eide*, then there is no real relationship among concrete sensible things, but only a mental interrelation among *eide* by a way of their combination or subordination.[56] The question then of the existence of the universal in the individual concrete things disappears, and the explanation of the real things is replaced by an interpretation of subordination which takes place among the *eide* themselves and their eternal *eidos*, an interpretation by a process of a gradual collection and division of differences between species and genus. Consequently, the universal is identified with the *eide* which has a mode of existence *a parte rei*, and Plato's reference to *methexis* of things in their *eide* becomes superfluous.[57]

In fact, then, Plato's *synagoge* is a deductive reasoning rather than inductive, and this theory of the universal in particulars enjoys only a noetic status. Consequently, Plato's *synagoge* with its *diairesis* and *diaphorai* instead of explaining how individual things are related to universal conceptions, leads in conclusion to the denial of things themselves.

Criticizing Plato for hypostatizing the universal,[58] Aristotle describes it (*katholou*) as "that which by its nature is capable of being predicated of several subjects."[59] The universal so understood is not a substance, but it is found in the form of things. In this view Krapiec observes:

> This is precisely what Artistotle's form achieves: owing to form as a unifying and organizing factor, the relations between the constitutive elements of a given thing develop analogously, that is, closely alike, in a number of beings, which we later apprehend as belonging to one class-species. This 'alikeness' of relations, [that is,

in fact that the transcendental relations which constitute a thing take place 'at the same angle', so to speak], causes us to perceive through induction, in a few or a great many concrete things, a common content which we express as the 'general'. It is clear that these relations are not actually identical in the particular cases, or else there could be no plurality of things; 'alikeness' simply means that we disregard existing minor differences, and consider things as to what the relations within them have in common, not as to what makes them different.[60]

However, if the content of the intellectual concept is derived from singular existing things and achieved through heuristic induction, then the universal does not exist *a parte rei*, and is in respect to its nature a product of our mind. In this way one can reach the objective source for our knowledge of both really existing things and their contents:

> Before I have had the slightest notion that I know, I first assert the existence of the world. The existence of the world, the existence of things, in other words a real, concretely existing entity is the datum prior to my self-awareness of knowing. Therefore, what I analyze first in philosophy is not knowledge and the content thereof, but being. Awareness and self-awareness appear and grow along with the apprehension of being. In fact I am not aware of knowing until I begin thinking reflectively. As long as knowing proceeds spontaneously, self-awareness [that is, the appearance of the self as knowing] comes in as secondary, partial and, as it were, in the middle of the distance.[61]

But if concepts are derived from the heuristic induction of sensibles, and if the universals are products of our mind as existing not *a parte rei*, then the certitude of human knowledge is based primarily on transcendental relationships, and secondarily on categorical ones. Such a solution gives us "a basis for hierarchical classification of concepts, on the one hand, and for setting up mental discourse, on the other hand."[62] In other words, the origin of concepts from the sensibles and the content of universals conceived as a result of the heuristic induction of the forms of things processed conceptually by our mind, can give a solid foundation for the objectivity of human knowledge, establishing thus the source for certitude of the first principles in philosophy in which "the concept of being is the first object of intellectual knowledge."[63]

Resolving the problem of the origin of concepts and establishing the objective character of our knowledge, the final question connected with

Intelligible Order of Investigation 71

inductive reasoning in philosophy is: what is the basis of certitude of the first principles of metaphysics? Distinguishing between *per se nota quoad omnes et in se*, St. Thomas writes:

> A thing can be considered in either of two ways; on the one hand, self-evident in itself, though not to us; on the other, self-evident in itself, and to us. A proposition is self-evident because the predicate is included in the essence of the subject, as 'Man is an Animal', for animal is contained in the essence of man. If therefore the essence of the predicate and subject be known to all, the proposition will be self-evident to all—as is clear with regard to the first principles of demonstration, the terms of which are common things of which no one is ignorant, such as being and non-being, whole and part, and such like. If, however, there are some to whom the essence of the predicate and subject is unknown, the proposition will be self-evident in itself, but not to those who do not know the meaning of the predicate and subject of the proposition.[64]

In view of this text it would hardly be expected that induction can explain all human knowledge. Although inductive heuresis can only give our knowledge objective foundation, it is unable to explicate the whole of knowledge. The reason seems to be obvious by the fact that at the very foundation of human knowledge "there are actually many cognitive events, many real ontic constructions which *qua* entities are intelligible in themselves. For anything that exists in any way is intelligible in itself inasmuch as it proceeds from the Prime Intellect."[65] Not going further into details Krapiec summarizes:

> The conception of the proper object was thus constantly revised and modified, so as to bring it to explain adequately the phenomena occurring in the real world. The successive constructions were basically carried out by virtue of intellectual intuition, that is by virtue of what might be called heuristic induction, guided not only by the philosopher's own vision of the world, but conditioned also by a heuristic vision of reality.[66]

Accepting, then, both the necessity and limits of heuristic induction in the philosophy of being, Krapiec advances the following points:

[There is]

> a. ... continuous intuition of reality, intuition elicited in an original form as existential judgment, and also in a derivative one in the

transcendental concept of being; the latter concept consists of existential judgments, too, together with the perception of the proportionate contents revealed in the concepts in their perfect states, that is, that of reversion to representations;

b. Also continuous reflection on one's own acts of cognition, and one the contents thereof;

c. This deepening of the intuitive knowledge of reality through reflection upon the acts and content of cognition, leads in turn to fresh intuition, a new vision enriching prior cognitive states. The new vision thus enlarged with fresh conceptual contents—which were already present, though obscurely, in the earlier vision [that is, in the intuition now reflected upon]—yields a new transcendental concept which is equivalent, as to content, to the primary intuition.[67]

In other words, metaphysics cannot be "induced" so to speak by simple heuresis of our sensibles, because induction itself presupposes metaphysics as such. Referring to the concept of the natural order which any scientist takes for granted, L. Monko writes:

> To the forefront of metaphysics emerges not induction as such, but reflection, not an experiment, but intellectual insight into the nature of things which are the object of experiment. On this basis we can penetrate the reality much further and deeper. The results obtained in such a way are no less concise than the scientific one; they constitute, moreover, the necessary foundation, supplement, and, in a way, give the finishing touches to science. Consequently, then, although generally speaking metaphysics today is outmoded, it is, in fact, a path which they often trod. Our conviction about the existence of an order in nature is a conviction reached in this precise way.[68]

2. Deductive Demonstration

Realizing the limitations of inductive reasoning in reaching the philosophical truth of being *qua* being, Aristotle resorts to deductive reasoning, and tries to establish a proper order between the two ways of explaining reality by using the following methods:

> It is clear that the loss of any one of the senses entails the loss of a corresponding portion of knowledge, and that, since we learn either

by induction or by demonstration, this knowledge cannot be acquired. Thus demonstration develops from universals, induction from particulars, but since it is impossible to come to grasp universals except through induction...nor can we get it through induction without sense-perception.[69]

Following Aristotle, Aquinas defines "demonstration" either by its final or material cause: in the former, demonstration is described as a syllogism productive of science,[70] and in the latter, it is considered under specific conditions of our reasoning, and says: "Demonstration is a syllogism that proceeds from premises that must be true, primary, immediate, better known and prior to the conclusion which is farther related to them as effect to cause."[71]

However, these rigid demands on deductive reasoning jeopardize the possibility of such a type of demonstration at all. Limiting himself only to the last requirement of deduction Krapiec observes:

> Attempts were made to establish a link between syllogistics and thinking bent on the discovery and investigation of causes; with that view, both *a priori* and *a posteriori* knowledge were put in the form of syllogisms. Those attempts were doomed to failure in many cases, particularly in the field of natural sciences, and even more so in metaphysics: in the field of natural science, because it was difficult to find out the truly essential elements of things (eventually, the scientists became more aware that they were not concerned at all with that which is or is not, with essence, but only with 'measuring' whatever measurable elements there exist and establishing relationships between the results thus obtained); in metaphysics, because the very conception of metaphysics had not yet been determined with precision and was rather based on pre-scientific intuitions of natural classes. Another point——and most important of all——is that Aristotle did not believe syllogistic deductive demonstration to be of any use in metaphysics since metaphysics employed primary concepts.[72]

In establishing primary philosophy and proving its main conceptions, "Aristotle himself would not make use of syllogistic deduction" but he would use a kind of demonstration which is based "on the analysis of the necessary states of reality—on the pointing out of necessary interdependence between states of things represented in knowledge"[73] However, the necessary relations of things viewed in terms of causality and effect cannot be explained by a formal demonstration as it has been pointed out, but in a real one. In this respect both Aristotle and St. Thomas distinguish two types of demonstrations, namely: *demonstratio propter quid* (proof by means of causes) which consists in *demonstratio ex causis rei procedit et primis et immediatis* (proof from the cause of a thing which proceeds from both the primary and from the immediate principles), and *demonstratio quia* (proof from the fact);[74] the former is an explanatory demonstration which shows not only how things are but also why something is as it is,[75] and the latter constitutes a factual demonstration which directly points to the very existence of beings. Following Aristotle, Aquinas makes a further distinction with regard to factual demonstration, namely that in which we proceed from direct and changeable effects to their causes "for effects are often better known and are more easily accessible to our knowledge (sensible knowledge especially) than causes," and that in which we proceed from indirect and remote causes to effects, for "if there be effects, then there exists a cause, but we do not know why a certain fact is precisely as it is."[76]

Summarizing St. Thomas's theory of twofold *demonstratio quia* Krapiec argues: "It follows that one cannot equate *propter quid* knowledge with *a priori* knowledge, on the one hand, and *quia* knowledge with *a posteriori* knowledge, for, as we have seen, *quia* demonstration is twofold: *a posteriori* and *a priori*."[77]

In view of those distinctions in philosophical demonstration, St. Thomas insists that both *demonstratio quia* and *demonstratio propter quid* belong to both scientific and philosophical knowledge.[78] As a matter of fact, explanatory demonstration presupposes the factual demonstration, because first you have to know *that* something is, and then, you can investigate *what* it is. But, 'existence' has two aspects: (1) a real presence in the world, that is, factuality; and (2) a constitutive element of being which makes a thing perfect, that is, actuality; in the former we are using the demonstration *quia*, and in the latter demonstration *propter quid*. However, although demonstration *propter quid* and *quia* are mutually interrelated, they must be supported by some negative reasoning; especially, as Krapiec stresses, by "*reductio ad absurdum*, elentic proof and systematic argument. All these types [the author adds] usually work in association, as complimentary to one another."[79]

Intelligible Order of Investigation

The complexity of demonstration in the primary philosophy of Aristotle (*prote philosophia*) or St. Thomas Aquinas's metaphysics shows that philosophical wisdom understood as science and understanding is based on a specific deictic method of reasoning. The reason for this is that the central conception of metaphysical meaning of being *qua* being is taken neither in distributive nor collective sense but in its formal and constitutive element which makes a being *being* (*esse*). Consequently, the conception of being so understood cannot be elaborated either in *a posteriori* or *a priori* way, but only by pointing to such processes of thinking which would elicit the formal aspect which constitutes being in its beingness. In this view Krapiec concludes:

> What we call the concept of being is the symbol of a living act of thinking, unable, by virtue of its structure, to part from the correlative, concrete reality. Abstraction is possible wherever universal concepts occur exclusively (*de iure*); it cannot be carried out where transcendental concepts are involved. This is so because the proper object of metaphysics is reality (being) *qua* existing, and every transcendental concept contains the intellectual affirmation of existence. Now metaphysics is the only cognitive discipline to apprehend reality in the aspect of existence (and not merely as an essence of existing), being susceptible to more or less generalization, that is, of being subjected to higher and higher degrees of abstraction; therefore metaphysics cannot, without losing its identity, abstract from its cognitive aspect, from its formal object, in short: from its specificity. It is by virtue of this specificity that metaphysics asserts existence, that is, always takes into account the semantic aspect of language, always employs——to use the traditional phrase——the eidetic side of language; though strictly speaking, it be not really eidetic, because existence as it is affirmed by metaphysics, cannot be translated into any picture or concept. It is only an act of assertion of existence in concrete substance.[80]

* * * * *

In his doctrine on *via ascensionis et descensionis*, St. Thomas evaluates the office of the wise man as a discovery of the due order of reasoning through which he can impose a rational order on his own acts.

However, the wise man, in discovering and imposing this natural order seeks not only an order which is inherent in reality, but also an order by which he will be able to investigate this reality. Since the process of human knowledge is an effect of a work of mind, there is a specific order of reason. In this respect, St. Thomas says: "The progress of the sciences is the accomplishment of reason, and it is the proper role of reason that it should put things in order: hence, in each and every work of reason there is certain order, especially from one to another."[81]

The reason is concerned with the order in two ways: in the way in which reason only considers the order, and in the way in which reason not only considers but also subordinates this order to the higher one. Keeping in mind this twofold order of reason Aquinas distinguishes between the natural order of the philosophical wisdom and the supernatural order of theological wisdom.

In the natural order of the philosophical wisdom, the highest and the most perfect science is, according to St. Thomas, that which is concerned with the knowledge of the order of being. To discover this order and to reflect its order in the human soul, is also the ultimate end of the philosophical wisdom.[82]

Above the natural order of philosophical wisdom there is also the supernatural order of theological wisdom. Between these two orders there is no opposition, but rather a mutual harmony according to the analogy of proportionality. As a matter of fact, both of them are derived from the divine wisdom, and as such they are coordinated with each other: "grace and virtue imitate the order of nature, which has been instituted by divine wisdom."[83]

The harmony and coordination of the natural and supernatural order St. Thomas considers in terms of formal and final causality. In regard to formal causality, the natural order is subordinated to the supernatural order of grace, because "the perfection of grace is more worthy than the perfection of nature."[84] In regard to final causality, the natural order is subordinated to the supernatural order of grace, because the glory of spiritual creatures "is the end of operations of assistent grace."[85] In this way the supernatural order of grace is the ultimate consummation of all created beings.[86]

But, in the knowledge of the supernatural order St. Thomas distinguishes two kinds of wisdom, namely, mystical and theological. Mystical wisdom is a result of infused grace given by the Holy Spirit, and as such is supernatural *formaliter*. Theological wisdom, however, is a result of studying the revealed truth given by faith, and as such is supernatural *radicaliter* and *originative*.[87] In other words, the object of mystical wisdom is God as such according to the mode that is suprahuman and supernatural, and the object of theological wisdom is God as revealed and believed.[88]

II: RATIONAL ORDER OF CREATED THINGS

St. Thomas Aquinas in *Summa Theologiae*, 1a.13.6c writes:

> Whenever a word is used analogically of many things, it is used of them because of some order or relation they have to some central thing. In order to explain an extended or analogical use of a word it is necessary to mention this central thing. Thus you cannot explain what you mean by a 'healthy' diet without mentioning the health of the man of which it is the cause; similarly you must understand 'healthy' as applied to a man before you can understand what is meant by a 'healthy complexion' which is the symptom of that health. The primary application of the word is to the central thing that has to be understood first; other applications will be more or less secondary in so far as they approximate to this use.

This text of the Angelic Doctor can serve us in the proper understanding of St. Thomas's doctrine on analogy of being and help us to find the proper order of *magis* and *minus* which takes place among things in reality. In view of Aquinas, however, the analogy of being itself shows that things constitute an order of *magis* and *minus* in multiple way, establishing thus various modes of predication of the order of being as such. In other words, if among things there are *greater* or *lesser* degrees of being, then the order of predication of real being must itself be based on analogical conception of being as such.

The problem of establishing the proper order of *magis* or *minus* of real things, requires then finding the metaphysical foundation for analogy of being *qua* being, both in its essential and existential mode of predication. Generally speaking, the essential mode of predication of being analogically conceived shows the *horizontal* dimension of things as being in various ways composed of various parts, and constitute an immanent order of being; the existential mode of predication by analogical reasoning points to the *vertical* perspectives of things in their mutual subordination, which takes place between the lowest and the highest things, and establishes a transcendental order of being as such, leading by the same token to the discovery of the ultimate Being — *Maximum ens, Summum Esse*, namely, God.[1] But, since essential and existential characteristics of being are not separated from within but are united from without as two distinct ontic elements of being, then the analogical predication of being, both in its immanent and transcendental perspectives establishes an order of *magis et minus* of things according to the proportional degrees of their perfection: *secundum modum suae perfectionis*.[2]

The question then, is: what is the metaphysical foundation of the order of being? How to understand being *qua* being in its analogical composition and proportional ascension and descension of the plurality of things and their unity? In other words: what is the metaphysical principle through which reality constitutes itself as an analogical order of being in its very beingness?

A.: Order and Relation

The very foundation on which the order of being is based, consists, according to St. Thomas, in the plurality of things and their mutual relationship.[3] Using interchangeably the words *ordo* and *relatio* Aquinas states "that things themselves have a mutual relation and order."[4] In view of this "mutual relation and order of things," reality displays the analogical structure of things which found themselves on various levels of being, and constitute a proportional order of *greater* and *lesser* degrees of perfection of their entity. However, before going into a detailed analysis of the analogical structure of the order of *magis et minus* of beings, it is necessary to realize in what way St. Thomas understood the interdependency of the notion of 'order' and 'relation'.

In delineating the nature of relation, and in describing the mode of its being, many difficulties were encountered. St. Albert the Great said in this respect that "between philosophers, there has always been dispute about relations."[5] Generally speaking, all those difficulties arise from the differences in concepts of being.[6] Interpreting St. Thomas's theory of relation in view of his doctrine of being, we have to look at his main predecessor, namely, Aristotle.

Aristotle was the first to lay the foundations for the doctrine of relation,[7] and gave the first systematic definition of relation as a reference between two or more things.[8] The broad definition of relation is according to Aristotle as follows: "Those things are called relative, which, being either said to be *of* something else or *related* to something else, are explained by reference to that other thing."[9] To relative beings so conceived belong such things as: possession, habit, perception, knowledge, position, etc.[10]

Having established the definition of relative things, Aristotle considers the nature and properties of relation itself. Relation is a particular mode of being and is designated by the term *to pros ti* (relation).[11] Relation so conceived must realize two important conditions for the doctrine of order, namely: (1) That the relative can have contraries; (2) That the relative things can admit of variation of degree. However, these conditions are not the mark of all relations, because such relative things like 'double' and 'triple' have no contrary nor degree.[12]

St. Thomas accepted the Aristotelian doctrine of relation and applied it to new speculations both of metaphysics and theology, especially to those which are devoted to questions of creation,[13] the Trinity,[14] and the Incarnation.[15] In this respect St. Thomas excelled many other mediaeval philosophers and avoided many theological errors by eliminating some misinterpretation of the Aristotelian doctrine of relation.[16]

The very structure of relation St. Thomas considers in two ways: namely, *ratio relationis* and *esse relationis*:

> In relation, as in all accidents, there are two things to consider, namely, its being [*esse*], according to which it is based in a subject, according to which [the subject] posit something in itself, inasmuch as it is an accident; and its relation according to which it [the subject] refers to another, on account of which it is placed in a determined genus.[17]

By *ratio relationis* St. Thomas means a reference of one thing to another: "The meaning of relation is that it refers to another."[18] This reference, however, can be expressed — as Cajetan correctly observed[19] — by the preposition *ad*.[20] In this sense relation is one of the categories of being and since relation belongs to such a category it is an analogical concept.[21]

However, this reference of one thing to another and respect to something else requires a foundation. St. Thomas defines the foundation of relation in terms of causality: "relation is found and based upon something as upon a cause, as similarity is based upon something as upon a subject, as in things which are similar."[22]

Relation so conceived signifies a particular mode of being which apart from subject implies a definite and external end and can be expressed by the preposition *inter*. The question which might arise here is, how to determine the *esse relationis*? Where is the foundation of relative things? St. Thomas enumerates five categories in which relative things can be grounded, namely: substance,[23] quantity,[24] quality,[25] action,[26] and passion.[27] We can divide all these categories into two groups, namely, the remote and the proximate. Substance and quality constitute a remote foundation of relation, and as such they are the subject of relative things. Quantity, action and passion belong to the proximate foundation of relation, and as such they are the measure of relative things.[28]

In summing up, in any relation expressible as xRy there are three elements: [x]: a *subject*, that is, the fundament of relation; in the subject as in the fundament of relation there is inherent the whole content of any reference, namely, in the father as in a subject there is the whole content of fatherhood; [y]:a *term of reference*, for example, son is a term in reference to father; [R]: a *reference between two things*; this reference is a cause through which a subject is ordered to its own end, namely, procreation is a cause of being a father or a son.

Now, having established the very meaning of the notion in relation, St. Thomas applies it to the concept of order. The basic element which constitutes the essence of order is according to St. Thomas relation, both the real and the logical: "Just as a real relation consists in the order of a thing to a thing, so a relation of reason consists in the order of the intellects."[29] In view of this St. Thomas uses interchangeably the words *ordo* and *relatio*. The interdependency of *ordo* and *relatio* Aquinas expresses by using the following conjunctions: *aut, vel, sive*, etc.[30] However, all these conjunctions we can reduce to one principal, namely, to the conjunction *et*.[31]

The interdependence of the concept *ordo* and *relatio* is so complete that St. Thomas explains each of them in terms of the other. A typical case of using interchangeably the words *ordo* and *relatio* we find in the

De Potentia. In article nine of question seven St. Thomas, considering the relation between creatures and God, uses the term of *relatio* as a generic term of order, and says: "in things themselves there must be a certain order; and this order is a certain relation."[32] But in response to objection seven of the same article, the Angelic Doctor uses the term *ordo* as a species of relation, and says: "this order is nothing other than the order of one creature to another."[33]

Even though the concept of order if so closely tied to the concept of relation, there are some very important distinctions between them. In general, all distinctions between *ordo* and *relatio* we can consider in regard to extension and comprehension.

First of all, there is a difference between the concept of order and that of relation in regard to the way they are understood. In the very nature of relation St. Thomas distinguishes two essential elements, namely, that of accidents and that of order. Having in mind this twofold element of relation Aquinas says: "The proper account [*ratio*] of relation is not taken by way of comparison to that in which it is but by way of comparison to something beyond."[34] In view of this text the concept of order is identified with the concept of relation as far as the element of ordering is concerned. As a matter of fact, the concept of order cannot be identified with the concept of relation as an accident, because it transcends all particular categories.[35]

Secondly, there is a difference between the concept of order and relation in respect to their extension. The concept of order contains all those relations in which correlative things are related to each other according to a definite succession of priority and posteriority. Having recourse to the division of static and dynamic relations, we can say that order is constituted by all such relations which have a particular principle of succession according to place, time, dignity or to any kind of particular cause.[36]

Now the order considered in respect to its plurality exists in the pattern of relations between the perfections of different things and which can be characterized by real relations. In his *Commentary on the Metaphysics*, St. Thomas simply says: "The relation which is in things consists in a certain order of one thing to another."[37] This mode of arrangement Aquinas describes by the relative pronoun *ad* or *secundum*. In fact, both relative pronouns are equivalent, because they express simply an act of referring one thing to another. The only difference that exists between those expressions is what we like to emphasize in a particular relationship, the end or principle of reference. The relative pronoun *ad* is used when one wishes to indicate the term of relation, for example, *ordo ad finem, ordo ad invicem, ordo ad totum, ordo ad ultimum, ordo ad principium*, etc. Accordingly, the relative pronoun *secundum* would be used to point to the principle of reference, for example, *ordo secundum generationem, ordo secundum accidens*, etc.

In the order considered in some plurality there are various connections of perfections of being which depend not only on one particular relation, but on a tissue of many different kinds of relations. However, all relations which can exist among perfections of being Aquinas reduces to the three following species:

1. An arrangement that occurs among quantitative perfections: in this kind of order the quantity of one being is compared and measured with the quantity of the other being;
2. An arrangement that appears among active or passive perfections: in this kind of order the active or passive power of one being depends on the active or passive power of another;
3. An arrangement that can be found among the perfections of being in regard to existence itself: in this kind of order the existence of one being depends on the existence of another.[38]

B: Order and Analogy

In view of the interdependency of *ordo* and *relatio* conceived as two ontic characteristics of being, the very nature of reality displays that things are mutually referred to each other, although not in the same way. St. Thomas argues: if relation consists in reference of one thing to another, and if order constitutes an arranged unity of things referred to each other, then, in reality there must be a specific diversity that establishes among things various degrees of perfections of being. However, the various degrees of perfections of being indicate that, if there is among them some similarity, things are ordered and related to each other. For Aquinas *similitudo* means *proportio*, namely *analogia*. Thus the various degree of perfections of being show that reality constituting an order of mutually related things to each other, is by itself *analogically* structured as well.

The analogical structure of reality manifests itself in both cognitive and entitative order. Cognitive order points to the fact that references of things are found among logical relations, and in the entitative order references of things are based on real relation. The basic difference between the real and logical relation consists in that the reference of a real relation must have a real foundation and a real term, and the reference of logical relation can belong to different orders.[39] In other words, the real relation requires a real distinction, whereas the logical relation only logical ones.[40]

In the very structure of logical relation there is such a composition and reference that it is in a category of order by itself: "relation of reason consists in the order of the intellects."[41] But logical relation so considered belongs to the order of intentional beings which exist in the intellect alone.

Having an intentional nature logical relations are subjected to a particular order of intentional beings according to the principle "second intentions depends upon first."[42] In this order St. Thomas distinguishes two kinds of concepts, namely, the concepts created by the human mind, and the concepts discovered in the procedure of the human understanding. The concepts of the first kind belong to the order of first intentions, and as such they signify a mental attention to the things themselves. But the concepts of the second kind belong to the order of second intentions, and as such they signify the attention of the mind to something in the mind as the object of knowledge.[43]

On the other hand, the real relation consists in an ordering of one thing to another, wherein the following conditions obtain: (1) a subject is a real being; (2) a subject has a real foundation; (3) a term of reference is a real being; (4) a term of reference is distinct from the subject; and (5) a reference is of the same order ("things which are relative are of the same order").[44] The essence of the real relation St. Thomas defines as follows: "In order for [two] particular things to possess [one] order, each of the two must be a being and each one must be distinct (for there is no order of the same thing to itself) and each one must be able to be ordered to the other."[45]

In general, the real order consists in real relations whereas we can distinguish a twofold arrangement, namely, that of predicamental and transcendental relations. The distinctions of these two classes of relation consists in the distinction of their relationship. The relationship of the predicamental relation occurs between two or more complete beings, and as such it is a principle of external order. The relationship of the transcendental relation can arise within the elements and parts of one and the same being, and as such it is a principle of internal order.

The predicamental relation St. Thomas defines as an accident, whereby its *esse* consists in an ordination *ad*: "an accident whose whole being is in relation to another."[46] The real order considered as a predicamental arrangement would consist in a reference by which one being is related to another.[47] In this sense St. Thomas writes:

> Relation has one meaning in as much as it is an accident, and another inasmuch as it is in relation. Inasmuch as it is an accident, it is in a subject, not however in as much as it is relation or order, but only because it is to one thing as if it becomes the other thing, and, in a certain sense stands in for the related thing.[48]

The transcendental relation St. Thomas expresses by such terms as *habitudo*,[49] *respectus*,[50] *ordo*;[51] by this kind of expression Aquinas would like to stress the absolute character of the transcendental relation. The absolute character of the transcendental relation consists in the general nature of relationship, which occurs in every being. In general, the relationship of the transcendental relation belongs to the intrinsic structure of any created being, and can be defined as a principle of being that lies in an ordination of particular elements of being to one another.[52] In other words, in contrast to necessary relation which occurs between constitutive parts of beings (for example, soul-body), the transcendental relation takes place among the ontic elements of being, for example, essence-existence, cause-effect, medium-purpose, exemplar-imitated thing, etc.

The relationship of transcendental relation considered as an intrinsic arrangement belongs to the nature of the whole being (*totum ens, entitate sua dicit ordine ad*). Goudin, one of the first systematizers of St. Thomas, defines the transcendental relation as: "an order which is enclosed in the essence of a thing, or the very entity of an absolute being which, by reason of its essence, is bound to another ... an absolute entity which encloses a reference to itself."[53]

The intrinsic arrangement of being must be mutual. In view of this, St. Thomas defines the transcendental relation in terms of proportion that exists among the particular elements of being itself. But the mutual arrangement among the particular elements of being means the proportion of essence and existence, substance and accidents, cause and effect, etc. In other words, the mutual arrangement among the particular elements of being means the proportional ordination of act and potency: potency is related to act, and act is related to potency.

The transcendental order, then, consists in a proportional arrangement that exists within the being itself. But, since in reality *esse* is diversified in many different kinds of being, there is a specific order of being. In this order St. Thomas distinguishes a twofold arrangement, namely:

1. *ordo inaequalitatis entium;*
2. *ordo aequalitatis entium.*[54]

The real order, then, consists in a real relation of both the predicamental and the transcendental kinds. However, since the principle of priority and posteriority could be attributed to either the origin or the perfection of things, the real order can be considered in two ways, that is, according to the mode of procession and the mode of perfections. The real order considered according to the mode of procession is based on the principle of dependence, which constitutes a mutual influence among things related to each other. But the real order considered according to the mode of perfections is based on a principle of any series, which constitute a specific sequence and comparison between degrees of certain characteristics of being, for example, *ordo secundum locum, tempus, dignitatem,* etc.[55]

C: *Analogy of Being*

In view of the two types of real relations, the order of *magis et minus* which takes place among things can establish twofold analogy of being, namely, categorical analogy based on predicamental relations according to the principle of composition of real beings, and metaphysical analogy based on transcendental relations according to the principle of subordination of beings to necessary one, namely, *Maximum Ens.* But, since in St. Thomas being reveals two entitative aspects, namely, that of existence (*id unde nomen imponitur*) and that of essence (*id quod significandum imponitur*),⁵⁶ the categorical and metaphysical analogy describes the order of *magis et minus* of things in their beingness according to the essential or the existential mode of predication of being.

In the essential mode of predication *esse* is analogically predicted of being as something that is added to a thing as its determining principle. In the existential mode of predication *esse* is absolutely predicated of being, because, since every nature is essentially being, nothing can be added to being as an extraneous nature in the manner in which a difference is added to a genus or an accident to a subject.⁵⁷ Hence, the proper application of St. Thomas's theory of analogy to the order of *magis et minus* of things corresponds to and depends on the appropriate interpretation of the modes of predication of being in its essential and existential characteristics.

In the factual development of St. Thomas's metaphysics, however, the followers of the Angelic Doctor overemphasize either the essential or existential characteristics of being, misinterpreting thus the Thomistic understanding of the analogical predication of being as such. In this respect the contemporary leading Polish Thomist and the founder of the so-called Lublin School, Albert Krapiec, referring to Cajetan and Sylvester of Ferrara as to the main classical commentators of Aquinas, makes the following remarks:

> [Cajetan] overemphasized the difference of essence and existence in being as a subject of metaphysics, and consequently he took into consideration only the essential aspect of being abstracted from its actual existence. . . . Understanding the danger of Cajetan's theory, Sylvester of Ferrara in opposition to it, stressed the fact, that in real being it is impossible to abstract existence from essence. Essence is a subject of metaphysics but only as actually existent. . . . The different concepts of being of those two commentators of St. Thomas Aquinas provided the foundation for two different theories of analogy.⁵⁸

1. Being and Analogy

The Latin word *ens* is taken from the verb *esse*: "nomen entis ab esse imponitur" (the name of being is taken from to-be).⁵⁹ St. Thomas, following Avicenna, describes being as it is expressed by *esse*.⁶⁰ The reason for this kind of procedure seems to lie in the fact that our intellect derives the very notion of being from the concrete apprehension of sensible qualities: "We express a thing in a manner of how we conceive it by our intellect. Our intellect, however, which begins the process of knowledge through the senses, does not pass beyond the manner which is found in sensible things, in which form and that which has form are distinct."[61] Hence, for St. Thomas the very nature of being has at least two entitative characteristics: existential and essential.[62]

In view of this twofold aspect of being, Krapiec argues for the primacy of existence over essence in the conception of being. First of all, if the very notion of 'being' is derived from the concrete sensible apprehension of real beings, then in the intellectual comprehension of being the stress should be given to the existential characteristics of being as such: "in the existential judgment 'A-exists', senses present to us the concrete essence of 'A' and intellect affirms its concrete existence" and as such it "forms afterwards the concept of being as existent essence."[63] Secondly, referring to the distinction between *ens ut nomen* and *ens ut participium*,[64] Krapiec points to the fact that "existence is the entitative act of essence, which cannot be omitted in real being when considered as a subject of metaphysics."[65] Finally, if one takes into consideration the fact of diversity of perfections of being, then existence as an actuality of being " is more perfect element in being than essence," because "essence of being is real only when existent."[66] Existence then, as the most perfect element in being, is not only prior to any essence, but it can itself constitute being in its totality, as it is in the case of the First Being, that is Pure Existence.[67]

Proclaiming, however, the priority of existence over essence in being, one should neither reduce one element to another, nor separate one aspect of being from the remaining one; in the former, being would be univocally considered as a universal and abstract concept formed by the mind, and in the latter "a danger of deviation from realism in metaphysics" could arise.[68] But, if being as being contains existence and essence as two inseparable aspects, then the problem arises as to the very mode of predication of being in its existentiality. In the words of Krapiec:

> Should being as being be only essence it could be apprehended in the process of abstraction. As concrete existent essence, however, it cannot be apprehended in that process which passes beyond exis-

tence and many individual, though real elements. It is necessary, then, to elaborate the knowledge of being as existent.[69]

In elaborating "the knowledge of being as existent" one should realize that since in reality there are two aspects of being which cannot be separated from each other nor reduced to one another, then between these elements there must be a specific ontological difference or "more precisely the real non-identity of essence and existence."[70] The principle of priority of existence over essence in being should therefore be understood not as a simple opposition, but as a mutual subordination of both from within and between things, according to which their essential elements, in conformity with their own proper nature, enter into composition with their existential ones, constituting thus a particular order of ontological determination and establishing various modes of being. In other words, although 'essence' and 'existence' are found in being *qua* being, as really distinct ontic elements, they are based on multifarious "net of ontological relation" which determines particular being in their various composition:

> [C]ompositions of integrant quantitative parts, of essential parts of matter and form, of personal parts of nature and subsistence, of ontological parts of essence and existence, also substance and accidents. These compositions multiply in different beings, because particular accidents or integrant parts possess their own determination of matter and form or essence and existence. Though particular being is an ontological unity, it appears to us as composed of a large, almost infinite number of various 'parts' which in respect to each other and to the whole are bound in necessary relations of 'this' individual being. Consequently, individual being appears to us as a 'net of ontological relation' being to each other as act to potency. This is nothing else than an analogy of concrete being.[71]

The real non-identity of essence and existence in being indicates to the fact that all contingent beings always constitute some composition of various entitative elements according to different relations which take place between them, establishing at the same time in regard to both immanent disposition between themselves and transcendent subordination between them and the Necessary Being, two ontological orders of being, namely, an internal order of particular being from within itself, and an external order of all contingent beings from without each other. In view of this basic composition of essence and existence

Rational Order of Created Things

on one hand, and the primacy of existence over essence on the other hand, the order of being can establish a twofold mode of understanding the entitative components of beings, namely, as they are in themselves, and in regard to their reciprocal relations. If one considers the entitative components as they are in themselves and independently from the way they are realized in concrete composition of their being, then the essential parts of being can be apprehended univocally, because particular being can have the same qualitative characteristics with other beings, becoming thus a common predicate for all things which belong to the same class of beings. Yet, if one examines the entitative components in regard to their reciprocal relationships and mutual interdependence within a being and between beings, then the essential parts as ontological determinates of composition of being as such can be comprehended *analogically*, because in each particular instance every individual being has different proportions and a unique set of its own inner connections, constituting thus a separate nature and distinct self-identity. In conclusion Krapiec writes:

> Obviously, every type of composition is a basis for more or less univocal concepts, concerned with this concrete being. Pure univocity of concepts is concerned mainly with integrant parts of being; all other types of composition require analogical apprehension. They also form the background for analogy of physical and ethical laws.[72]

2. Metaphysical Analogy of Being as Being

In view of the principle of primacy of existence over essence in being, on one hand, and the principle of real distinction between essential and existential characteristics of being, in their various compositions and proportions, on the other hand, the metaphysical knowledge of being as existent requires that its ontological determination will also be understood as such, namely as based on the fact of real nonidentity of the constituent elements which make being *qua* being. The reason for this is that metaphysical understanding of being is taken neither in distributive nor collective sense, but in a formal meaning. The formal meaning of the composition of essence and existence of being indicates that their proportion and relation which take place between them as analogous terms are subordinated to the act of existing as to the main entitative constituent which makes being as being. Consequently, the metaphysical knowledge of being as existent calls for a special type of analogy which Krapiec calls metaphysical analogy.

Although the analogy of being can be formulated either by categorical or predicamental relations, nevertheless, according to Krapiec, the realistic metaphysics demands that the analogical structure of being *qua* being should be sought in transcendental and existential characteristics of being as such: "The problem of analogy in philosophy is invariably connected with reality, with existence. For analogy is an expression of reality itself."[73] The reason for basing metaphysics not on predicamental relations is the very fact that they can only give us "an univocal concept of relations abstracted from its concrete subjects."[74] As a matter of fact, the categorical analogy based on predicamental relation is unable to reveal the real proportion of essence and existence in being *qua* being, showing thus "only a 'quasi-analogy' of proper proportionality, for one can define its univocal and identical relations which sometimes can be recognized even directly without any analogy."[75] Moreover, the categorical analogy, as based on predicamental relations can give us not a knowledge of being *in se* but only *ad aliud*. Metaphysics then, if it wants to attempt to elucidate on the analogical structure of being as it is in itself and not only as something which is simply related to others, must be based on transcendental relations and proportions.

The proportional structure of being *qua* being could be reached in its real order of being only if it is based on transcendental relations since, in order to know being as it is in itself (*in se*), it must be known in its wholeness:

> The constituent parts of a particular being are in some way subordinated to one another if they form, in a given aspect, an appropriate whole. The subordination of these parts, whether to the whole or to one another, is not something at random in being, but it forms necessary bonds, that is relations which are transcendental; for they cannot be separated from existence of the parts, if these are constituents of the whole which they form.[76]

However, since proportions and relations "never occur(s) according to one fixed pattern," then our cognition is analogical in regard to the entire entity of all beings.[77]

The analogical structure of being can be, however, understood in its wholeness either as a structure which includes the entire range of existence without limits, or as one which is manifested in some limited group of all existing beings. In view of this twofold aspect of being in respect to its existentiality, the analogical structure of being can establish two types of analogy based on transcendental analogy and analogy of general proportionality. The former forms a basis for a new knowledge obtainable through the exact transcendental concepts, the latter--a basis for more universal concepts which are transcendental only in a wider sense."[78] In order to reveal the proportional structure of being *qua* being in its unlimited and unrestricted existentiality, the metaphysical analogy should be sought in transcendental relations, understood, however, not in a sense of general proportionality, but in terms of transcendental proportions of being which are convertible with being itself, namely, in a form of transcendental concepts such as unity, truth, good, beauty, etc.: "Consequently, when we deal with a concrete existent thing we can speak about analogy of good, truth etc. The existent content is in itself a being which further forms an analogy of good, truth, or other principal properties of being."[79]

3. Principal Analogate as the Ultimate Source of Analogy of Being

The question which may arise here is: what is the reason for the analogical proportion of essence and existence in being? Why should the metaphysical analogy be based on pure transcendental properties of being? In other words, does the analogical structure of being understood metaphysically require an existence of any principal analogate which would form such Being in which there could be a complete identity of essence and existence? Again, in respect to these questions there is among the Thomists a serious controversy between the followers of Cajetan and those of Sylvester of Ferrara.[80]

Stressing the harmonious composition of being in its subordination to essence (*ens nominaliter sumptum*), Cajetan maintained that in the very structure of analogy of proportionality there is no need to have a reference to the principal analogate as a sufficient reason for the existence of analogical beings, because essential being is intelligible by itself and sufficient to determine the very nature of any being. Moreover, emphasizing the essential being as the subject of metaphysics, Thomas del Vio formalizes the concept of being, depriving thus all beings of participation in and relation to the *Maximum Esse* as to their ultimate source; in such a case analogy of being has only a proportional unity:

> The essential being appears to us as a pure essence when the relation to a *Maximum* results from an existent being. Consequently, Cajetan's concept of being possesses only a proportional unity without references to a numerically one *Maximum* being. The knowledge of essence in limits of analogy is only a source of a proportional unity.[81]

The proportional unity of being, however, can never give us the knowledge of the principal analogate, namely, God, and *de facto*, would mean ordering of things *ad infinitum*, destroying thus the whole order of *magis et minus*.

On the other hand, Sylvester of Ferrara, accepting "the concrete actually existent beings as a subject of metaphysics"[82] stressed the hierarchical structure of being and analyzed it under being of actual existence ("*sub esse actualis existentiae*").[83] In view of being so conceived the various proportions of things require the necessity of existence of the principal analogate as the ultimate source of participation of all beings, since if there is some gradation among things, then in their mutual ordering there must be a greater or lesser degree of being, then there ought to be an ultimate reference to *Maximum* Being, as the fundamental source which makes various degrees of being among things possible. Consequently, "every analogy results in a knowledge of principal analogate with reference to which analogical elements are graded. This principal analogate enters the definition of other, minor analogates."[84]

The controversy on the metaphysical analogy of being between the followers of Cajetan and those of Sylvester of Ferrara, consists, according to Krapiec, in making a sharp separation between essential and existential predication of being *qua* being, resulting "either in a step 'upwards' toward an absolute pantheistic monism, or in a step 'downwards' towards some kind of nihilistic existentialism."[85] In order to avoid in the metaphysical understanding of being *qua* being those reductionistic dangers, one must keep in mind that "a real order of essence has always implicit in it an existential order, and vice versa."[86]

In view of this mutuality of essential and existential order of reality, the metaphysical analogy of being cannot be based on the proportions which take place between things, but between their beings.

Referring to St. Thomas Aquinas *SCG* II.15, one is reminded that in perceiving a given really existing being:

> [W]e can distinguish in it the constituent elements as well as the ones that play no part in the constitution of that being. All that which constitutes a given thing may become the subject of definition and should be exhausted in a formal definition of an object.... All other, non-constituent elements demand an explanation why they should be present rather than absent in a particular thing.[87]

In other words, the constituent elements of a thing which enter into its definition do not need any further explanation, but any other non-constituent elements which, in fact, do appear in a thing require some additional explanation as to the very cause of their presence; in the former case things are unique and unrepeatable "for anything that does not differ in its constituents from a given thing must be that thing itself,"[88] but in the latter case, since the elements as non-constituents are found in many instances of things, they are contingent to them and come not from within but from without. Now from the metaphysical point of view, if being *qua* being is considered as a composition of essence and existence, and if the essential being is intelligible by itself, independently whether it exists or not, then the very act of existing which is found in any real thing requires causal justification for its own presence in reality.

The recognition then of the act of existing as a really real element of a concrete thing, on one hand, and its non-cognoscibility as a non-constitutive element which does not enter into a definition of thing, on the other hand, leads us to the necessity of conceiving metaphysical analogy in terms of variety of essences, considered, however, "*sub esse actualis existentiae.*" But, if things constitute a hierarchical order of *magis et minus*, and if this hierarchical order of *magis et minus dicuntur ad maximum*, then "the fact of existence of variety of essences is incomprehensible in metaphysics, unless we accept pure existence as *summum* of being forming a basis for relative, proportional state of existence in real, contingent beings."[89]

Our search for the ultimate source of the order of *magis et minus* of beings brings us finally to the conclusion that the proportional structure of being in its composition of essence and existence requires our accepting the existence of the principal analogate which justifies all the analogical perfections in individual analogates of contingent beings, and which becomes thus the ultimate cause of all things, not only in respect to the essential but also to the existential characteristics of their beingness, namely, the intrinsic as well as the extrinsic causes. Referring to the fact that plurality of things in the world needs predication *per analogiam*, St. Thomas summarizes his doctrine on God as the ultimate cause of everything in the following way:

> That which belongs to a thing by its nature, and not be some other cause, cannot be diminished and deficient therein. For if something essential be subtracted from or added to a nature, there will be at once another nature: even as it happens in numbers, where the addition or subtraction of unity changes the species. And if the nature of quiddity of a thing remain entire, although something is found to be diminished, it is clear that this does not depend simply on that nature, but on something else, through the absence of which it is diminished. Wherefore that which belongs to one thing less than to others, belongs to it not through its nature alone, but through some other cause. Consequently, that thing will be the cause of all in a certain genus, to which thing the predication of that genus belongs above all; hence that which is most hot is seen to be the cause of heat in all things hot, and that which is most light is the cause of all things that have light. Now God is being above all, as we have proved in the First Book. There He is the cause of all of which *being* is predicated.[90]

III: THE EXISTENTIAL ORDER OF BEING

Having established the analogical structure of natural things according to the order of *magis et minus*, it remains to analyze the notion of being as it is related to and constituted by the act of existing.

Being, according to St. Thomas, can be considered in two ways: as it is in itself or in relation to its manifold instances. Being considered in itself is a common predicate of all things and constitutes a specific order of community. Yet being considered in relation to its manifold instances is a subject of a particular thing and as such constitutes a definite order of diversity. In other words, being considered in itself is a principle of community and being considered in relation to its manifold instance is a principle of diversity. For this twofold characteristic of being the question is, what is the proper way of predication of being in regard to its diversity and community?

A: The Order of Diversity and Community

Two things sharing the same quidditative characteristics coincide with each other in regard to their essences, but they are diversified according to their being; for example, two men coincide with each other insofar as they have the same human nature, but they are opposed insofar as they constitute two different individuals. In *De Ente et Essentia*, the Angelic Doctor writes: "The quiddity of anything in a genus must be other than its act of existing, since the different beings within a genus or species have the same generic or specific quiddity or nature, whereas their act of existing is diverse."[1]

As a matter of fact, the opposite characteristics of being follow from the distinction which takes place between the essence and the act of existing. In the context of this distinction, essence is regarded as something which unifies different things by attributing to them the same nature and by constituting a specific order of community of things, both according to their real and cognitional being. The species 'man' and 'horse' in their cognitional being are different from each other, but in regard to their quidditative natures they are the same and constitute the genus animal. In reality, since only individuals exist, particular things are different according to their being and common according to the quidditative nature of their classes.

This function of being both a principle of diversity and of community, St.Thomas states as a necessary condition for predication.[2] Things have the same quidditative characteristics of their natures and as such they can constitute some community of essences. However, without difference in their being, this community of essences would be reduced to one and the same generic nature, and all things would lose their own identity and as such they would be reduced to one simple quiddity. This conclusion, which stays in an evident contradiction to the normal observation of things, can be avoided if we would accept that every particular thing realizes the common nature according to its own diverse way.

In which way are diversity and community of being a necessary condition of predication? Obviously predication requires a plurality of subjects according to which one nature can be predicated of another, such as the humanity of Socrates and Plato, etc. However, this plurality of subjects cannot be granted by the quidditative characteristics of things, because in the very structure of essence there is something which is common to many things. It remains then, that the plurality of subjects belongs to the act of being. On account of its actuality, being is a principle of the subjects in which it inheres according to different modes in particular things. In this sense, being as a principle of subjects is also a principle of diversity. Being is a principle of diversity because, in any individual case, being is that by which one thing is different from another. Two things cannot have the same being, no matter how much they would be similar to each other. In other words, being of a particular thing is incommunicable of itself.[3]

Predication, however, requires always some kind of universality. So, if being has to be predicated to all things, and if the intellect attributes to things not only the quidditative but also the existential characteristics of its being, then being itself must be considered as something universal and common to all things.[4] Consequently, being appears as the most common characteristic of all things, and as such it is the widest predicate of all that is. The being by which everything formally is, is common and is the ultimate principle of community of things.

What is the reason according to which being is the common predicate of all things that exist, and yet is to be diversified in each particular instance of being? These opposite characteristics of being seem to consist in different ways of predication of being. However, since the order of predication follows upon the order of being, and since in the order of being there is a twofold aspect of being, we have to distinguish a twofold mode of predication of being, that is, the predication of quidditative and existential characteristics. In a word, the difference which takes place between community and diversity of being lies in the fact that predication of being in its quidditative characteristics is concerned with the definition of thing, and the predication of being in its existential characteristics is indifferent to any definition.

The predication of being in its quidditative characteristics is accomplished by a definition of a thing, and as such is concerned with the question of what a particular thing is. The human mind, in predication of the quidditative characteristics of being, considers a thing independently whether or not it exists, and it can deliberate only that which is possible; for example, we can understand what is meant by humanity without knowing whether a man exists. This indifference in regard to the act of existing is a necessary requirement for a predication of being in its quidditative characteristics. St. Thomas proves this from the property of the act of existing as something ultimate in being.

The act of existing denotes actuality of a thing, and as such can belong only to an individual substance. Individual substance, however, in its individuality is, according to St.Thomas, inconceivable for the human mind, because our intellect is unable to understand and grasp that which is concrete as such. Even in sensible cognition we cannot cross over the apprehension of accidents. Therefore, the act of existing, belonging only to the individual substance, cannot be defined but only described and indicated as something that is. In other words, the act of existing does not include the universality which is needed for a definition of thing. In conclusion we might say that being predicated in its existential characteristics is indifferent to any definition of any kind.

Being predicated in its existential characteristics is not only indifferent to any definition of thing, but also undefined in itself. Otherwise, actuality by which the act of existing is meant would belong to all things in the same way, that is, to the thing and to its property, to the whole and to its parts, etc. In reality, however, there are different kinds of being. The multiplicity of being and the most common character of *esse* indicate that the act of existing is the greatest perfection of any thing, and as such it can be communicated to and included in all things intrinsically. But, since the actuality is the basis and foundation of everything that exists, it is prior to all particular beings. In a word, the act of existing, as the most general and universal property of being, cannot enter into the definition of thing either as a genus nor as a difference.

The notion of being is too simple to admit of definition. For a definition requires placing that which is to be defined into its genus and difference, being which is attached to all things cannot be enclosed within any particular genus nor be restricted by any specific difference.[5] Moreover, being cannot be a genus for every genus, because whatever is in a genus differs as to existence from the other things contained within the same genus.[6]

To sum up, a being as such can be considered in two ways: in regard to its quidditative and existential characteristics. Being considered in its quidditative characteristics is the most common predicate of all things and as such is attributed and communicated to everything that exists in whatsoever way. Yet being, considered in its existential characteristics constitutes many diverse subjects which in their actuality are incommunicable to each other. The order of diversity and community so considered can be analyzed according to its extension and comprehension. In the order of extension, being is considered as diversified in different instances of things according to the actuality of particular subjects: the more actual a thing is the more it has being. In the order of comprehension, being is considered as something common to all things according to the intelligibility of any thing that exists: the more being is, the more common is its range of intelligibility. In other words, being is considered in its diversity and community according to the reciprocally inverse *ratio* of extension and comprehension.

The Existential Order of Being

How is it possible for being to express both the diversity and community? What is the principle according to which being has these different characteristics?

In the very structure of any being, St.Thomas distinguishes between the act of being and that to which the act of being belongs. The act of being is the ultimate formal constituent of being as such (*esse*), and that to which this act of being belongs consists in being a subject of a particular thing. Whatsoever is the ultimate formal constituent of being as such, it is also the most proper principle of intelligibility of being, that is, *ratio entis*. But that which is a subject of a particular thing is also its own actuality. Now, being as it is considered in regard to its intelligibility is a principle of community, and being as it is considered in regard to its own actuality is a principle of diversity. In a word, being is the most diversifying principle of everything that has being, and is the most common principle of everything that is being. In conclusion we might say that being is the most common, because it is the most diverse thing in the whole reality.

Being, since it is a principle of both diversity and community, consists in an order of particular and universal *esse*. On the one hand, if being is considered in its diversity, it indicates that it is related to *esse* as to something which is diversified in each individual thing, and as such it establishes an *ordo ad esse particulare*, that is, as it is found in each particular being.[7] On the other hand, being, if considered in its community, is seen to be related to *esse*, but as to something which is universal in every being, and as such it establishes an *ordo ad esse universale*, that is, as it is found in every being.[8] In a word, being is an order both to particular and universal *esse*. Now, since in being there is an identity of common nature and the subject of which it is predicated, *esse* in a particular being signifies its act of existing, but as something which is qualified and limited by some specific determinations. The reason for this is that *esse* in a particular being is considered as something by which one being is diverse from another. But, to be different from another, *esse* must have something specific which would diversify it from all other being. These diversifying characteristics cannot come from *esse* itself, because *esse* as an act of existing cannot be differentiated as such. Yet *esse* can be diversified, but only by things other than itself. However, since in the very structure of any being there is only a composition of essence and its existence, and since *esse* itself cannot be diversified, it follows that the diversification of being comes from its essence. Consequently, *esse* can be diversified and distributed among beings as related to essence, and determined by some quidditative characteristics.[9]

Esse considered in its particularity accrues to being in a diverse way. Yet, since *esse* cannot be diversified as such, it is in itself indifferent to any limiting determinations. Moreover, *esse* itself is appropriate to natures that are diverse in species, but in itself it can be predicated of everything that is. *Esse* so considered is the widest predicate of all, free from all limiting determinations. But, predicable of every class, of every individual, *esse* exceeds all genera and species, and as such it is regarded as something universal and common in every being which is conceived by the intellect in its transcendentality.[10]

In view of the diversity and community of being, St. Thomas describes *esse* as something which can be attained by our intellect in a twofold way, namely, the way of composition and resolution. Being in the way of composition is "that which the intellect conceives first," so that "all other concepts are attained by adding to being."[11] Being in the way of resolution is that which the intellect conceives last and in which the intellect resolves all other concepts. In the former case, being is considered in its diversity, and in the latter in its community. Being attained by our intellect in the way of composition is considered in its diversity, because that which the intellect conceives first is being as found in particular things, and from which different modes of existing are expressed by adding to it something which is not expressed in the notion of being itself. Being attained by our intellect in the way of resolution is considered in its community, because that which the intellect conceives last is being to which a rational consideration terminates as to something which is common and universal to all beings.[12] But, since that which is ultimate in resolution is first in *esse*, being as something which is ultimate in the intellect must be first in reality.[13]

B: The Order of Community and Transcendentality

The order of diversity and community shows that being is predicated of things both in regard to their quidditative and existential characteristics. Now, the question which might arise is how to combine these opposite characteristics of being. What is the ultimate principle of the order of being? To understand St. Thomas's position we have to consider the notion of being as it is expressed by the relation of essence to existence. In general, essence is considered as the principle of unity, and being as the principle of plurality. Unity expresses being as it is individual in itself and diversified from all others, and plurality expresses being as it is universal and common to all things. Accordingly, the order of being would consist in a disposition of unity when being expresses the diversity of things by having something common, and it is a disposition of plurality when being expresses the community of things by diversifying it according to particular subjects.

Because unity and plurality follow upon being, the order of being has to be considered according to the modes by which being can be expressed in reality. Being considered in its plurality means an act of existing which is due to a determined subject and specified by having some quidditative characteristics. Being considered in its unity means an act of existing which is indifferent to any limiting determinations and can be predicated of everything that is. Now, this twofold characteristic of *esse* is a necessary condition for the predication of being in its transcendentality. To understand the reason why being should be considered under the aspect of both unity and plurality we have to consider the ways by which being *qua* being is attained by our intellect.

In the order of apprehension St. Thomas distinguishes two ways according to which being comes to our intellect, that is, by the acts of affirmation and negation. From these two follows the notion of being as conceived in its division and indivision: by division being is considered as *many*, and by indivision being is conceived as *one*.

Being, then, considered in itself can be described as some unity and plurality. The unity and plurality are the primary differentiae of being according to which being is considered in itself as *one* and *many*.[14] However, *one* and *many* signify being as the same, but under two different aspects. As signifying the same reality *one* and *many* are related to each other, but, as expressing being under two different aspects, *one* and *many* are opposed to each other.[15] Let us consider this twofold characteristic of being.

One and *many* include in their concepts being in general and add, over and above being, certain intelligible notes by which being is conceived as divided and undivided: "for just as thing is said to be one because it is not divided, so things are said to be many because they are divided."[16] Now *one* and *many* so considered are opposed to each other according to their intelligible essences (*rationes*) by which different modes of being are expressed.[17] *One* and *many* are opposed to each other because of a twofold kind of negation of division: the notion of *one* expresses a negation pure and simple, while *many* includes a negation which results from the fact that one thing is not another.[18]

One and *many*, however, as opposite notions do not exclude each other.[19] On the contrary, *one* and *many* correspond to each other[20] and express being in its division and indivision according to a specific order of intelligibility. In this order, being is understood as divided and undivided depending upon the intelligible aspect which our intellect can grasp, both in being's essence or things extrinsic to its essence: in the former, being is considered absolutely and, in the latter, relatively. In view of this distinction, St. Thomas can establish a twofold order of unity and plurality by which being can be considered as *one* and *many*:

1. As undivided absolutely and divided relatively, being is *many secundum quid* and *one simpliciter*, for example, as what is *one* in subject may have *many* accidents;
2. As undivided relatively and divided absolutely, being is one *secundum quid* and *many simpliciter*, for example, as what is *one* in species may be *many* in number.[21]

One and *many*, then, express being in diverse ways: by *one*, being is expressed as undivided, while *many* involves a division. Now, these two opposite notions of *one* and *many* signify the same reality and are included in the notion of negation.[22] In this way we can say that *many* follows on *one* which must be placed in its definition but not vice versa.[23] The reason for this is that *many qua many* cannot express being as divided unless each one of the divided things is conceived as being *one*.[24] Consequently, *one* and *many* are two intelligible aspects of being, but as contained under some unity: "For multitude itself would not be contained under being unless it were in some way contained under unity."

In view of the fact that being is either simple or composite, *one* expresses indivisibility of being in diverse ways "according to more or less."[25] Simple being is undivided both actually and potentially, while composite being is predicated as undivided after the fashion of the order which takes place between different elements of a particular being.[26] On the basis of the diversity of composition, St.Thomas establishes a specific order of unity and plurality: "It is apparent that the diversity of things requires that not all be equal, but that there be an order and gradation among things."[27] Consequently, being is a plurality, because of the varying proportions of essence and existence, and being is a unity, because of the similarity of all being in *esse*.

Having established the order of unity and plurality of being, the question which arises now is how being *qua* being can be analyzed in its community of *esse*. The community of being when it is related to the plurality of *esse* establishes an *ordo ad esse commune* according to different grades of entity which correspond to diverse modes of existing and by which the diverse genera of being are obtained. The community of being when it is related to the unity of *esse* establishes an *ordo ad esse commune* according to which some general modes of being are expressed and by which being is more clearly described under what is already contained in the very nature of being itself. The community of being considered in its plurality describes *esse* in a way according to which things have being, and the community of being considered in its unity describes *esse* in a way according to which everything that is, *is* being.

The community of being can be described as a plurality of *esse*, because things do not have being in the same way.[28] *Esse* is attributed to things according to a specific order. Because in a real being there is a composition of essence and existence, to *have* being means to *be* being according to the order which takes place between essence and existence of a particular being. The reason for this is that one element of being is in proportion to another: essence is ordered to an act of existing, and vice versa. Thus to *have* being means to *be* this or that being but as determined by the very subject of a particular thing. Hence, to *have* being means to *be* being according to various quidditative determinations of *esse*. In a word, being considered in its community is a plurality of *esse*, because among real beings there are many various proportions of essence and existence.

The community of being can also be described as a unity of *esse*, because every being insofar as it exists is similar to other beings. The similarity of all being in regard to the existence is the most general characteristic of being and by which the ultimate reality of *esse* is expressed. This is clear from the modes of existing under which being *qua* being is realized.

To *be* being *qua* being does not mean to *be* this particular being, because there are many other beings. To *be* being *qua* being is not also to be some definite genus or species, because besides one genus there are many other genera, for example, material and immaterial beings. Moreover, to *be* being *qua* being does not mean to be related only to some specific form of being, because being as such extends to everything that is. Hence, being *qua* being transcends all forms, genera and species, and describes the manifold modes of existing under the aspect which is common to every being, that is, that which is, *is*. Thus, being *qua* being is related to everything that is, because it surpasses any particular mode of existing. Being so considered is the most common predicate of everything that is, because it is the most transcendent characteristic of that which exists.[29]

The community of being considered in its unity and plurality of *esse* displays the transcendental structure of being *qua* being.[30] In this sense we can say that *esse commune* is *esse transcendentale*.[31] Now the question is, how being can be expressed in its transcendality. What can be said of being considered as something which is common to everything that is? To answer this question we have to analyze the way in which *esse commune* is attained by our intellect.

Esse commune as the ultimate principle of everything that is cannot be thought in a direct way by addition of some extraneous nature, in the way that a species is formed from a genus, or an accident given to a subject. The reason is that every nature is essentially being. And so being would be as a concept completed by being itself rather than by a *differentiae* outside itself. To avoid this tautology, St. Thomas describes *esse commune* as something which in its notion neither includes nor excludes any addition.[32]

This indifferent character of *esse* to any particular determinations is a necessary condition under which being can be predicated in its

The Existential Order of Being

transcendentality. Being itself contains the full range of transcendentality, because it is the first object envisaged by the intellect without which nothing can be apprehended by it. In the very nature of being so considered we can distinguish, however, some general modes of existing by which being *qua* being is described under certain intelligible aspects. These intelligible aspects, known as transcendental concepts of being, are common to all being, and are related to being in respect to its existential characteristics.

The question which may occur now is, how being can be described by particular transcendentals in its existential characteristics. In what way are being and the transcendentals related to each other? In other words, how are transcendentals found in the very structure of being, and yet can be compared to each other? In his *Commentary on the Sentences,* St. Thomas distinguishes two manners of explanation according to which being can be analyzed by transcendentals, namely:

1. With respect to subject(*suppositum*);
2. With respect to their concepts.[33]

Transcendentals considered with respect to their subject are seen to be mutually convertible because, as expressing the same thing under different aspects, they are identical in their subject (*ens*). But being identical in their subject, transcendentals are as broad as being itself. Consequently, whatsoever is said of being must be said of every transcendental. In this sense we might say that the transcendental *one* is being inasmuch as it is undivided, *true* is being as it is related to intellect, and *good* is being as it is related to will. In a word, transcendentals are identical with being as with something which expresses its existential characteristics through all kinds of being.[34]

Transcendentals, however, when analyzed with respect to their concepts are related to each other as expressing the different marks, viewpoints, and aspects of being according to a specific order of transcendentality. This order seems to lie in the propinquity of particular transcendentals to being because, as contained virtually in the concept of being, transcendentals emanate from being itself and reflect being from different angles either as proximate to or remote from the very structure of being itself. In this sense we might say that *one* is among all transcendentals the closest to being, because *one* expresses being in its absolute signification, that is, as it is expressed through an essence. After unity comes *true* and *good*, because they express being in its relative signification, that is, as when it is related to something external by which being is considered as participating certain positive perfections of the intellect and the will.[35]

To sum up, we might say that *esse commune* is the ultimate principle of the existential characteristics of being and consists in a specific order of unity and plurality. The reason for this is that *esse commune* is divided into *one* and *many*. Now, *esse commune* considered as an order of unity and plurality is seen to be *esse transcendentale*, because the order of unity and plurality of *esse* is something which surpasses all particular instances of being and contains everything that is, in whatsoever way. In a word, *esse commune* consists in an order of transcendentality.

C: *Transcendental Order of Predication*

Being consists in a disposition of *esse* in respect to both its diversity and community. Being so considered is a basis from which all transcendentals follow, according to a specific order of predication.[36] In this order we can distinguish a twofold kind of signification, namely, absolute and relative. Being considered in its absolute signification means an act of existing which is indifferent to any limiting determinations and can be predicated of everything that is. Being considered in its relative signification means an act of existing which is due to a determined subject and specified by some quidditative characteristics. Consequently, being when considered absolutely is a disposition of *esse* in respect to its community, and when considered relatively it is a disposition of *esse* in respect to its diversity. But, since the absolute signification is prior to the relative, and since the plurality presupposes the unity, the transcendental characteristics of being should be derived from the act of existing and not from that to which the act of existing is due.[37]

Although being itself cannot be defined, it can be described as that by which everything really exists, and can be known as something which is universal to every thing. Every being insofar as it exists is similar to every other being. This similarity of all being in regard to

The Existential Order of Being

their existence is the ontological foundation of the transcendental order of being. The question arises, how being can be expressed in its transcendentality. In the first article of the first question of the *De Veritate*, St. Thomas states that being can be expressed in two ways, namely:
1. As that which follows upon every being in itself;
2. As that which follows upon every being in relation to something else.

In view of this twofold way of expressing the general mode of being, let us consider more precisely the transcendental order of being according to the threefold element of any order.

1. The Order of Priority and Posteriority

The transcendental *one* is the first property of being, because it refers to being absolutely. The priority of *one* over all other transcendentals we can consider inasmuch as there are modes according to which the indivisibility of being is expressed. Because there are only two entitative constituents of being, *one* expresses its indivision either as considered in relation to existence or essence. This twofold way by which the indivision of being is expressed, St. Thomas derives from the fact that *one* considered in itself is indifferent to both essence and existence: "It makes no difference to the *one* whether it be referred to essence or to existence."[38] On the basis of this fact we can say that *one* expresses the indivisibility of being in two ways according to the order which takes place in the very nature of being between essence and existence. Consequently, the order of indivisibility as expressed by *one* is the same as the order of being considered in itself.

One is the transcendental predicate by which being is described in its existential characteristics as something undivided in itself.[39] In this sense St. Thomas insists against Avicenna[40] that *one* does not add to being any reality, because *one* simply means indivision of being itself: "*One* does not add any reality to being, but is only a negation of division; for *one* simply means undivided being."[41] *One* expressing the indivisibility of being is related to *esse*, because any division of being in respect to its existential act would turn being into nonbeing.[42] Hence, *one* is a mode by which being is preserved.[43]

One is a transcendental predicate which bespeaks being as undivided also in regard to its essence. In this sense St. Thomas can say that essence of a thing is *one* of itself, and not because of its act of existing.[44] However, *one* is expressed through essence, but when it is related to and realized by existence: "It cannot be absolutely called one essence, except where there is one existence; and this is where it is numerically the same essence."[45] Only through existential act can essence be one, because essence considered in itself does not have any being and unity whatsoever. In a word, *one* can be attributed to and expressed through essence, but only as when actuated by existence.[46]

One, then, is a transcendental predicate which bespeaks undivided being both as when expressed by existential act of being or through its essence. As expressed through being's essence, *one* has the meaning of substance itself.[47] But, as when considered in its relation to the existential act of being, *one* is more common than substance and transcends any category.[48] *One* so considered is really the same as being predicated analogically of everything that exists according to the principle: the higher and simpler a being is, the more it is *one*. Consequently, inasmuch as there are different grades of being there are various modes of unity.

The order of priority and posteriority can also be considered in regard to the modes of existing upon which the transcendental properties of truth and goodness follow. The transcendental *true* is a predicate toward what the intellect tends, and the transcendental *good* is a predicate toward what the appetite tends. Hence, the transcendental *true* reveals being in its relation to the intellect (*ordo ad intellectum*), and the transcendental *good* reveals it in its relation to the appetite (*ordo ad appetitum*).[49] In view of this order St.Thomas concludes that being is expressed by the transcendental *true* as something which is knowable, and by the transcendental *good* as something which is desirable.[50]

The transcendental *true* and *good* are related to each other and follow upon being according to a specific order of priority and posteriority. This order we can analyze either in respect to the existential act of being or in respect to its perfections. In the order of existential act, *true* precedes *good*, because "the true regards being itself absolutely and immediately."[51] In the order of perfections, however, *good* has priority over and above *true*, because the *good* perfects many more things than the *true*.[52]

The transcendental *true* is prior to the *good*, because "the true is more closely related to being which is itself prior to the good."[53] The priority of *true* over *good* the Angelic Doctor proves in two ways:
1. As considered in respect to the mode according to which *true* and *good* follow from being;
2. As considered in respect to the order as found between cognition and appetency.

On the one hand, *true* is prior to *good*, because of the different modes according to which they follow from being: *true* follows from *esse simpliciter*, and *good* from *esse secundum quod est aliquomodo perfectum*. Now, since *esse simpliciter* precedes *esse secundum quod*, *true* following from the primary perfection of *esse* is considered by our intellect as prior to *good*, which expresses being only in its secondary perfection of *esse*. Consequently, *true* precedes *good*, but insofar as it is related to and grounded in the very actuality of being.

The priority of the transcendental *true* over the *good* can also be proved by the difference between the cognitive and appetitive powers, namely, that of intellect and will. Analyzing the very nature of the cognition and appetency, St. Thomas states that the intellect is higher than the will. From the superiority of the intellect over the will, the priority of *true* over *good* follows. *True*, which corresponds to the order of cognition, is prior to *good*, which belongs to the order of appetency, because knowledge naturally precedes appetency. In the conclusion of the argument St. Thomas says: "Since the true is related to knowledge, and the good to the appetite, the true must be prior to the good according to reason."[54]

The transcendental *true* and *good*, however, can be analyzed not only in respect to the specific content of being, as when the conformity of being to the intellect and the will is expressed, but also in respect to the modes of general perfections by which being is considered in itself. For *good* is more universal than *true*, the perfection conferred by the *good* on being precedes that which comes from *true*. Hence, in the order of perfection *good* is shown as prior to *true*, because it expresses many more perfections of being than *true* according to the principle: each thing is perfect insofar as it is in act. In view of the different modes by which general perfections of being can be expressed, the transcendental *true* and *good* establish a specific order of priority and posteriority. This order St. Thomas considers both in their mutual reference and in their relation to being, namely:

1. When the perfections of *true* and *good* are conferred to each other;
2. When the perfections of *true* and *good* are conferred to being.

In each case the *good* appears to us as more important than the *true*, and more included in being itself. Hence, the transcendental *good* must be conceived as prior to *true* both in respect to the modes of perfections considered in themselves and in regard to the reference which they have to being.

The transcendental *good* precedes the *true*, because the perfection of *good* is more common than that of *true*. The perfection which corresponds to the transcendental *true* is not the perfection inherent to all beings, but a perfection which is received by way of perception. This kind of perfection we can find only among such beings which have some capacity for immaterial cognition, that is, the intellectual substances. Now, the perfection which is included in the transcendental property of *good* is proper to all beings and extends to all categories of being, because *good* is what pertains to being according to its immanent constitutive principles and its final cause.[55]

The priority of *good* over *true* can also be shown when their perfections are compared to being itself. The perfection appropriate to *good* is derived from participation in the very act of existing, and the perfection of *true* from participation in knowability of being. But, since cognition is posterior in the act of existing, it follows that, in the order of perfections, *good* should be prior to *true*.

In the order of *true* and *good* then, there is a mutual reference in which one transcendental stands to another: *true* is conceived as some *good*, and *good* as some *true*. This mutual reference of *true* and *good* is based on the different order according to which the intellect tends to truth as to some *good*, that is, *good* under the aspect of truth, and the will tends to goodness as to some *true*, that is, under the aspect of goodness. In the order of cognition the intellect precedes the will, and in the order of appetency the will precedes the intellect. A similar order happens between the transcendental *true* and *good*, because the intellect is perfected by *true*, and the will is perfected by *good*.

2. The Order of Distinction

The order of priority and posteriority always requires a definite distinction. The transcendentals following upon being according to a specific order of priority and posteriority must display some differences. But, since particular transcendentals express the general modes of existing as some intelligible aspects of being, the required distinction for the transcendental order of being is based on the different modes of signification. To understand, then, the order of distinction which takes place among particular transcendentals, we have to recall St. Thomas's doctrine of signification.

In the very structure of signification St. Thomas distinguishes between name as signifying something subsisting or simple. To signify something as subsisting we must use a name which is concrete, that is, that which is first of all and primarily the name of a *compositum* or *concretum*. To signify something as simple we have to use a name which appropriately belongs to the form whereby a *concretum* is what it is: such forms do not subsist by themselves. In view of this distinction, something is signified by a name either as contained in the very nature of a thing (*res significata*) or as related to the different modes of signification (*modi significandi*). Now, with reference to the mode of signification there is in every name a signification as of something which is abstracted from things according to the different intelligible aspects which our intellect can find in reality. Name, however, as signified of the nature of a thing has signification as something which is related not only to the intelligible aspects of a thing but also to its entitative properties.[56]

Now, transcendentals are the most common names under which our intellect considers the general modes of being in many different ways. But, since by means of a name we express things in the way in which the intellect conceives them, we ought to distinguish in the transcendental order of being a twofold mode of signification, namely, the logical and the ontological. In the logical mode of signification, being can be described inasmuch as there are different aspects under which our intellect can express being in itself. In the ontological mode of signification being is described in regard to its entitative properties which follow upon the existential act of being.

In the logical mode of signification, transcendentals are names which express being according to a twofold order of explanation, namely, absolutely and relatively. Being as considered absolutely expresses something either affirmatively or negatively: if affirmatively, being would be expressed by the transcendental *res*; if negatively, being would be expressed by the transcendental *unum*. Being as known in relation to every other being expresses something either in separation from another or in conformity with the mind: if being is considered in separation from another, it is expressed by the transcendental *aliquid*; if being is considered in conformity with the mind, it is expressed by the transcendental *verum* (when analyzed in conformity with the intellect) and by *bonum* (when considered in conformity with the will).[57]

In view of the logical mode of signification, transcendentals express being by adding a certain intelligible aspect, and signify different facets of being. The transcendental *res* expresses the intelligibility of being's essence, by which being has something positive in reality. The transcendental *unum* expresses the intelligibility of indivision by which being is conceived as undivided. The transcendental *aliquid* expresses the intelligibility of division, by which being is conceived as divided from others. The transcendental *verum* expresses the intelligibility of conformity of being to intellect. The transcendental *bonum* expresses the intelligibility of conformity of being to will.

In the ontological mode of signification, however, transcendentals express not only the intelligibility of being in abstraction, but also the intelligibility of being in concretion, that is, as expressing some entitative properties of being. [58]The reason for this seems to lie in the very fact that the transcendental properties of being follow upon the existential act of being and its essence. Now, the transcendental properties of being which accompany being wherever being is found follow upon its existential characteristics from the transcendental *unum verum*, and *bonum*. In the order of transcendentals so considered, *res* would be understood as identical with *ens*, and *aliquid* with *unum*. The transcendental *res* differs from *ens* in this, that the former expresses the quiddity of being, while the latter is taken from the very act of existing.[59] The transcendental *aliquid* is, on the other hand, identical with *unum*, because what is signified by "something" in an affirmative way is contained in what is signified by "one" in a negative way.[60]

Now, the transcendental properties of being are distinct from each other virtually and constitute a specific order of opposition, by which being is understood as having different intelligible notes. The reason for this order seems to lie in the manner of understanding being by which the intellect distinguishes in the very notion of being different modes of existing. In this sense we can say that unity, truth, and goodness are found in being as opposites, because they express *esse* in its integrity, conformity, and activity. Consequently, the order of the transcendental characteristics of being can be considered in regard to *one*, *true*, and *good* as they are contrasted to each other. First of all, the order of the transcendental characteristics of being can be considered in regard to the transcendental *one*, and then it consists in the integrity of *esse*, by which indivision of being is expressed. Secondly, the order of the transcendental characteristics of being can be analyzed in respect to the transcendental *true*, and then it consists in the conformity of *esse*, by which being is conceived as something knowable. Finally, the order of the transcendental characteristics of being can be traced in regard to the transcendental *good*, and then it consists in the activity of *esse* by which being is conceived as something desirable. In view of this threefold mode of existing, under which being is considered in itself and in relation to another, it is clear that the order of the transcendental characteristics of being is expressed and established by the principle of identity, sufficient reason, and finality.[61]

3. The Principle of the Order of Transcendentals

The transcendentals signify being in its existential act, but under different aspects. These different aspects are common predicates by which the transcendental characteristics of being are described in their diversity and community. The reason for this is that the transcendentals are the widest concepts of being in extension, and the most complete in comprehension. The transcendentals are the widest concepts of being in extension because they are attributed to everything that exists whatsoever. The transcendentals are the fullest concepts of being in comprehension because they are predicated of all things as notions which are included in the very act of being.

The *ratio* of the transcendental order of being consists of the very notion of being itself. But, since the notion of being bespeaks essence with relation to existence, the *ratio* of the transcendental order of being is established when being is considered in its *ordo ad esse*. Hence, in searching for the *ratio* of the transcendental order of being, we must consider its transcendental characteristics inasmuch as there are manners of understanding being by which different intelligible aspects of *esse* are expressed. But, since *esse* is a principle of both diversity and community, the *ratio* of the transcendental order of being can be analyzed in either way. The *ratio* of the transcendental order of being can be considered in respect to the diversity of *esse*, because the various transcendentals can be verified by every particular instance of being as found in reality. The *ratio* of the transcendental order of being can be considered in respect to the community of *esse*, because being is the first object found by the intellect in reality. Consequently, transcendentals are found in reality according to the manners of understanding being in its *ordo ad esse*.

Now the question which arises is, what is the principle of predication of being in its transcendentality? How is being *qua* being found in reality? In a word, what is the *ratio* of the transcendental order of being?

The *ratio* of the transcendental order of being has to be considered as it is expressed by and related to *esse*. But, since *esse* signifies both existential act of being and a subject possessing existential act,[62] the *ratio* of the transcendental characteristics of being can be considered in its relation to *esse* absolutely and relatively. The *ratio* of the transcendental characteristics of being is related to *esse* absolutely, as when they express some entitative properties which follow upon being as something which is expressed through essence, because essence is that by which being is a subject possessing the act of existing. The *ratio* of the transcendental characteristics of being is related to *esse* relatively, as when they express some entitative properties which follow upon being as something which is participated, because in the very structure of any created being the existential act is something which is received as a part of the whole being and as something which belongs to its very essence. In a word, the *ratio* of the transcendental characteristics of being is described in its relation to *esse*, which they follow upon existential act whether expressing the very nature of being *per essentiam* or *per participationem*.[63]

The very notion of being is the basis from which all transcendentals follow according to a specific order of succession. The successivity of transcendentals from being can be considered in two ways:

1. In respect to the various conceptual contents which transcendentals express in being;
2. In respect to the common element according to which transcendentals follow from being.

Now, the *ratio* of the transcendental characteristics of being would be established as an order of succession if the very nature of being and the transcendentals are found both in the manner of understanding and in the modes of existing.

In the order of succession there is a common element according to which all transcendentals follow from being. This common element consists in the existential act of being. The transcendentals follow upon the existential act of being, because essence considered in itself has no being whatsoever. But, since *esse* is predicated of things analogically, the transcendentals are following upon the existential act of being in different ways depending on the properties of the nature of being. Hence, the transcendentals are notions, the meanings of which never remain exactly the same in every instance of being and which are applied to things in a sense which is partly the same and partly different. In this sense we can say that all transcendentals admit of degree in their application to being, for example, one thing has more unity than the other, one thing is more true than the other, and one thing is more good than the other.

The transcendental characteristics of being are common predicates which contain different conceptual contents by which being is expressed in its existential characteristics in different ways. The diversity of conceptual contents of being constitutes an intentional order which arranges all transcendentals in a specific hierarchy of succession. This hierarchical ordering of transcendental characteristics of being can be considered in two ways:
1. As a hierarchy of ascent according to which particular transcendentals are successively derived from being: being--one--true--good;
2. As a hierarchy of descent according to which particular transcendentals are convertibly integrated to each other: the one is the identity of *esse*, the true is the conformity of undivided *esse* to the intellect, and the good is the actuality of undivided intelligible *esse* in relation to the will.[64]

*****

The *ratio* of the transcendental order of being, then, is established by the various ways of understanding the succession of the transcendentals relative to the act of being. This order of succession can be established both in regard to a harmonious proportion to the nature of being of which transcendentals are said to be, and in regard to a hierarchical ordering of ascent and descent of transcendentals to or from being. Finally, since transcendentals are predicated of being in the same way as *esse,* the *ratio* of transcendental characteristics of being consists in the order of proportion which is found between the essential and existential characteristics of being.

To sum up, the *ratio* of the transcendental order of being is related to *esse* as to something which expresses some actuality. The *ratio* of the transcendental order of being so considered can be attained by our intellect in a judgment in which being is conceived in its general modes of existing as *unum, verum, and bonum.*

IV: METAPHYSICAL ORDER OF BEING AND TRUTH

In the order of being and truth there is, according to Aquinas, a mutual reference based on their transcendental characteristics of reality. The Angelic Doctor analyzes this mutual reference of being and truth considered in their transcendentality not only in the cognitive but in the ontological order as well. In his analysis of the mutual reference between being and truth in their twofold order, however, Aquinas gives the priority to being over truth, if it is considered in the ontological order; but then he attributes the priority to truth over being if it is considered in the cognitive order.

This ontological interpretation of the classical description of truth as mutually related to being has received a contemporary and new existential explanation. This chapter presents the existential and ontological foundations of being and truth as exemplified in the metaphysics of *esse* by Aquinas and the ontological phenomenology of *Dasein* by Heidegger.

A: The Connotations and Meaning of Being

The term 'being' has many connotations and can be used in many ways. In general, we can distinguish two basic connotations, namely, nominal and original. The nominal connotation of being can be used either distributively or collectively, and the original connotation of being points to the formal meaning of being. The distributive connotation of being expresses its particularity, the collective its totality, and the original its constitutive element as it is expressed in itself.

The distributive connotation of being expresses the division found among individuals or individual groups of things, and it is expressed by adjectives such as: "each," "every," "either/or." Being, understood distributively, is taken in its full intention, that is, each man, each thing, each fact is some kind of being. Being, so understood, can - according to St.Albert - be applied to everything which exists either in reality or in the mind, thus establishing a specific order of transcendental characteristics of being in its oneness, truth and goodness.[1]

The collective connotation of being expresses a whole composed of individual things, namely, 'man' understood in the collective sense. Being, understood collectively, is taken in its full extension, that is, all things have "being" in common. Being, so understood, is the common characteristic of individual things which form some universality; St. Thomas comments:

> We use that which is called 'all' or 'every' when we are talking of discrete things; for example, as when we speak of 'every man' we use this expression [all] in speaking of these things which are continuous, which are closely linked to division, as for example when we speak of 'all water' and 'all air'.[2]

Distinguishing between distributive and collective connotations of being can help to disclose methodological difficulties in establishing the nature of metaphysics as both a particular and as a universal science of being. On the one hand, if 'being' should be taken only in its distributive sense, then reality would be viewed as some diversity, and metaphysics as such would be the most concrete and particular science of each individual being. One can find this in Bergson's treatment of intuition, which leads to the examination of someone's self as a pure duration of multiplicity and "by which one places oneself within an object in order to coincide with what is unique in it and consequently inexpressible."[3] On the other hand, if 'being' should be taken only in the collective sense, then reality would be viewed essentially as some unity, and metaphysics would become the most abstract and universal knowledge. This can be found in Hegel's idea of Mind, which represents the unity of Absolute Spirit.

Being, as a starting point for metaphysics, cannot be taken in its collective sense, because reality would be limited to conceptual unity as it is formulated by the human mind. Nor can being be taken only distributively, because it would be considered only in its particularity, namely, as it is found in each individual thing. Consequently, metaphysics based on being, understood either distributively or collectively would, from the very beginning, lead to some ambiguity between unity and plurality, community and diversity, between Parmenides's "all is one" and Heraclitus's "one is all."

This twofold logical connotation of the term 'being' demonstrates only the nominal definition of being, namely, how this word is used. However, the starting point for metaphysics should be being but as it is expressing itself, not as it manifests itself either in mind or in reality. The analysis of 'being as being' indicates that 'being' is understood as something by/through which being is *being*. In other words, metaphysics is concerned with the disclosure of the formal element of being which constitutes the very beingness of being.

In the notion of 'being as being', the formal element through which being is described in its beingness points to the very *origin*, the very source of things (*arche*). In a word, the formal meaning of being as expressing being's beingness becomes the original meaning of 'being' as it is expressed in/by itself. In searching, however, for the most original meaning of 'being', two different descriptions of being have been offered, namely:
1. A description of being as something which is taken from the very 'whatness' of things and expresses the factual essent of things;
2. A description of being as something which is taken from the very 'thatness' of things and expresses the actual existent of things.

A question now arises: which of these two descriptions of being explains the most original meaning of being? What is the most inner structural element of being through which reality is really real? In general, Heidegger has recourse to the intellectual experience of the Greek language and stresses the *factuality* of reality in being (the presence of being in things is taken for granted, namely, the 'thereness' of being in Being); while St. Thomas refers to the intellectual experience of the contingency of things and stresses the *actuality* of reality in being.

B: The Priority of Being

Heidegger derives the notion of being from the Greek verb *to einai* and says: "The first meaning of 'to on' refers to 'ta onta' (*entia*), the second to 'to einai' (*esse*)."⁴ Consequently, Heidegger gives priority to the element of preservation of things by which being can be something *factual*. Factuality of being does not mean existence because, as Heidegger points out, the Greek word:

> *Existasthai*, 'existence', 'to exist', meant for the Greek precisely nonbeing. The thoughtless habit of using the words of 'existence' and 'exist' as designations for being is one more indication of our estrangement both from being and from a radical, forceful, and definitive exegesis of being.⁵

Heidegger derives the meaning of 'being' from '*ta onta*' and not '*to einai*', because by the infinitive form of the latter, being is a vague concept: "the vagueness of this meaning finds its explanation: (1) in the blurring characteristics of the infinite, (2) in the mixture into which all three of the original stem meanings entered."⁶ In order to avoid the vagueness of the meaning of being we must start with concrete things which Heidegger calls *Daseiende*: "It starts from the essent and is oriented toward it. It does not start from being and does not enter into the questionable nature of *its* manifestness."⁷

Being, as indeterminate in itself, becomes determinate in a particular essent, that is, essent of people in a busy street, essent of Bach's fugue, essent of Strassburg cathedral, essent of Hölderlin poems. But being of essent is something which is discovered in opposition to nonbeing: "essents are always confronting us. We differentiate between their being-so and being-otherwise, we make judgements regarding being and non-being."⁸ To know, then, being as it is found in essent, we must compare its beingness with its nothingness.

For St. Thomas, however, the notion of 'being' is derived from the Latin verb *esse*: "nomen entis ab esse imponitur."⁹ St. Thomas, following Avicenna, describes being as it is expressed by *esse*, because our intellect derives the very notion of being from concrete apprehension of sensible qualities. So considered, being reveals two entitative aspects, namely, that of existence and that of essence.¹⁰ Consequently, St. Thomas gives priority to the element of emergence of things by which being is something *actual*. Actuality of being means existence, because *esse* means 'to-be', that is, something actually existent.

Esse, however, expresses being not only as something which is actually existent, but also as something which makes being factual essent, namely, as something by which being is so or otherwise. In other words, factuality reveals the essential characteristics of being by which it is found in different categories. Consequently, being is expressed as a composition of essence and existence.

Comparing St. Thomas's philosophy of *esse* and Heidegger's theory of *Sein*, one can conclude that basically both agree that the beingness of being should be the starting point of metaphysics. In his *Was is das — die Philosophie?*, Heidegger is quite close to Aquinas when he writes: "Philosophy seeks what being is, insofar as it is. Philosophy is en route to the Being of being, that is, to being with respect to Being...."[11] St. Thomas expresses the beingness of being as follows: "'being' does not signify 'quiddity' but only the act of existing."[12] However, the difference between St. Thomas and Heidegger consists in how each understands the very source of beingness in being, namely, in the original meaning of being.

For Heidegger, *Sein* is taken from *Seiende*; there is no basic difference between them. In *Vom Wesen des Grundes* Heidegger says: "Ontological 'difference' is the Not between being and Being."[13] Consequently, the very beingness of being is grounded in 'what-is', and in that which is identified with being itself, namely, as that through which a being is understood and found in reality.

For Aquinas, on the other hand, *ens* is taken from *actus essendi*, namely, from *esse* by/through which a being is really actual in reality. The link between *ens* and *esse* is so close that Aquinas describes being as "that whose act is to be,"[14] "that which coincides with to be."[15] In other words, being means that which is or exists (*esse habens*).[16] Consequently, *esse* as the *ratio entis* is not something which is identified with 'what-is', but it is the constitutive principle which, together with that 'what-is', makes things 'being-so' or 'being-otherwise'. Again, being as being is expressed by *esse* as a real composition of essence and existence.

The basic difference between St. Thomas and Heidegger consists in the way they treat *ratio entis*, that is, the beingness of being. Another question now arises: is this difference so significant that it makes these two metaphysical positions irreconcilable?

In Heidegger's doctrine on being there is some distinction between *Sein* and *Seiende*. *Sein* means Being as such, that is, as it is manifested to *Dasein*. *Seiende* means the same as Being but as it is involved in different kinds of beings:

All being is in Being. To hear such a thing sounds trivial to our ear, if not, indeed, offensive, for no one needs to bother about the fact that being belongs in Being. All the world knows that being is that which is. What else remains for being but to be? And yet just this fact that being is gathered together in Being, that in the appearance of Being being appears, that astonished the Greeks.[17]

But, this distinction between *Sein* and *Seiende* as the relation which takes place in regard to the position of being in Being has been, according to Heidegger, somehow evaporated from the human mind and has lost its original meaning. This, Heidegger calls *Seinvergessenheit*. This has also happened in regard to the distinction between essence and existence:

> The origin of the distinction between essence [*essentia*] and existence [*Existentia*], as being exactly the same as the origin of the distinction between various beings, has been hidden, or as expressed by the Greeks, 'forgotten.' Forgetfulness of being means this: the origin of the ontic distinction between 'whatness' and 'thatness' had been forgotten help Being, due to which each being comes to light as Being, but as Being it remains unquestioned. The distinction between 'whatness' and 'thatness' was not just another piece of learning in metaphysical thinking, this demonstrates also an achievement in the history of Being.[18]

Heidegger's *Seinvergessenheit* is, in fact, nothing else than St. Thomas's *Vergessenheit* of *esse*. A further question now arises: how to explain this obscurity of *esse* in being. In general, the forgetfulness of *esse* in being is due to the nature of metaphysical thinking.

In the very nature of metaphysical thinking there is some ambiguity in regard to the question of being.[19] Historically speaking, this ambiguity can be shown in Aristotle's uncertainty about the kind of knowledge of which metaphysics is comprised. On the one hand, his books of *Metaphysics* Aristotle calls *prote philosophia*, because they consider the first principles and first causes. On the other hand, the Stagirite calls it *teologike episteme*, because they treat the "most divine beings," namely, the substances which are separated from matter, especially the Pure Act or the Prime Mover.

The ambiguity of metaphysics in regard to being consists in some duality of its function, that is, as a science of being in itself and in its totality. But, since philosophy is a knowledge through ultimate causes, being in itself can be understood only in its relation to its totality. Consequently, metaphysics of *to on he on* (being as being), leads to the *trimiotaton genos* (the highest kind of being). In other words, metaphysics contains some ambiguity because it is a science about the connection between relative and absolute being.

In order to understand the connection between relative and absolute being, we must realize the situation of *esse* in being. Generally, *esse* is *in being* either as *esse ut actus* or *esse in actu*. On the one hand, if *esse* is in being as something which is as its own act, then such being is completely of its own nature, namely, as pure act. On the other hand, if *esse* is in being as something which is not of itself but through something else, then *esse* participates in being as in act. This same distinction is also found in Heidegger's *Nietzsche* where he writes: "*Esse* in distinction to *essentia* is *esse in actu*."[20]

C: The Authenticity of Truth

The two different metaphysics of being posited by St. Thomas and Heidegger result in two theories of truth, for truth follows being. If being is to be derived from factual essents (*das Seiendes*), then the truth of their beingness is to be discovered in the immanent order of human subjectivity, that is, in the existential structure of man's *Dasein*: "There is truth only in so far as *Dasein* is and so long as *Dasein* is."[21] In contrast, if being is to be taken from actual existents, then the truth of their beingness is to be found in the transcendent order of things themselves: "Truth is found more in being of things, than in quiddity."[22] In spite of this distinction, we find that the difference between the immanent and transcendent order of truth found in Heidegger and Aquinas respectively, does not pertain as much to the *"ratio veritatis"* as it does to the *"locus veritatis."*

1. The Order of Intelligibility of Being as Taken from an Actual Existent

St. Thomas defines truth as a disposition of being in which *esse* is expressed in its transcendentality: "The true is the order of a being, not as if adding some nature, nor as if expressing some special manner of being; but something which generally found in a being, which is not however expressed by the name of being."[23] Truth, however, expresses the transcendental characteristics of *esse* by adding to being some conformity by which there is a mutual reference between the knower and the thing known: "This is what the true adds over and above being, precisely conformity, or the adaquation of the thing and the intellect."[24] Consequently, truth defined as *adaequatio rei et intellectus*, consists of an order of intelligibility in which a threefold element can be distinguished: thing, intellect and relation. Thing and intellect constitute the material element of truth, while relation constitutes its formal element.[25]

This order of intelligibility (as it is expressed by transcendental truth), may be analyzed both in regard to the knower and in regard to the thing known. The reason for this is the fact that truth can be found both in the thing and in the intellect.

> The true is in things and in the intellect. However, the true which is in things is convertible with being according to substance, but the true which is in the intellect is convertible with being, as convertible with that which is manifested. This belongs to the meaning of the true. Although it could be said that a being is in things and in the intellect as the true, granted that the true is principally in the intellect, indeed being is principally in things. And this is the case because true and being differ in meaning.[26]

Thus, truth, considered in respect to the thing known, constitutes an *ordo cognitionis*, expressible by the principle: *modus cognoscendi sequitur modum essendi*. But, truth, considered in reference to the knower, establishes an *ordo intellectuum*, expressible by the principle: *modus operandi sequitur modum essendi*. In view of this distinction, the order of intelligibility can be considered in the two following ways:
1. as an order of cognition (*ordo cognitionis*);
2. as an order of intellectuality (*ordo intellectuum*).

a. *Ordo cognitionis*

Cognition consists in a relation which takes place between the knower and the thing known: "Every cognition happens through the union of the thing cognized and the one cognizing."[27] This relation occurs when a thing becomes known by the knower according to his manner of knowing because "the mode of cognition follows the mode of the thing which cognizes."[28] There are many different manners according to which a thing may be known by the knower.[29] St. Thomas further distinguishes the twofold order of cognition as:
1. the order of sensible cognition; and
2. the order of intelligible cognition.[30]

As such, this twofold order of cognition is now examined in view of the threefold element of order: priority and posteriority, distinction, and principle.

The order of priority and posteriority in cognition is twofold, and is considered both in reference to reason and to the senses. But, since a thing is known through its principles and according to its nature, the priority and posteriority in cognition should be understood in an absolute sense rather than in a qualified way.[31] In a word, in the order of priority and posteriority, what is essential is always prior to what is only accidental. St. Thomas now considers three ways by which something is prior in cognition:
1. in regard to singularity and universality of things;
2. in regard to intelligibility of things; and
3. in regard to attributes of things.

First of all, in the order of cognition the act of reason is prior to that of sensation, because reason first knows universals, and the sense singulars. In this order the senses know universals only accidentally inasmuch as they know the singular of which the universals are predicated; for example, the senses know man inasmuch as they know Socrates, who is a man, while reason knows Socrates inasmuch as it knows man.[32]

Secondly, in the order of cognition reason is prior to sensation, because reason first comprehends the attributes of things, and senses first perceive a composite. In this order reason first knows the attributes of things, because in the order of intelligibility, an attribute is prior to the whole; for example, 'musical man' cannot be known without understanding the meaning of the part 'musical'. Accordingly, senses first perceive a composite, because composite things are first offered to the senses;[33] for example, looking at the landscape the eye first sees a generalized impression, and only later it is able to determine various details.

Finally, in the order of cognition reason is prior to sensation, because reason first recognizes the attributes of prior things and senses discern the character of the attributes of a composite. In this order reason first comprehends attributes of prior things, because they are prior to that of composites; for example, straightness is said to be prior to smoothness, because straightness is an essential property of line while smoothness is a property of surface; thus, a line is naturally prior to surface. But from the viewpoint of grasping by the senses, surface is prior to line, and the attributes of composite things are prior to those of simple ones.[34]

Having established the priority and posteriority of sensible and intelligible cognition, St. Thomas considers the distinction which occurs between different cognitive powers. As a matter of fact, a man does not apprehend anything through his own essence, but through the faculties of his soul. The faculties of his soul, however, are distinct from man's essence. In this sense St. Thomas says: "Intellect is a certain power of the soul, and the very essence of the soul."[35] St. Thomas derives the reason for this from the relation which occurs between cognition and being. In general, cognition is related to intellect as existence is to essence, because cognition is an act of intelligence as existence is an act of essence.[36]

In the structure of the soul there are several faculties which are subordinated to particular objects. Between the object and the corresponding faculty there is a specific order of passive and active powers of the soul. If the object is the active principle and the cause of some movement, the corresponding faculty is passive and a subject of its activity; for example, light is the source of sight in the eye. But, if the object is a term and an end of some activity, then the corresponding faculty is active and principal cause of this activity. Applying these principles to the faculties of the soul we would have the following gradations:

1. The vegetative powers are active, because they change the food into nourishment;

2. The sensitive powers are passive, because they are changed by their objects; and
3. The spiritual powers are either passive or active, because the intellect itself is partly passive and partly active.[37]

But, cognition consists in a specific order of cognitive powers according to the principle: "to the degree that a given form is more noble and simple, to the same degree it will possess greater ability."[38] This order constitutes some unity and plurality of powers in which the higher faculty governs and rules the lower one.[39] The reason for this order seems to lie in the fact that every being, besides God, is composed of act and potency. But, since potency is related to act, all cognitive powers are diversified by and dependent upon each other inasmuch as there are different objects: "It is still the case therefore that the distinction among the powers of the soul is in accordance with the distinction of objects."[40]

Summing up, it can be said that the order of cognition consists of a mutual relation between the knower and the thing known. This order of cognition results in a specific arrangement of cognitive powers in which there are gradations of being and knowing. St. Thomas establishes the order of cognition according to the distinction which takes place between sensible and intelligible ways of apprehending.[41]

b. *Ordo intellectuum*

Transcendental truth, when considered in respect to the intellect, constitutes a specific order of intellectuality. Intellectuality itself is defined by St. Thomas as a rational knowledge: "intellectuality results from immateriality."[42] In general, the order of intellectuality consists of a relation which takes place between the subject and the object of knowledge.[43]

All knowledge takes place through the assimilation of the knower and the things known: "knowledge is the assimilation of the knower and the thing known."[44] As the result of the assimilation process there is a description of a thing known in the intellect: "knowledge is nothing other than the description of things in the soul, for knowledge is said to consist in the knower and the thing known."[45] But, since knowledge is in the intellect, assimilation which takes place between the intellect and the thing known consists in a disposition of the subject and the object of knowledge:[46] "[knowledge] is the ordered collection of the species of those things which exist in the intellect; they are not according to completed act, but found only between potency and act."[47]

In the very nature of knowledge, then, there is a mutual relation of the knower and the thing known according to a specific order of assimilation.[48] The question which might arise now is: what is the principle of the order of assimilation? To answer this question, one must consider the conditions under which the integration of the subject and object of knowledge takes place.

In the very structure of knowledge there is a specific order of intelligible species:[49] "the disposition found in the intellect appear to be nothing other than the species of intelligibles with it."[50] The reason for this order seems to lie in the manner of understanding by the intellect:

> one cannot understand a given thing unless he is assimilated to it through the intelligible species. Hence intelligible species must be added over and above, so that the intellect passes through them into act; the disposition of species must be brought about by some act of ordering.[51]

However, an intelligible species consists in a disposition of the intellect and the thing known in two ways:
1. as considered in regard to the subject of knowledge; and
2. as considered in regard to the object of knowledge.

An intelligible species, when considered in regard to the subject of knowledge, is some entitative modification of the intellect itself; while considered in regard to the object of knowledge, it is a formal aspect of the thing known by the intellect.[52] From this, another question arises: what is the principle of the order of knowledge when considered as a disposition of intelligible species?

Knowledge constitutes some unity out of plurality in which the thing known is related to and integrated with the intellect in many different ways: "the knowledge of one who understands is integrated from many things which are known."[53] Distinguishing between material and immaterial *esse*,[54] St. Thomas states that knowledge constitutes a unity of the knower and the thing known in a way of immaterial being. The reason for this is that matter is a principle of individuation by which perfections of one being are separated and excluded to others.[55]

Intelligible species, then, consists in some unity of the subject and the object of knowledge according to a specific order of immateriality.[56]

In this order the intellect and the thing known are related to each other in many different ways. St. Thomas distinguishes two kinds of operation by the intellect in regard to the thing known, namely:
1. the operation by which the content of a thing is expressed in a concept; and
2. the operation by which the intellect reflects on its action.[57]

On the basis of this twofold operation of the intellect, St. Thomas now distinguishes two kinds of intellectual order:
1. that which is discovered by the intellect in things themselves; and
2. that which is included in the intellect as such.

The order considered as discovered by the intellect consists of such relations as those which the intellect attributes to external things as they are found in the consideration of the reference of one thing to another, for example, the relations which occur between species and genus. The order considered as included in the intellect itself consists of such relations as those which follow from the manner of intellectual cognition, for example, the relations which occur between things as conceived by the intellect.[58]

2. The Order of Comprehensibility of Being Taken from a Factual Essent

Being, understood as predicated from an actual existent, reveals its truth as a result of the mutual disposition of the intellect and the thing known according to the principle that "the intelligible in act is the intellect in act."[59] Acknowledging the view of truth as some disposition of the knower and the thing known, Heidegger, however, wants to be more specific as to the very *locus veritatis*. Referring to Aristotle's doctrine on truth, Heidegger defends the Stagirite from a narrow understanding of truth as a simple judgment (*hypolepsis*) and says: "Aristotle never defends the thesis that the primordial 'locus' of truth is in the judgment."[60] The *locus veritatis* is, according to Heidegger, *Dasein*.

For Aristotle, *logos* has a double function, namely, both to uncover and cover up human existence (*Dasein*), and in this way making Being to be true. But in his interpretation of *noesis*, Aristotle reduces *logos* to *aisthesis* and stresses only the function of *dianoein*, omitting the element of *noein* itself. In view of this, one must distinguish in the order of *noesis* between *nous* and *noein*, both of which enable *logos* as *dianoein* to function in uncovering truth in Being. *Nous*, Heidegger renders by the German noun *Vernehmung*, *noein* by the verb *vernehmen*. In the English translation of *Einführung in die Metaphysik*, the aforementioned terms have been translated as follows:

> *Noein* means *vernehmen* (to apprehend), *nous* means *Vernehmung* (apprehension), this in two senses that belong together. To apprehend means to accept, to let something (namely that which shows itself, which appears) come to one. *Vernehmen* means also to bear a witness, to question him and so determine the facts, to establish how the matter stands. To apprehend (*vernehmen*) in this twofold sense means to let something come to one, not merely accepting it, however, but taking a receptive attitude toward that which shows itself. When troops prepare to receive the enemy, it is the hope of stopping him at the very least, of bringing him to stand (*zum Stehen bringen*). This receptive bring-to-stand is meant in *noein*.[61]

Linguistic analysis of *noein* and *nous* allows Heidegger to interpret *noesis* as a process of occurring of being, which is also the most dominating element in the whole realm of apprehension. And, although man is not included directly in the process of *noesis*, then, in order "to participate in this appearing and apprehension, he must himself be, he must belong to being. But the essence and the mode of being-human man can only be determined by the essence of being."[62]

Dasein, however, apprehends not only being but also Being. In order to understand this twofold apprehension by *Dasein*, the following questions must be raised:
1. What is the ontological difference between being and Being;
2. What kind of being belongs to *Dasein*; and
3. How are beings and Being uncovered by *Dasein*?

a. What is the Ontological Difference between Being and Beings

By 'ontological difference', Heidegger understands a negation (*das Nichts*), which takes place between being and Being. Negation, which here is taken as a constitutive element of an ontological difference, is not just a privation; on the contrary, it is a condition which allows Being to appear in beings. The 'not' in the constitution of an ontological difference is, then, the negation that beings are not Being. Nor is the 'not' a separation since Being is taken from beings. Consequently, the 'not' as an ontological difference between beings and Being is "merely a distinction of the intellect (*ens rationis*);"[63] but one which enables *Dasein* to apprehend things as beings in opposition to Being; the former constitutes the ontical order of reality and the latter the ontological order of reality. In Heidegger's words: "Nothingness is the Not of being and thus is Being experienced from the point of view of being. The ontological difference is the Not between being and Being."[64]

The ontological difference between beings and Being conceived as a twofold negation is, according to Heidegger, the precondition for truth, that is, by making our thinking about beings and Being possible:

> We speak of the *difference* between Being and beings. The step back goes from what is in thought, from the differences as such, into what gives us thought (*Das-zu-Denken*). That is the *oblivion* of the difference. The oblivion here to be thought of is the veiling of the difference as such, thought in terms of *lete* (concealment); this veiling has in turn withdrawn itself from the beginning. The oblivion belongs to the difference because the difference belongs to the oblivion. The oblivion does not happen to the difference only afterward, in consequence of the forgetfulness of human thinking.[65]

But, if the Being of beings consists in an ontological difference as such, then what is the very foundation for truth? Answering this question Heidegger says:

> Being manifests itself as thought. This means: the Being of beings reveals itself as the ground that gives itself ground and accounts for itself. The ground, the *ratio* by their essential origin are the *logos*, in the sense of gathering of beings and letting them be. They are '*hen panta*'.[66]

However, Being as the ground for beings is by the same token the ground for their concealedness and unconcealedness, namely, truth:

> Being shows itself in the unconcealing overwhelming as that which allows whatever arrives to lie before us, as the grounding in the manifold ways in which beings are brought about before us. Being as such, the arrival that keeps itself concealed in unconcealedness, is what is grounded; so grounded and so generated, it in turn grounds in its own way, that is, it effects, it causes.[67]

This "double" status of truth leads to the question of the ground for the transition from concealedness to unconcealedness. In Heidegger's view, this ground requires a specific "realm of transcendence"[68] which he founds in the uniqueness of human *Dasein*.[69]

b. What Kind of Being Belongs to **Dasein**

Defining 'transcendence' as 'surpassing' (*Überstieg*), Heidegger does not understand by it a characteristic which could possibly be a property either of objective or subjective beings, and as such, it cannot be described as a 'subject-object relationship': "Transcendent *Dasein* (a tautological expression in itself) surpasses neither a 'boundary' which stretches out before the subject and forces it to 'remain in' (immanence) nor a 'gap' which separates it from the object."[70] Consequently, *Dasein* is the *locus veritatis*:

> Transcendence can be understood ...as signifying what is unique to *human Dasein* — unique not as one among other possible, and occasionally actualized, types of behavior but as a *basic constitutive feature of Dasein that happens prior to all behavior.*[71]

More questions arise: how is transcendence interwoven with *Dasein*? In what sense is transcendence the constitutive element of *Dasein*? More precisely, how does *Dasein* disclose its own being?[72] These questions presuppose a twofold order of human reality: the ontological order of *Dasein* and the phenomenological order of *Dasein*. Since ontology and phenomenology are not separated from each other for Heidegger, then his philosophy "takes its departure from the hermeneutic of *Dasein*, which, as an analytic of *existence*, has made fast the guiding-line for all philosophical inquiry at the point where it *arises* and to which it *returns*."[73]

The hermeneutic of *Dasein* points to its two constitutive elements, namely, the "essence" and the "issue of which *Dasein* constitutes its entity." The "essence" of *Dasein* must be sought in its "to-be" (*Zu-sein*), which Heidegger defines as *Existenz*: "*The essence of Dasein lies in its Existenz.*"[74] *Existenz* is exclusively an attribute for the human *Dasein* by which Heidegger does not understand a simple property or pure quality but a unique state of human *Dasein*, that is, a state "towards-to-be." In a word, *Existenz* is understood as such as an ecstatic essence through which *Dasein* is "standing out" in a sense of being open to Being itself.[75]

Existenz, the very "essence" of *Dasein*, also constitutes an issue for *Dasein's* entity in which its own being is revealed and through which I am myself. Mineness, as an issue for the entity which comports itself to its being, indicates that *Dasein* consists of its own possibility (*Möglichkeit*).[76] But, since *Dasein* can also realize its own possibility, it is its own transcendence:

> In surpassing, *Dasein* first attains to the being that *it* is; what it attains to is its 'self'. Transcendence constitutes selfhood. On the other hand, not only transcendence, but also surpassing, touches on a kind of being that *Dasein* 'itself' is not. More accurately: only in and through surpassing can we distinguish and decide, within the realm of being, who and how a 'self' is and what it is not.[77]

The hermeneutic of *Dasein* leads to a phenomenology of truth. The ontological difference of *Dasein* between how its "self" is and what it is not, is the foundation for establishing *veritas transcendentalis*. But, since transcendence indicates that *towards which* surpassing happens, then the question is what is in *Dasein* that is transcending? Heidegger answers:

> That *towards which Dasein* transcends, we call the world; and we can now define transcendence as *Being-in-the-World*. World goes to make up the unified structure of transcendence; the concept of world is called *transcendental* because it is part of this structure.[78]

"Being-in-the-World" as the transcendental characteristic of human *Dasein* is, by the same token, the transcendentality of the world which "reveals itself to *Dasein* as the actual totality of what exists for the sake of *Dasein*."[79] In other words, not only *Dasein* itself is transcendental, but the world in which *Dasein* is has transcendental characteristics within *Dasein's Existenz*. However, if both *Dasein* as "being-in-the-world" and the world itself have transcendental characteristics in their ontic and ontological foundations, then transcendence conceived as surpassing is essentially freedom: "Surpassing to the world is freedom itself."[80]

Heidegger defines freedom as causality, but understood as "the origin of reasons (*Ursprung von Grund*)"[81] and their mutual relationship as *Gründen* (grounding). *Dasein's* freedom has "many ways of grounding"[82] both beings and Being; so understood, Heidegger calls grounding *Be-Gründung* (foundation). Grounding as foundation reveals beings in an order of ontical truth, and Being in an order of ontological truth.[83] In the conclusion of his understanding of grounding as the foundation for both ontical and ontological truth, Heidegger says:

> Thus we see that the 'birthplace' of the principle of sufficient reason lies neither in the essence of the assertion nor in its truth, that is, in transcendence itself. *Freedom is the origin of the principle of sufficient reason.* For founding, expressing itself as ontological truth is grounded in freedom, the unity of outstripping and deprivation.[84]

c. How Beings and Being are Uncovered by **Dasein**

The classical theory of truth defines it as the rightness of a thing. This rightness of a thing is based on the principle of the intelligibility of being, namely, every being to the extent that it exists is intelligible. In view of this principle, the more being is, the more intelligible it is. However, this principle of intelligibility requires a representation of this rightness of a thing to a human mind. Representation of the rightness of a thing to the mind demands an openness on both sides which consists of a mutual possibility of communication between the knower and the thing known. For Heidegger, such a possibility is nothing else but freedom: "The essence of truth is freedom."[85]

As the very essence of truth, freedom can be shown in the original understanding of the Greek word *'aletheia'*. *'Lethe'* means: hiddenness, concealment, coveredness, veiledness; and *'a-'* means 'privation'. In translation, truth as *'a-letheia'* means un-hiddenness, un-concealedment, disclosure, discovery, re-velation. Truth, then, is basically an un-covering of that 'what-is'. Un-covering of that 'what-is' means 'letting-be' of being as it is, allowing 'to-be' in its right way of being. Allowance of something 'to-be' in its right way of being is nothing else but leaving it free as it is in itself, namely, freedom.[86]

Thus, truth is an existential dimension of *Dasein*: "Being-true as Being-uncovering, is a way of Being for *Dasein*."[87] Heidegger analyzes the phenomenon of truth as an un-covering of *Dasein's* "Being-in-the-World:" "Uncovering is a way of Being for Being-in-the-World."[88] By un-covering, "*Dasein* is in the truth."[89] In view of the identity between truth and *Dasein*, truth is not disposed by man but man is disposed by truth.

In view of the fact that truth follows being, the search for an ultimate foundation for freedom would depend on the way of understanding being itself. As we saw, there are two ways of understanding the meaning of being, namely, as factual essent (Being taken from being), and as actual existent (Being taken from 'to-be'). If we understand Being as a factual essent, this indicates that the presence of beings in Being is self-evident and taken for granted, that is, as the 'thereness' of beings in Being. Whereas, if we understand being as an actual existence, this indicates that the contingency of beings in Being is the sufficient reason for their 'to-be'. Consequently, truth following Being, understood as factual present in reality, consists of the immanent characteristics of being in human subjectivity, namely, in human *Dasein*. Whereas, truth following Being, understood as actual existent points to the transcendental characteristics of Being as such.

* * * * *

As the above comparison between Heidegger's and St. Thomas's doctrines on being and truth has shown, there are many similarities in these two great philosophers. To begin, both of them stress the necessity of finding "the ground of truth of Being" in transcendence; each bases his respective philosophy of being on one perennial question: What is all that which is? Moreover, Heidegger seems to follow Aquinas's stand that "the soul in a certain sense is all things"[90] by stressing the immense possibility of human *Dasein* in "opening-up" the infinite realm of beings which are "gathered together in Being."[91] Furthermore, Aquinas would agree with Heidegger that in the process of 'un-covering' Being in beings, we must enter into our own *Dasein* when he says that the true and false are part of the inner structure of *Dasein*.[92] Heidegger is in complete agreement with St. Thomas who, following Aristotle,[93] says:

> Since the true and the false are opposed, and opposites concern the same thing, it is necessary to first seek for falsity in the intellect;

neither falsity nor truth is in things, except through order to the intellect.[94]

By contrast, however, when comparing Heidegger and St. Thomas, one cannot overlook the differences between their views on the ultimate foundation of truth. The Angelic Doctor argues: "truth is in the divine intellect properly and primarily, it is in the human intellect properly and secondary; it is in things as not being proper to the things and in a secondary way, since there is no truth except of one in respect to other."[95] For Heidegger, however, such a metaphysical position has *"onto-theologische Verfassung"* which "becomes questionable for thinking, not because of any kind of atheism, but from the experience of thinking which has discerned in onto-theo-logy the still *unthought* unity of the essential nature of metaphysics."[96] Any student of Heidegger is familiar with his uncertainty as to the very structure of metaphysics and his various attitudes toward the philosophy of God. Nevertheless, insofar as the question of Being and beings is concerned, Heidegger admits:

> The onto-theological constitution of metaphysics stems from the prevalence of that difference which keeps Being as the ground, and beings as what is grounded and what gives account, apart from and related to each other; and by this keeping perdurance is achieved.[97]

PART C:

THE IMMANENT ORDER OF BEING

INTRODUCTION

Unity and plurality of things follow upon their being, which St. Thomas analyzes as a composition of essence and existence. The order of unity and plurality of being, then, would consist in a disposition of essential and existential characteristics.

The usual term used by Aquinas for being is *esse*. But *esse* expresses real things analogically according to different modes of being, either in regard to its harmonious constitution or hierarchical gradation. The natural order of unity and plurality of things, then, will depend on finding the proper disposition of immanent and transcendent characteristics of being.

I: THE ORDER OF BEING AS HARMONY AND HIERARCHY

In view of St. Thomas's doctrine of the real composition of essence and existence, the order of being both in its harmonious constitution and hierarchical gradation of things would lead the Angelic Doctor to emphasize the existential and transcendental character of reality while Duns Scotus would insist on the essential and immanent order of being. In order to see the different ontological position of St. Thomas and Duns Scotus, one has to compare their appropriate doctrines on being as expressed by the relation of essence and existence according to the threefold element of any order, namely: (1) that of priority and posteriority, (2) that of distinction and composition; (3) that of principle and foundation (*ratio ordinis*).[1]

A: The Primacy of Esse

That which is the most formal in every being St. Thomas describes as *esse*: "that which is the most formal of all things is being itself."[2] The Angelic Doctor calls *esse* then what is innermost in each and every thing, and that which is deepest in them all, because it is formal in respect of all that is in a thing.[3] In this sense Aquinas considers *esse* as including in itself every perfection of being: "being is the most perfect of all things."[4] The reason for this is that *esse* of itself is free from every determination and does not imply any restriction in being. But *esse*, as the most formal and the most perfect in being, is nobler than everything that follows upon it.[5]

The reasoning which establishes the absolute priority of *esse* over essence can help us to discern a similar distinction in the cognitive order. Again, that which makes being knowable is not its essence but its existence. If a thing would not have an act of existing, it would not be known at all. Consequently the human intellect grasps the very nature of being through the aspect of *esse* conceived in its priority over essence.[6] In conclusion we might say that *esse* is absolutely prior to essence, because it is the ultimate formal constituent of being and the principle of intelligibility.

Esse, however, expresses being as its ultimate formal constituent only as an actual existent: "that which I call being is the actuality of all acts, and for this reason it is the perfection of all perfection."[7] The reason seems to lie in the fact that when *esse* is predicated of everything it must be free from any kind of limiting determinations. As a matter of fact, that which constitutes being as being must extend to all species, kinds, and modes of being. But that which is the ultimate formal constituent in all that is, cannot be essence, because essence involves potentiality which is the source of limitation in being. In a word, *esse* is the ultimate formal constituent of being, because it is the being's act of existing.

Esse considered as some actuality is the principle of intelligibility of being because as St. Thomas says: "A thing is intelligible insofar as it is in act . . . , hence the nature or quiddity of an object can be understood precisely because it is an act. For the act is that because of which a nature obtains its intelligibility."[8] But, since that by which a nature is constituted, and that by which a nature is understood, have a relation to each other, it follows that this nature cannot be understood without the other.[9] In view of this it is clear that the intellect cannot understand one element without the other, because that by which the nature is understood is that by which the nature is constituted. But, since that by which the nature is constituted is the act of existing, it follows that it is also that by which being is understood.

For St. Thomas then, the notion of being is derived from the act of existing: "The term 'being' is taken from the act of existing."[10] Whatsoever is said about being, it is necessarily related to its act of existing: "being does not mean 'quiddity' but only the act of existing."[11] The link between *ens* and *esse* is so close that Aquinas describes being as "that whose act is 'to-be',"[12] "that to which belongs being."[13] In a word, being means that which is or exists.[14]

Now *esse* can express the very nature of being at least in two ways, namely, as something which comes first in everything that is, and as something which makes a thing an actual being.[15] *Esse* expresses being as something which comes first in every thing that is, because it is something which is presupposed by all others: "the very first effect is being itself, which is presupposed in all other effect, and which itself does not presuppose any other effect."[16] *Esse* expresses being as something which makes a thing an actual being, because it is something which is the very act of subsisting forms: "Being itself is the act of a subsisting form."[17]

When we turn now to Duns Scotus we can see that in the doctrine on being the Subtle Doctor identifies *esse* with essence: "being is really the same as essence."[18] The identity of *esse* and essence is so close that there is between them only a mental distinction: "essence and being differ only in reason."[19] Moreover, the intelligibility of being is possible if it is accessible to our intellect in its essential characteristics: "everything which is *per se intelligibile* either essentially includes the reason [*ratio*] of being, or is contained either virtually or essentially in the reason [*ratio*] of being."[20] Identifying *esse* with essence Duns Scotus proclaims the primacy of essence over existence both in the cognitive and entitative order of being.

In the cognitive order Duns Scotus agrees with Aquinas that the very first object of human intellect is being *qua* being: "the first object of our intellect is being."[21] The Subtle Doctor agrees also with St. Thomas that the adequate object of the intellect is being as such. But, being *qua* being as the very first and the most adequate object of human intellect Duns Scotus understands in terms of essence, because essence only can be the most proper intelligible object of human intellect: "the first object of the intellect cannot be anything except what is essentially included in whatever is *per se* intelligible."[22] The intelligibility of being *qua* being in our intellect consists in understanding of reality "under the reason of common being,"[23] namely, "by the ascending and abstractive process" of intellection.[24] In this abstractive process our intellect can establish an actual distinct knowledge of various quidditative characteristics of being and as such an essential order in which there is a certain hierarchy of concepts of things known to us.[25]

In predication of being *qua* being, Duns Scotus distinguishes two types of cognition, namely, abstractive and concrete.[26] Now the abstractive knowledge based on essential characteristics of things is, according to Duns Scotus, superior to the concrete knowledge of reality, because the former gives us knowledge of being "in actu distincte" and the latter "in actu confuse."[27] Moreover, although our intellect originally grasps being as exercised in material things, the highest knowledge of being as such can be found if it is conceived "sub ratione entis communi,"[28] namely, "sub ratione aliqua communiori, quam sit ratio primi obiecti sensibilis."[29] The reason for this consists in the fact that between the faculties and their objects there is a specific proportion and a natural order of potentiality and actuality.[30] Now, although the object of our intellect is the material being, in its operation, however, it is independent from the particularity of *materia singulari*.[31]

The quidditative character of *esse* and the priority of essence over existence is also evident in the entitative order of being in respect to the ontological predication of being considered in its univocity. Duns Scotus insists that human intellect stands in the focus of the content as it is signified in the very concept of being itself, namely as if it would have some common entity independently from any particular being in reality. The reason for this seems to lie in the fact that the univocity of being can establish the *"communitas entis"*[32] and consequently be applicable to any instance of things. Moreover, univocity of being indicates that in the very conception of being there is some basic unity of meaning which enables our intellect to predicate being to various modes of things, avoiding thus any confusion: "Every understanding which is certain of one concept and doubtful of various [others], contains a concept of what is certain, and another concept from the concepts from which the doubtful one arises. . . . Therefore the concept of being. . . is univocal."[33]

But, if *esse* is taken from essence, and if essence can be grasped by our intellect in abstraction, then the question arises: how being understood in its univocity can explain and establish the order of unity and plurality of beings. In other words: how is one being different from another? To answer to this question we have to analyze the principle of distinction between essence and existence.

B: The Real or Formal Distinction

The classical text in which St. Thomas proves the distinction between essence and existence is in the *De Ente et Essentia*.[34] Discussing the various composition of being Thomas Aquinas argues:

> Whatever does not belong to the notion of an essence or quiddity comes from without and enters into composition with the essence, for no essence is intelligible without its parts. Now, every essence or quiddity can be understood without anything being known of its existing. I can know what a man or a phoenix is and still be ignorant whether it exists in reality. From this it is clear that the act of existing is other than essence or quiddity, unless, perhaps, there is a being whose quiddity is its very act of existing. And there can be only one such being, the First Being. For nothing can be multiplied except: (1) through the addition of some difference, as the generic nature is multiplied into species; or (2) by the form being received in different parts of matter, as the specific nature is multiplied in different individuals; or (3) by one thing being separate and another thing being received in something--for instance, if there were a separated heat, by reason of its very separation it would be different from heat which is not separated. But, should there exist some being which is simply the act of existing, so that the act of existing be itself subsistent, a difference cannot be added to this act of existing. Otherwise, it would not be purely and simply the act of existing, but the act of existing plus a certain form. Much less can matter be added to it, because then it would not be a subsistent, but a material, act of existing. So we conclude that there can only be one such being which is its very act of existing. With this exception, in every other thing existing is other than its quiddity, nature or form.[35]

In view of the real distinction between essence and existence it is clear that the human intellect conceives the very nature of being as some order in which one element cannot be known apart from another.[36] The human intellect cannot have a direct and immediate perception of being as an essence prescinded from existence, because essence itself is considered apart from both actuality and intelligibility.[37] Nor is the human intellect able to consider being as pure existence, because existence as the most perfect and formal principle of being transcends any limitations and determinations, and as such cannot be at the focus of the human mind.[38] The very structure of being then, can be expressed either by essence as it is related to existence or by existence as it is contained in the quidditative substrate of being. The former constitutes an essential order of being, and the latter an existential order of being.

On the basis of the twofold manner of understanding being we can say that *esse* subsists in reality in many different ways according to the order of distinction which obtains between essence and existence. The very notion of *'subsistere'* St. Thomas defines as *determinatum modum existendi*.[39] But, since in reality there are manifold modes of existing, being subsists in many different ways.[40]

In the very structure of being so considered, St. Thomas distinguishes a twofold order *ad esse*, namely, that of simple and composite substances. In the order of simple substances there is only one kind of composition, namely, that of its essence and existence. But in the order of composite substances there are at least two compositions, that is, that of form and matter, and that of thus-composed substance and its own existence.[41]

As it is well known, Duns Scotus rejects entirely St. Thomas's proposition of the real distinction of essence and existence: "I do not know this fiction, that being is something over and above essence."[42] Duns Scotus remains consistent to his quidditative metaphysics and positively negates any real distinction of essence and existence: "the being of essence is never in reality separated from the being of existence."[43] Furthermore, identifying *esse* with essence *Doctor Subtilis* applies only a rational distinction between them, and by the same token, making being *qua* being immune and neutral to any real distinction among ontological co-elements of being as such: "this second way seems probable, and most probable, if it states that essence and being differ only in reason."[44]

Rejecting the real distinction of essence and existence, Duns Scotus resolves the question of unity and plurality of being according to his doctrine of the essential composition of individual and common nature of things. As a starting point of the essential composition of things Duns Scotus asks the question: whether or not the nature is of itself a this? In order to answer this question Duns Scotus considers many propositions and gives a negative answer: "in relation to itself, nature is not exclusive and proper to any particular thing."[45] If the nature could be of itself a this, it would not be in others, so as the divine essence cannot be multiplied in other beings, because the divine nature exists of itself as a *this*.

Generally speaking, in the essential composition of things, Duns Scotus enumerates two "realities" or "formalities" which constitute every being in its unity and plurality. Not going into details, those two "formalities" are known as *haecceitas* and *natura communis*. While *haecceitas* is the principle of individuation of things, common nature is the principle of community of being: "community of itself is in harmony with nature, singularity on the other hand is in harmony with nature through something, in a thing, which unites it."[46] However, both *haecceitas* and common nature must fulfill the following two conditions:

1. They must constitute a positive entity, because otherwise *haecceitas* would not add anything to the individual nature, and common nature would not be a real unity but a numerical one;
2. They must be present in each particular thing, because otherwise *haecceitas* would not be the ultimate principle of individuation and common nature would not be the principle of community of being.

Every being, then, has, according to Duns Scotus, more than one entity[47] and as such it can constitute an essential composition of individual and common nature. But, not having the same signification, on the one hand, and requiring each other, on the other hand, the individual nature is only formally distinct from common nature, and as such they are not *primo diversae,* but *proprie differentiae.*[48] But, being united by common nature and differentiated by individual nature, the essential composition of things may be establishing a specific order of perfection: "one grade of perfection determines all the preceding ones to the ultimate unity, just as one specific difference determines all preceding perfections to unity in a species."[49] Summarizing then Duns Scotus's view on the order of perfections, one can conclude that *haecceitas* as a principle of individuation constitutes a specific hierarchical order of particular things, because nature in this instance is meant to be more singular than universal, and *natura communis* as a principle of community establishes a particular harmonious order of various being, because nature in this case is meant to be more universal then singular.[50]

C: Omne ens ordinatum est

For St. Thomas the *ratio* of the order of being understood as a composition of essence and existence seems to consist in a disposition of actuality and potentiality, because every composition of being requires something which is actual and something which is potential;[51] the Angelic Doctor argues that the philosophers "examine various essences according as they have existence in things. Consequently, wherever they discover a different habitude of potency to act, and therefore diverse modes of existing, they conclude that they are diverse genera of being."[52]

Now the order of being considered as a mutual reference of potency and act St. Thomas describes in terms of a proportion,[53] on the account of which there is in being a mutual order of reference according to which potency is related to an act, and act is related to potency: "act and potency are described in reference to each other."[54]

The order of being, however, considered as a reference of potency to an act, can be established inasmuch as there are different modes of perfections in being. The reason for this seems to lie in the fact that potency is determined by an act in many different ways: "potency is called perfect inasmuch as it is determined by act."[55] In this order actuality is conceived as a principle of perfection, and potentiality as a principle of imperfection: "each and every thing is perfect to the degree that it is in act, for potency without act is imperfect."[56] In view of this principle we can establish in being the following hierarchy of perfections: the perfection of potency united to an act is higher than that which is not united to an act.[57] In other words, the order of perfections and imperfection depends on the type of reference of potency to an act: the more perfect act is, the less it is limited by potency.[58]

In the mutual relation of actuality and potentiality there is a specific order of priority and posteriority: "Some things participate in one particular thing according to the order of priority and posteriority, as for example potency and act participate in the reason [*ratio*] of being."[59] The order of priority and posteriority which obtains between actuality and potentiality shows that in the very nature of being act is absolutely prior to potency. This absolute priority is the ultimate *ratio* of the order *ad esse*. But, since *esse* is found in reality in many different ways, being consists in an order *ad esse* insofar as it is some disposition of actuality and potentiality expressible by the following principle of limitation: "no act is found to be limited except through a potency that is receptive of that act."[60]

Duns Scotus, on the contrary, proclaiming the primacy of essence over existence, seems to reverse the order which takes place between actuality and potentiality, and says: "Then it appears necessary to concede that potency is to essence as its foundations, and to being as to an end."[61] The quidditative composition of things establishes specific order of potentiality and actuality in terms of the essential order: "But although potency refers to the order of something in which [potency] is related to act, according as such an order is varied, potency is proportionately distinguished."[62] In view of this essential order Duns Scotus makes distinction between two divisions of potentiality: "some [potency] which is appropriate to its own being, namely insofar as it is simply in potency; and other potency which is oriented towards other external being as if it were in accordance with that which is in potency to that being."[63] In conclusion Duns Scotus says:

> And this is most properly the difference of being, and it is called the objective potency, inasmuch as the whole is in potency to existence, and not in act, both its subject and its end. . .The second difference is not of every being, for it is only of that, which beyond its proper being arises to take on another being from another; and thus insofar as it does not have this, it is in potency to something else, for example, a body is not white in potency, as such, not simply, but in order to be white, which is being *secundum quid*, and which is also extrinsic. And so potency can be called subjective.[64]

The *ratio* of the essential order consists, according to the Subtle Doctor, in subordination of potentiality to actuality. Duns Scotus's doctrine on the essential order of being can be synthesized with his own words:

> All creatures because they are limited are parts of the whole universe; that is one by the unity of order, as it is said by Aristotle in 12 *Methaph.*; and so each of them [*creatura*] is potential to that form which consists in being an order; so that each has an order to another part, either with respect to the eminence which is in various natures in the universe, or with respect to equality which is the disposition of both equal and unequal things according to St. Augustine, or with respect to actions and passions, or with respect to

causality, and so each created agent producing an effect is potential because the order among them can follow upon itself and its effect.[65]

* * * * *

The priority of existence over essence in St. Thomas, and the primacy of essence over existence in Duns Scotus, led those two great medieval masters to establish two kinds of metaphysical synthesis, in which the stress is given either to existential or essential characteristics of being. But, if the stress is given to the unity of things, then the order of being is based on the principle of **harmony**, and as such it means some integrated unity. However, if the stress is given to the plurality of things then the order of being is based on the principle of **hierarchy**, and as such it consists in arranged plurality. In view of this distinction, I may conclude that St. Thomas Aquinas is following the hierarchical structure of reality, with emphasis on transcendental and existential order of being, while Duns Scotus's doctrine intends to interpret being in its harmonious structure of reality, with emphasis on immanent and essential order of being.

II: USIADISTIC ORDER OF BEING

In the development of metaphysics, its object of investigation, which is being *qua* being, has been expressed differently in various theories of being. In general, the main criterion of interpretation of being *qua* being depends on whether a particular metaphysical system stresses the unity of being (Parmenides) or its plurality (Heraclitus). Now, if the stress is given to the unity of being, then being *qua* being is understood intrinsically and as such identified with some "superreality," without a sufficient explanation of the diversity of things in reality. But, on the other hand, if the plurality of being is overemphasized, then the metaphysical understanding of being *qua* being is quite often dissipated into some kind of logic of becoming and, by the same token, such a theory of being must deny the existence and reality of any unity and any order which take place among concrete things.

At the basis of the dispute on the unity and plurality of being lies the unresolved problem which Aristotle created by trying to explain being *qua* being in terms of twofold substance, that is, primary and secondary substances (*prote* and *deutera ousia*), thus involving a certain tension among them in respect to their proper metaphysical status of being. This metaphysical tension between primary and secondary substances, the scholastic masters tried to overcome by the doctrine of essence and existence as two ontic elements of being. By concentrating in this chapter only on St. Thomas's and Ockham's metaphysical systems, the author will attempt to show that the former, by accepting the real distinction between essence and existence, saves the integrity between being and becoming. The latter, by identifying essence and existence, inevitably reduces metaphysics to specific logical theory of becoming, thus losing the balance between unity and plurality of being. In other words, distinguishing between essence and existence in being as its two distinct ontic elements of composition of real things, St. Thomas saves not only the balance between unity and plurality of being, but he also gives a cogent order of explanation of being and becoming, while William Ockham's stringent realism of individually existing things prevents him from explaining reality in its unified order of being in its totality.

A: Usiadistic Theory of Being

The classical understanding of metaphysics consists in a conviction that there is a specific philosophical discipline, the subject matter of which is being *qua* being. In the opening sentence of book Gamma of his *Metaphysics*, Aristotle writes:"There is a science which investigates being as being and the attributes which belong to this of its own nature."[1] Defending the superiority and supremacy of metaphysics over/against the other scientific disciplines, the Stagirite repeats his understanding of metaphysics, and says: "It will belong to this [sc. first philosophy] to consider being *qua* being--both what it is and the attributes which belong to it *qua* being."[2]

However, in order to explain metaphysics so conceived, Aristotle comes to the conclusion that being *qua* being ought to be analyzed in terms of substance (*ousia*), because "that which is primarily being and not any particular being, but being simply and absolutely, must be substance."[3] For Aristotle, then, "what being is, is just the question, what is substance."[4]

But, by explaining being *qua* being as substance, Aristotle recognizes individual (*tode ti*) as the only ontological principle by which any being can really be a real being. Therefore, this individual concrete existent is substance in the primary sense; such individual beings the Stagirite calls "primary substances" (*prote ousia*). However, individual beings cannot be known by our intellect directly, because, taking into consideration the multiplicity of things in reality, we have to know the proper nature through which each being can be identified as such. This cognitive identity with their own nature can be known by our intellect only through that which they have in common, that is, universal (*katholou*) because our intellectual power, in grasping reality, can recognize either generic or specific characteristics of being, that is, *genos* and *eidos*; the universals Aristotle calls "secondary substances" (*deutera ousia*).[5]

The universal, however, which Aristotle defines as "that which by its nature is capable of being predicated of several subjects,"[6] gives us only a predicational entity of a mental nature, which consists in supplying our intellect with the definition of being, and by which we can reach the true science (*episteme*).[7] In fact, therefore, by explaining being *qua* being by substance, Aristotelian metaphysics creates a tension between the way the individual beings exist and the way our intellect can identify their proper nature in their universal characteristics, a tension between primary and secondary substances.

Although realizing the logical difficulties in his interpretation of being *qua* being through substance, Aristotle in defense of his *prote philosophia* refers to the principle of intelligibility, and insists that it must apply to both being and thinking, for they are equally real reality. On the one hand, each and every being by having an individual nature must be considered as a primary substance, because in order to save the integrity of its nature "substance cannot admit of more or less."[8] But, on the other hand, our intellect in its way of grasping the proper nature of being cannot stop at the "individualness" of being, but it must also work out some unifying principle which will be common to all other particular beings as that by which particular existent being can be knowable in its nature.[9] In conclusion, then, Aristotle insists that both being and thinking must have ontically the same status of being intelligible, otherwise any *episteme* would be impossible in regard to anything.[10]

The Aristotelian solution of basing the object of metaphysics on being *qua* being in terms of substance met with different reactions among various philosophers. First of all, the Peripatetic proposition of solving being *qua* being by substance encountered severe criticism and radical rejection as a contradictory theory, for example, Plotinus.[11] Secondarily, some philosophers, although more sympathetic to Aristotle's attitude in explaining being *qua* being by substance, introduced an essential modification in its understanding, for instance, William of Ockham, who, in fact, reduces the entire reality of primary substance to the individual existent being alone. Finally, some of his followers tried to resolve the apparent deficiencies of the Peripatetic primary philosophy by discerning in the concept of being such an ontic moment which would allow for lessening internal tension between primary and secondary substances. As a matter of fact, such an ontic moment which gradually led to overcoming, in Aristotelian metaphysics, of the discrepancy between the primary and secondary substances will be--in the medieval ages--the teaching on existence as a co-element with essence in being, for instance, St. Thomas.

B: Being as Becoming

In order to oppose many existing scholastic tendencies to treat mental or logical category as real entities, endowed with some metaphysical reality, William of Ockham attempts to explain being by substance in terms of Aristotelian doctrine on *ousia*. However, following the Aristotelian theory of the twofold substance, the Venerable Inceptor interprets the primary substance as being realized in individual and particular things while treating, at the same time, the secondary substance only as a universal abstract notion without any extramental reality and which does not even express the essence and nature of things. In the words of Ockham:

> In the first place, it must be noted that every substance, which is a real thing contained in the genus of substance, is absolutely and simply a first substance, individual and singular, so that genera and species and the most general genus itself are not true substances which exist outside the mind. Neither are they of the essence of particular substances because they are certain intentional beings which have no existence outside the mind or they are some kind of other signs referring to real substances.[12]

In spite of the fact that Ockham accepts *verbatim* Aristotle's distinction between primary and secondary substances, he nevertheless accepts only partly Aristotle's teaching on secondary substances; he stresses only those texts of the Stagirite where the latter hesitates to attribute ontic status to secondary substances. In other words, although desiring to be in agreement with the Aristotelian teaching on *ousia*, Ockham neglects, nevertheless, the whole teaching of Aristotle on substance. He even denies that secondary substances can express the essence of things without any sufficient reasons. The only objection, as far as attributing any ontic status to secondary substances is concerned, is Ockham's suspicion that should a secondary substance represent extramental reality, then it would be necessary that primary substances also be composed not only of some individual existent, but they would also possess a universal nature, a theory which, according to him, is untenable, for in such a situation we would have to accept differing orders of general and universal nature as applied to various individual things.[13]

However, if the reality of things was to be sought only in primary substances, then it would be impossible to establish metaphysical understanding of being *qua* being in terms of substance. The reason for this is that being *qua* being can, according to Aristotle, be expressed by substance only through that what is primarily in reality, but taken without any qualifications, that is simply and absolutely.[14] In other words, if being is analyzed in terms of substance but not in all its senses, then we accept an equivocal or univocal concept of being, and consequently we would not be able to establish one unitary science of being *qua* being, as Aristotle argues in the third chapter of Book Kappa of *Metaphysics*.[15] Contrary to Aristotle, the Venerable Inceptor seems to follow both Aristotelian presuppositions but comes to the contrary conclusions, namely, that univocal/equivocal concept of being can establish one consistent metaphysical system. First of all, Ockham denies that the subject of metaphysics can be predicated simply and absolutely, that is, as having one specific subject-matter of its investigation. The reason for this is the fact that if only primary substances really express reality, and if there are many different substances, then metaphysics must be a science which must embrace all individual existing things predicated in a multiple way. Being, therefore, is, according to Ockham, not an exclusive subject matter which describes real things in their community and transcendentality; being *qua* being has priority only in the order of predication among many other subjects of metaphysics.[16] Consequently, metaphysics so understood would be deprived of any true unity and, as such, it would consist not only of a material but also of formal multiplicity of its subject matter:

> Among all the subjects of the different parts of metaphysics, being is first with a priority of predication. And there is a similarity between the question, what is the subject of metaphysics or of the

book of Categories and the question who is the king of the world or who is the king of all Christendom . . . so nothing is the subject of the whole of metaphysics, but here the different parts have different subjects, though these subjects may have a relation to one another.[17]

But even if Ockham admits that there must be some unity in metaphysics among its various subject-matters, their unity is unknown to us and its being has only conceptual nature: "I say that a particular being can be known, although those general concepts of being and unity are not known."[18]

However, if being is really only as one among many other subject matters of metaphysics enjoying exclusively the priority in the order of predication and not in reality, then being so understood can be only a predicational entity.[19] But, as a predicational entity which does not have any extramental reality, being can either be a univocal or equivocal concept. Being is a univocal concept if it is predicated in a collective sense and, it is equivocal if it is predicated in a distributive sense. Now, distinguishing between *praedicare in quid* and *in quale,* that is, predication in regard to what and to how of being,[20] Ockham arrives at the conclusion that being is purely a logical concept which is transcendental in nature and universal in character:

> 'Being' can assume two meanings. (1) In the first sense, the noun 'being' is associated with a concept which is common to all things and can be predicated of all things in the manner of quiddity. . . . (2) Notwithstanding there is a concept thus common to every being, the name 'being' is equivocal. For it is not in accordance with one concept that it is predicated of all its possible subjects taken in their significative function. Rather, to the name 'being' there correspond diverse concepts. . . .[21]

Reducing reality to primary substances, on the one hand, and attributing to being only a conceptual character lacking any extramental reality, on the other hand, Ockham not only negates the validity of metaphysics as a unitary science of being, but he also rejects the medieval teaching on the distinction of essence and existence. In his *Summa totius logicae* (3,2,27) and *Quodlibetum* (2,7), Ockham poses several objections against the doctrine on the distinction of essence and existence; he concludes that the only difference between them is semantic, and such a difference cannot add any knowledge to our metaphysical understanding of reality. Even if Ockham accepts Boethius's distinction between *quo est* and *quod est*, the Venerable Inceptor restricts this distinction to show the difference which takes place between divine and created beings. Moreover, to support his thesis that "existence is not a thing, different from the essence of a thing," Ockham refers to Grosseteste who, by distinguishing twofold predication of being by existence, namely, absolute and relative, states that in the former existence can be applied only to God, and in the latter it means only "an order and dependence on the first being, which exists of itself. And this ordering of dependence does not add anything to the dependent essence."[22]

By accepting the position that essence and existence are the same and that they have no different meanings, and by attributing to being univocity and/or equivocity, Ockham denies the validity of analogy: "There is no analogical predication, as contradistinguished from univocal, equivocal, and denominative predication."[23] Even when Ockham attributes some value to the analogical predication of being, the "proportion" will provide some resemblance to predicated things which are neither accidentally nor substantially alike.[24] But because they have no ontic likeness, things must of necessity be deprived of any real intrinsic proportion and, in reality, they can be related to each other only externally.[25] But, if things are deprived of any inner proportion and they are only externally related, then metaphysics based on univocity and/or equivocity will be dealing only with intentional being(s) which have a mental unity *sine fundamento in re*. Moreover, by negating the analogical structure of reality, we cannot know the real order of things according to their priority and posteriority because, for Ockham, real things can be really known as being expressed in primary substances, which are found in reality, only in plurality and not in unity. Since they are known only in their plurality and not in their unity, things cannot be known in their transcending relationship to each other, and metaphysics cannot establish any real order of being.

Metaphysics, then, as understood by Ockham, appears to be a certain science of plurality of things which lack real unity, because things can be known in their immanent order as being constituted of individual things according to their various species and genus. As a matter of fact, things which lack a concrete, real ontic unity can be found by our mind in various modes of realizations of their own nature, that is, in their order of becoming according to their species and genus. Such a conclusion seems to be in agreement with Ockham's theory of the real distinction between substance and quality.[26] Substance as a subject undergoes various modifications according to different qualities which are of things' primary ontic accidents, and which reveal the being of things in their process of changing, that is, in the order of becoming to be.

Ockham's metaphysics, then, by depriving things of their transcendental unity, replaces being by becoming, thus making the primary philosophy not a universal science but a science with many subject matters and branches of metaphysical investigation, and which treats them in a logical fashion. In other words, the instrumentalistic understanding of being *qua* being as some superconception without any extramental reality, forces Ockham to attribute the diversity of things to being, but understood as a term representing particular individual things, a term which, at the same time, does not express the real unity that takes place among things but a unity that is a product of our mind. Moreover, by making predication dependent on signification[27] and by accepting only a logical distinction between two modes of intellectual investigation, Ockham's philosophy of being comes close to the Heraclitean way of thinking on becoming.

C: Doctrine on Predication of Being

The usiadistic metaphysics of Aristotle and his followers leads either to an ambiguity in attempting to explain being in terms of a twofold substance, or to a tendency to reduce being to becoming. This is evident in Ockham's teaching that predication is basically dependent on signification. The failure to establish metaphysics of being *qua* being in terms of substance alone seems to stem from the ontic structure of being which requires to be explained both in unity and in the plurality of things. The shortcomings of a universal science of being, as it has been proposed by Aristotle, forced some of his followers to seek another resolution in the metaphysical explanation of being *qua* being. A new attempt of creating a metaphysics of being *qua* being has been initiated by Judeo-Christian philosophers.

1. Historical Note of Overcoming Usiadistic Predication of Being

One of the first philosophers who attempted to rescue the philosophy of being from the Aristotelian ambiguity of *ousia* as expressing the very nature of being, was a Jewish thinker, Philo of Alexandria. Philo was inspired by the biblical tetragrammaton expression of 'Jahve' which he translated (as also St. Jerome did much later on) as "I am who am" (*ego eimi ho on*). He sees human destiny as the final merging with God, because only God consists in being pure existence. But, if God is pure existence, then He must be Pure Being and absolutely simple.[28] Furthermore, if God as pure Being is absolutely simple, His pure existence is absolutely transcendent (*hyperousia*).[29]

Philo's conception of transcending the characteristics of existence will, in the future, not only enrich the Aristotelian metaphysics of *ousia* by contrasting it with *hyperousia* and give a transcendental interpretation of the Peripatetic doctrine of being *qua* being, but it will also allow the development of the notion of individual existence in terms of Plotinus's notion of *hypostasis*. For if man is created according to God's image, then his destiny is also to live as an existing being, which is realized in becoming Godlike. Consequently, through existence man is different from the essence of other creatures, as concluded by St. Gregory: "by essence man is different from horse, but by *hypostasis* Peter is different from Paul."[30] According to Teodoretus of Cypres, 'essence' and 'hypostasis' means existence (*to einai*).[31] This terminology becomes more precisely translated by Boethius who gave us the general distinction of being, that is, a distinction between *id quod est* and *id quo est*.[32]

Under the influence of the Boethian distinction between *id quod est* and *id quo est*, the medieval philosopher elaborates a doctrine on essence and existence and he applies it especially to the reinterpretation of Aristotelian metaphysics. On the one hand, Avicenna argues that existence is not included in essence,[33] and, on the other hand, Berengarius of Tours points out that there are different meanings of the verb '*est*,' that is, 'is' has a different meaning when it denotes 'existence,' and a different meaning when it denotes what something is.[34] In the Middle Ages, the distinction between essence and existence became commonly known, independently of whether or not it had been accepted and applied to the metaphysical theory of being. In any case, the distinction between essence and existence which became characteristic of the medieval philosophy of being made a tremendous impact on the development of the Aristotelian metaphysics.

2. The Predicamental Predication of Being

In finding the most appropriate name for the substance of God as the expression of the very 'beingness' of divine nature, St. Thomas consciously refers to the biblical tetragrammaton, saying that *qui est* is its most correct rendition. But, if God's substance is expressed existentially, then the act of existence should also serve in signifying any other created substances. In other words, instead of trying to express the real things in their "beingness" as realized in a twofold substance, the Angelic Doctor explains it by their *esse* conceived as an act of existing. Consequently, the order of predication of things should be based not only on the essential characteristics of real things, but also on their existential components, because *esse* is expressing fully and entirely *modus substantiae rei* of any thing.[35]

However, the question arises, how to predicate *esse* of being both in its essential and existential characteristics. In order to resolve this question, one should realize St. Thomas's interpretation of the Aristotelian doctrine on predication of being in both its logical and metaphysical order.

a. The Logical Order of Predication

Predication is the intellect's act of combining and dividing, having for its foundation in reality the very unity of those things, one of which is said of the other.[36] In this unity there is a specific order between the predicate (P) and the subject (S). Following Aristotle, St. Thomas distinguishes a twofold mode of predication, namely:
1. *Modus praedicandi per accidens;*
2. *Modus praedicandi per se.*[37]

In the mode of predication *per accidens*, St. Thomas distinguishes the following three instances of predication:
1. Predicating another accident of something already designated by another accident, for example, 'the righteous doer is musical';
2. Predicating an accident of a subject, for example, 'the man is musical';

3. Predicating a substance of something designated by accident, for example, 'the musician is a man'.[38]

In the mode of predication *per se*, St. Thomas distinguishes two kinds of instances, namely:

1. *Primus modus praedicandi per se,*
2. *Secundus modus praedicandi per se.*

The first mode of predication *per se* takes place when P expresses the essential parts of that which is expressed by S, for example, man is a being that has a sensitive life; in this mode of predication there is but a logical distinction between the intention of S and P. The second mode of predication *per se* takes place when P expresses a *proprium* which belongs to S, that is, S is included in P so that P expresses the *proprium* of S, for example, body which has surface is colored.

Having established the logical order of predication, the problem which now presents itself is how this twofold mode of predication corresponds to and expresses the very nature of being. In order to avoid any confusion in this matter, we have to realize that the division of predication into a twofold mode is not the same as that of the division of being into accidental and substantial *esse*.[39] To understand this twofold mode of predication of being we must enumerate the conditions under which the human intellect is ascribing *esse* of a particular thing.

Predication follows upon the activity of the human mind, taken in the sense of both, the agent and the possible intellect. Predication when considered as it is related to the agent intellect is an effect of its spontaneous activity, and when it is considered as it is related to the possible intellect it is a consequence of the activity of the intellect on that which is apprehended. Since the agent intellect does not have any activity apart from the possible intellect, predication as it is caused by the activity of the human mind is always related to the object of intellectual apprehension. In other words, since the human intellect is not producing anything unless it is in the act of comprehending something, in its act of predication it is always related to something objective either directly (if to the object itself) or indirectly (if through a particular faculty both cognitive and appetitive).

Predication depending upon the modes of cognition is accomplished by the intellect's act of combining and dividing. For in the human mind where there is a manifold composition of intellectual apprehension, the act of combining and dividing can be considered either from the intellectual content of the human cognition or from the natural dependence of the intellect upon the body in its operation. Hence the notion of predicability can be included in the notion of the intention, and as such it is accomplished by the universality which comes from the human mind, according to a twofold order:

1. The order of first intentions,
2. The order of the second intentions.

In the order of second intentions there is an arrangement of superior or inferior predicates according to greater or lesser universality, that is, an arrangement in which the superiors are predicated of every inferior. The order of second intentions so considered is brought about by the human mind, since the intellect is that which gives universality to things. St. Thomas proves his doctrine from the characteristics of a universal. In the notion of any universal there is some unity and community. But neither of these belongs to the nature of the thing considered absolutely. If community were included in the notion of man, in whatever being humanity were found community would be found. But this is impossible, because we do not find any community in a particular being, for example, the total reality of Socrates is individuated. Moreover, we cannot say that human nature as it exists in individual man has the character of a genus or species. We do not find human nature in them with a unity such as to constitute one essence belonging to all, which is required for the character of universality.[40]

The nature, then, if considered as it is found in the human mind, is universal. It is also evident from the consideration of the mode of existing of the essence in the intellect. Human nature itself exists in the intellect in abstraction from all individual conditions, and it thus has a uniform relation to all individual men outside the intellect, being equally the likeness of all and leading to a knowledge of all insofar as they are men. And from the fact that the nature has such a relation to all individual men, the intellect forms the notion of species and attributes it to that nature. But the nature existing in the intellect has the character of a universal from its relation to things outside the intellect, and not from the existence which it has in the mind, because it is one likeness of them all.[41]

However, the essence can be considered not only as it is related to the intellect alone,[42] but also as it is related to the act of existing in different individual things. The essence so considered constitutes an arrangement of many different predicates according to the plurality of perfection, that is, an arrangement of various degrees of being in which the higher perfection is predicated of the lower. It means that the order of first intentions follows from the hierarchical structure of reality itself.[43]

In the very structure of predication, then, considered as an intellectual act of combining and dividing there is a real foundation for different modes of expressing the very nature of a being. Since *esse* is both the act of existing and the ultimate reason for intelligibility of a thing, a question may arise as to how we combine the plurality of things, which comes from different acts of existing, and the universality which comes from the act of knowing. To understand St. Thomas's solution of this problem we have to analyze all the conditions under which *esse* can be predicated in its metaphysical order.

b. The Metaphysical Order of Predication

In his *Commentary of the Metaphysics*, the Angelic Doctor writes:

> Being which signifies a composition of proposition is accidental predicate, because composition takes place in the intellect in a determinate time. *Esse*, however, in this or that time is accidental predicate. But being which is divided into the ten predicamentals, signifies the very nature of those ten genera as they are in act and potency.[44]

In view of this text let us consider more precisely this twofold way of predication of *esse*.

Being is an accidental predicate, because it expresses something that is apart from or over and beyond the thing's essence. That, however, which can be predicated apart from and over the thing's essence, can express the accidental characteristic of being either in regard to the entity of a thing or the truth of a proposition. The principle according to which being expresses something accidental is in both instances a particular period of time. The accidental characteristic of being expressed by the particular period of time St. Thomas proves in two steps: from the fact that the composition of a predicate and subject in a proposition is made by the intellect, and this in turn is required by the specific function of temporal existence.

First of all, the accidental character of being follows from the fact that the composition of a predicate and subject in a proposition is made by the intellect in a definite period of time. Whatsoever has existence in a particular period of time is necessarily accidental to an essence that is eternal. The reason is that existence according to a particular period of time does not belong to the very structure of a thing, and as such it depends upon something which is external to the subject. In other words, being is an accidental predicate when it expresses a composition of subject and predicate in a proposition which is made by the intellect according to a definite period of time.

Secondly, the accidental character of being is expressed by means of the verb 'is'. Distinguishing a twofold mode of predication in time,[45] St.Thomas says that the accidental predicate expressed by the verb 'is', in each instance it expresses something that is apart from and over the thing's essence.

In contrast to accidental being *ens per se* expresses something that is contained in the very nature of a thing, that is, its essence[46] Since in the very structure of any thing the essence is contained in many different ways, there is a specific order of essential being. In general, this order can be considered in two ways, namely:

1. As an order in which essence expresses a potentiality to real being;
2. As an order in which essence expresses the being of a thing essentially as something that is related to its act of existing, that is, as an actual or potential being.

In other words, being *per se* is expressed by the essence of a thing either as something that is contained in the very nature of a thing as such or as something that is actuated in reality.

How to understand this twofold mode of expressing the very nature of being essentially? Is there any principle according to which being *per se* is predicated of a thing in two different ways? In searching for the answer to this problem we have to realize how we are using terms. The term 'being' St. Thomas uses in two ways:

1. As something existing in a soul, that is, something produced by reason;
2. As something existing in a thing, that is, a real being.[47]

Because a thing receives nothing from the intellect nor is it deprived of anything thereby, the order of being *per se* can be established only on the basis of the real being.[48]

Now, any being understood as something existing in reality St. Thomas describes in terms of, and reduces to, some determinate category.[49] The reason for this is the distinction between the essence and the act of existing in any created being.[50] In other words, the real being insofar as it is created and composed of essence and act of existing constitutes an instance of some determinate predicament.[51]

Being *per se*, then, is expressed by, and identified with, the essence of a thing as something that exists and constitutes an instance of some determinate predicament in reality. Given that real being is divided into ten categories, being *per se* constitutes a specific order of predicamental order of being[52] in which to predicate being of a thing essentially means to describe the nature of the ten genera according to their actuality and potentiality.[53] In this way St. Thomas classifies under the single heading of essential predicate the two Aristotelian modes of the predication of being, that is, being as it is expressed by the ten categories, and, as expressed by that which is actual or potential.[54] What is the background against which this kind of reduction of essential being could be justified? To understand St. Thomas's position we have to consider the essential order of being in respect to the order of substantial and accidental *esse*.[55]

The principle by which a real being is assigned to a determinate category is, according to St. Thomas, its essence.[56] Essence, however, can be expressed as a particular predicament depending upon its relation to its act of existing. In the second *Quodlibetum*, Aquinas, explaining how essence is related to the act of existing, says that being contains and expresses the very nature of a thing analogically.[57] Essence related to its act of existing expresses being as an instance of some predicament in not more than two ways, that is, *esse substantiale* and *esse accidentale*.[58]

Being *per se*, then, is an essential predicate and as such is designated by the essence of a thing that exists as either some definite substance or accident. For substance and accident are related to each other as something actual and potential, the order of essential being is the same as the order of the ten predicaments according to their actuality and potentiality. The reason for this is that the division of being into a twofold *esse* is not only adequate,[59] but in the very notion of substance and accident, expressed by their definitions, being is divided according to affirmation and negation.[60]

Essence, since it is something positive in reality,[61] expresses the very nature of a being in many different ways.[62] In his work *On Being and Essence*, St. Thomas gathers the different descriptions of essence depending on that aspect of being which is expressed. Essence, if it signifies something common to all natures, expresses being as divided into ten categories, through which natures or different beings are placed in different genera and species, for example, humanity is the essence of man. However, that by which a thing is constituted in its proper genus or species is what is signified by the definition expressing what the thing is, essence can be called *quiddity* and as such expresses 'what a thing was to be' (*quod quid erat esse*).[63] Finally, essence can be called a 'form' and 'nature': 'form' if it signifies the determinations of each thing, and 'nature' if it means the thing's essence as ordered to its proper activity.[64]

These manifold modes of expressing being by essence, as something positive that can exist in reality, St. Thomas reduces to the following two ways: as something *through* which a thing has being, and as something *in* which a thing has being: "per eam et in ea ens habet esse".[65] Essence as it is something *in* which a thing has being, is the subject of being. But essence as it is something *through* which a thing has being, is the principle of being and the part of the whole composite. How can one explain this twofold mode of expressing being by essence?

The term 'essence' denotes what is expressed by the definition of a thing..[66] Yet the term 'essence' can denote that which is expressed by the definition of a thing either as this is related to the intelligibility of thing, or as it is regarded as a part of the composite. On the one hand, the notion of essence is closely bound up with the notion of being, because essence as it is related to the intelligibility of a thing signifies that which the intellect first conceives, that is, being. On the other hand, since essence is one component of the whole composite, it can express the very nature of being if it is related to, and contrasted with, the second element of the composite, that is, the act of existing. In other words, essence can express the very nature of being either as a subject or as a part of being.[67] To understand this twofold way of expressing being by essence we have to consider the order of predication of essence as such.

Essence, as it is related to the intelligibility of a thing, can be considered either as a part of the real individual or as a whole. In the first case the notion of essence excludes any particular characteristics which belong to an individual being; for example, the word 'humanity' signifies the essence of man as a part, because it signifies only what belongs to man as man excluding all designation of matter. The essence, however, if considered as a whole, does not positively exclude the particular characteristics of an individual being though it does not contain them explicitly either; for example, the word 'man' signifies the essence of a man as a whole inasmuch it does not exclude quantitative designation of the matter. In conclusion, St. Thomas states that the essence of a thing must be predicated as a whole and not as a part, because if 'animal' were not the whole of what man is, but a part of it, it would not be predicated of it, since no integral part may be predicated of its whole.[68]

Now, since the order of intelligibility corresponds to the order of existence, the essence considered as a whole can be analyzed in one of the three following ways:

1. As it is related to this or that individual thing;
2. As it is related to the human mind; and
3. As it is related to itself.[69]

St. Thomas excludes the first two ways of predication and says that essence is properly predicated of an individual thing if considered absolutely, that is, abstracted from its existence in the thing or in the mind. The essence as a whole cannot be predicated of the individual thing as it exists in a particular being, because it would exclude the possibility of predicating the essence of many other things, and as such the essence would never exist outside the individual. In reality, however, there are many individual things having the same nature; for example, the essence of man is not predicated of Socrates alone, because it is attributed to all human beings. A similar reasoning St. Thomas applies to the predication of essence as it is related to the human mind. As a matter of fact, essence cannot be predicated of an individual thing as it exists in the intellect, because we would then attribute universality to an individual thing, and essence itself would be universal. But in reality nothing in a particular being is common or universal; for example, in Socrates his human nature exists, but only as individualized. Leaving aside the whole problem of individuation for the moment, it remains to conclude that the essence is predicated of individual being absolutely, that is, as it is considered in itself.[70]

To sum up, essence is properly predicated of an individual thing if it is considered as a whole and in itself. Yet essence so considered is abstracted from the very act of existing, both the real and the cognitional order. Whatsoever is abstracted from the act of existing can be considered only *in abstracto*, that is, as it appears in the act of the human cognition. Yet St. Thomas insists that essence as something positive in reality must express the very nature of being *in concreto*. The problem here involved is how to bind essence with being and to combine them in such a manner that the essence could be predicated of an individual thing as a whole and in itself, that is, *in abstracto*, and that the being expressed by essence would be still considered as it is related to the act of existing, that is, *in concreto*? To solve this problem we have to recall the Thomistic doctrine of designation.

The Angelic Doctor distinguishes two modes of designation, namely, determinate and indeterminate. This twofold mode of designation corresponds to a twofold mode of essence, that is, concrete and abstract. In the definition of essence as it is related to a concrete being, there must be included all particular characteristics which belong to that individual in a determinate way; for example, the definition of Socrates if Socrates as such could be defined would contain necessarily all the specific characteristics of his individual nature, that is, that of his flesh, bone, skin, hair, color, etc. Yet in the definition of essence as it is related to an abstract being, there are included all the particularities of an individual being, but in an indeterminate way; for example, in the definition of man there are all the specific characteristics of an individual but according to the different mode of particular human beings.

The same twofold mode of designation we can apply to the essence as it is considered in reference to the act of existing.[71] According to St. Thomas, the essence among individual beings has numerous acts of existing corresponding to the diversity of individuals. But the essence considered absolutely and in itself requires none of these acts of existing. Accordingly, one cannot say that the nature of man as such exists in this individual man, because, if existing in this individual belonged to man as man, it would never exist in this or that individual; human nature would never exist in it. The truth is that to exist in this or that individual, or in the intellect, does not belong to man as man. Considered in itself, the nature of man thus clearly abstracts from every act of existing, but in such a way that none can be excluded from it. And it is the nature considered in this way that the intellect predicates of all individual beings.[72]

The intellect, once it has established in the order of predication the proper relation of essence and act of existing, can predicate the nature of many individuals according to a specific order of universals, that is, genus, species, and difference.[73] In this sense St. Thomas can reduce the order of essences to the order of universals, because the universals accomplish all the required conditions of predication of being by essence, that is, as it is considered absolutely and as a whole. In conclusion, Aquinas says: "The essence has the nature of a genus or species insofar as it is expressed after the manner of a whole, for instance, by the word 'man' or 'animal', as containing implicitly and indistinctly everything that is in the individual."[74]

To sum up, in the essential order of being as it is considered in regard to the origin of the substantial and accidental *esse*, there are two kinds of form: accidental form which corresponds to the *esse accidentale*, and substantial form which corresponds to the *esse substantiale*. Now, since *esse* primarily is predicated of a substance and secondarily of an accident, substantial being is related to both kinds of determination: accidental and substantial *esse*. In other words, substantial being has *esse* from its very nature, and accidental being according to the mode of participation in substance.

* * * * *

The aim of this chapter was to present and to contrast two types of primary philosophy, that is, philosophy which understands being analogically and existentially, and philosophy which conceives being as a univocal/equivocal concept. The former is based on plurality and unity of things, and the latter stresses only the plurality of things. But a philosophy that conceives being univocally/equivocally lacks any internal unity of being, and must lead to a ceaseless process of becoming, "to the eternally Unchanging--of the myriad of inferior beings in constant flux, to the one, superior, and changeless Being."[75] However, by making created beings absolutely dependent on God, the natural order of individual things as presented in Ockham's philosophy resembles the Heraclitean philosophy of becoming, where any solid and substantial reality is dissolved and nothing is left but flux and a perpetual struggle (*polemos*) of all things against each other, as explained by Martin Heidegger.[76] But any temptation to follow the Heraclitean philosophy of becoming will ultimately lead to nihilism, as it has been so powerfully shown by Friedrich Nietzsche:

> The eternal and exclusive Becoming, the total instability of all reality and actuality, which continually works and becomes and never is, as Heraclitus teaches, is an appalling and awful conception. . . . Out of the war of the opposites, all becoming originates . . . the wrestling continues to all eternity. Everything happens according to this struggle, and this very struggle manifests eternal justice. . . . The Things themselves in the permanency of which the limited intellect of man and animal believes do not 'exist' at all.[77]

Ockham's metaphysics of being resembles Kotarbinski's reism, Russell's atomism, and Wittgenstein's neopositivism--as some scholars of the Venerable Inceptor pointed out.[78] Being *qua* being reduced to becoming changes metaphysics of being into philosophy of things and as a result Ockham's metaphysics becomes a pure logic, or rather his metaphysics is subordinated to the demands of logic. In the contemporary times, this subordination of metaphysics to logic will lead to treating metaphysical categories to be "recognized as productions of language,"[79] because "Being as Being is the kind of word that cannot be more than word."[80]

III: PREDICATIONAL ORDER OF NATURAL THINGS

From the time of Aristotle the philosophers try to explain the being of natural things through the notion of substance understood either in the essential or existential order of their ontic constitution. On the one hand, the essential order of substance points to the *genesis* of coming into being the natural things, and in this way they can be predicated in their permanent and absolute characteristics both in regards to their individuality and community as containing the same nature. On the other hand, the existential order of substance indicates in the very being of the natural things their actual status in reality as being realized in various modes of 'to-be'. Although St. Thomas knows both of these current tendencies in philosophy, he not only follows the existential order of understanding of substance as expressing the very being of natural things, but in his analysis of *esse* he attempts to integrate all human knowledge of reality centered in metaphysics as directing all other sciences.[1]

The classical understanding of substance as a subject of being whose entity requires it to exist in itself (*ens per se, ens in se*) has been primarily predicated of all natural things, and analogically only of the Absolute Being, that is, God. Such an application of substance, however, has been challenged by Descartes who by defining substance as absolute and independent existence, not only reverses the application of substance from created beings to Infinite Being, but by the same token he reduces substance to be only the attributes of natural things, thus destroying the possibility of the metaphysical knowledge of being as such.

The aim of this chapter is to examine the Cartesian new conception of substance, and to contrast it with the Thomistic existential understanding of the categorical order of being.

A: Ontological Order of Natural Things

The basis for philosophical truth of everything in reality is--according to Descartes--nature. Referring to Descartes's *Six Meditations*, Adam Zoltowski writes: "On this basis our philosopher is convinced that truth contains everything that teaches him nature."[2]

For Descartes, nature means God as well as all things created and established by God according to some order: "By nature, considered in general, I now understand nothing more than God himself, or the order and disposition established by God in created things; and by nature in particular I understand the assemblage of all that God has given me."[3] In view of this definition we must analyze and distinguish between the general and the particular meaning of nature.

1. Nature and Order

The general meaning of nature contains the order of natural things as established by God. Within the order of natural things, however, we must distinguish between the order of being (*ordo essendi*) and the order of discovery (*ordo cognoscendi*). Descartes defines order in terms of priority and posteriority: "Order consists only in this, that the things which are proposed first ought to be known without the aid of those which follow and that the latter ones ought to be arranged in such a way that they are demonstrated solely by what precedes them."[4] In the order of being, God is prior. In the order of discovery, one's own existence is prior. But, since Descartes is concerned with the order of discovery rather than with the order of being in his investigation of the complexus of things given by God to nature in particular, we must turn to our very own existence as proposed by the expression *cogito ergo sum*. In other words, it is in the *cogito* that I first discover that God exists. After this I discover that all other things exist and correspond to my clear and distinct ideas of them.

2. New Conception of Substance

It is in the *cogito* that I discover my nature in particular as substance. Descartes defines substance itself as follows: "By substance we can conceive nothing else than a thing which exists in such a way as to stand in need of nothing beyond itself in order to its existence."[5] With this definition, Descartes introduces absolute independence to the notion of substance. But, since absolute independence in existence can be applied only to the substance of God, all created substances can only exist by the concourse of God.[6] Taking this into account, Descartes comes to the conclusion that created substances cannot be known in their existence, but only in their attributes.[7] Consequently, in order to know substances, we must first discover their principal attributes: ". . . there is always one principal property of substance which constitutes its nature and essence, and on which all things depend."[8]

Nature, then, consists of substance's attributes. In the *cogito* I can discover that my nature is a thinking thing (*res cogitans*).[9] This is because thinking is the principal attribute of spiritual substances. As a matter of fact, a spiritual substance always thinks. In his discussion with Arnauld, Descartes argues:

> I have no doubt that the mind begins to think at the same time that it is infused into the body of an infant, and that it is at the same time conscious of its own thought, though afterwards it does not remember it, because the specific forms of these thoughts do not live in the memory.[10]

The analysis of *cogito*, my nature in particular, reveals that my thinking substance is intermingled with a body: "But there is nothing which that nature teaches me more expressly than that I have a body which is ill affected when I feel pain, and stands in need of food and drink when I experience the sensations of hunger and thirst, etc."[11] All of this information received by my nature in particular proves that my thinking substance is united with a body:

> Nature likewise teaches me by these sensations of pain, hunger, thirst, etc., that I am not only lodged in my body as a pilot in a vessel, but that I am besides so intimately conjoined, and as it were intermixed with it, that my mind and body compose a certain unity.[12]

There must be some unity between mind and body. Otherwise, my mind would not feel the pain when my body is hurt. In conclusion, Descartes says that "all these sensations of hunger, thirst, pain, etc., are nothing more than certain confused modes of thinking, arising from the union and apparent confusion of mind and body."[13]

In the *cogito*, then, I can discover that besides a thinking substance I also have a corporeal substance which is surrounded by many other bodies:

> And indeed, as I perceive different sorts of colours, sounds, odours, tastes, heat, hardness, etc., I safely conclude that there are in the bodies from which the diverse perceptions of the senses proceed, certain varieties corresponding to them, although perhaps, not in reality like them; and since, among these diverse perceptions of the senses, some are agreeable, and others disagreeable, there can be no doubt that my body, or my entire self, in as far as I am composed of body and mind, may be variously affected, both beneficially and harmfully, by surrounding bodies.[14]

3. Twofold Kind of Principal Attributes

After discovering the very existence of corporeal bodies by the *cogito*, my mind proceeds to investigate the very nature of things. However, since any substance cannot be known in its existence but only in its attributes, my *cogito* ". . .must accurately define what I properly understand by being thought by nature."[15] Whereas my *cogito* discovers that the very nature of body consists of extension: ". . . the nature of matter or body in its universal aspect does not consist in its being hard, or heavy, or colored, or any other way of affecting our senses, but solely in the fact that it is a substance extended in length, breadth, and depth."[16] All phenomena of nature, then, can be explained in terms of quantity. In the conclusion Descartes says: "I have described the earth and even the whole world after the fashion of a machine."[17]

This mechanistic interpretation of reality deprives the very nature of things of any finality:

> We will not seek reasons of natural things from the end which God or nature proposed to himself in their creation, for we ought not to presume so far as to think that we are sharers in the counsels of Deity, but considering him as the efficient cause of all things, let us endeavor to discover by the natural light which he has planted in us, applied to those of his attributes of which he has been willing we should have some knowledge, what must be concluded regarding those effects we perceive by our senses.[18]

The Cartesian interpretation of nature, however, requires not only mechanics, but also teleology. The reason for this is found in the sharp distinction between mind and body. In the mind there is freedom and finality, but in the body there is determinism and causality. How can this inconsistency of Descartes's philosophy be explained?

The inconsistency found in the Cartesian philosophy of *cogito* is due to the unsolved problem of the relationship between mind and body. In the *cogito* we discover two separate substances, mind and body. Now, this dualism of nature leads to the conclusion that I am a soul lodged within a body. This difficulty has been raised by Arnauld in his fourth objection to the Cartesian concept of man as a thinking thing: ". . . nothing corporeal belongs to the essence of man, who is hence entirely spirit, while his body is merely the vehicle of spirit; whence follows the definition of man as a spirit which makes use of a body."[19]

In his philosophy of man, Descartes tries to reconcile both the real unity and the distinction between soul and body. When soul and body are considered as related to each other, they are conceived as incomplete substances and as such united in reality: "Mind and body are incomplete substances viewed in relation to the man who is the unity which they form together."[20] When soul and body are considered by our *cogito* according to its clear and distinct ideas, they seem to be complete substances and as such separated in reality: "Taken alone, they are complete [substances]. And I know that thinking substance is a complete thing no less than that which is extended."[21]

This unsatisfactory explanation of man's nature leads inevitably to the dualism of spirit and matter. As the human being consists of two separate substances, it would appear to be very difficult to maintain that there is any intrinsic relationship between the two elements. Yet Descartes insists that this relationship can be compared to that of a pilot and his ship, but not in the sense that the spirit is lodged in the body which is used as some external vehicle or instrument. Consequently, they must also be very closed united and intermingled, and, in a sense, constitute some unity.

Descartes's doctrinal dichotomy between separation and unity of mind and body appears somehow contradictory. His attempted resolution of this dichotomy is seen clearly in his reply to Arnauld. In this reply, Descartes makes what appears to be a formal distinction between the substances, *cogitans* and *extensa*, taken in themselves and taken in relation to man. This point is in opposition to the fact when one argues that they are incomplete substances because they cannot exist by themselves. Descartes replies to this by saying that, because of the separation between mind and body, they are complete substances in themselves. But it is also true that insofar as they are substances they have no lack of completeness, and when they are joined in composition they form a single self-subsistent thing. But as such, the mind and body are not in this subsistent type of composition, because they do not constitute substantial unity.

In other words, on the one hand, Descartes demonstrates the real distinction or rather the separation between mind and body, and because of this he comes up with two different substances, each unique for itself. But, on the other hand, because of the fact that one has a clear and distinct idea of body as an extended and unthinking thing, how is one to deal with the relationship between an immaterial soul and a material body? As Descartes would not accept the implication of no interaction between the two separate and different substances, he established an uneasy and untenable position of their unity in man which rests solely upon a presupposition.

In conclusion, desiring to resolve the problem of the unity of the human being which arises from his separation of mind and body, Descartes excludes the doctrine of hylomorphism. He attempts to resolve this problem by certain ideas which are, at least, unclear and indistinct. But he goes not further in the explication of this problem nor in the solution of how the two substances, the mind and the body, can and do unite. Because of this unsatisfying answer, Descartes gave rise to the question of whether or not there was any real causal connection between mind and body. This point is resolved by some Cartesians through a theory of occasionalism, which itself has given less credibility to the idea of two separate substances interacting as Descartes presupposes.[22]

B: The Metaphysical Order of Natural Things

In contrast to Descartes, for St. Thomas being of natural things can only be defined in regard to their essential characteristics, but always as having some specific reference to the act of existing. The reason for this is that without having any reference to the act of existing, and being known only by our intellect in respect to their essential attributes, being of natural things would be known by us without any certainty whether or not those attributes exist really in things. Realizing, however, that the act of existing cannot be defined as such, Aquinas agrees that "every thing by its very nature is being,"[23] and can be defined by its essence alone, because "everything is being through its own essence."[24] In knowing, however, being of natural things through essential characteristics, our intellect knows them as something expressing the very content in conjunction with the appropriate acts of existing.

1. *Ratio* of the Metaphysical Order of Being

For St. Thomas, then, our intellect can define being through an essence of a given natural thing but as it is in its integral nature, that is, as having some particular act of existing. Generally speaking, in the order of metaphysical predication, being can be predicated of a given subject in no more than three ways, namely:
1. As pertaining to the essence of the subject;
2. As inhering in the essence of the subject; and
3. As a predicate drawn from some extrinsic entity and denominated as such.[25]

Now, applying this threefold ways of predication to the nature of particular beings, St. Thomas establishes a specific order among the categories. First of all, if being is predicated in regard to its essential nature, it constitutes the category of substance; for example, Socrates is a man, man is a living being. Sometimes, however, the predication is related only to the inherent nature of being both absolutely and relatively: if absolutely and in regard to matter it constitutes the category of quantity; if absolutely and in regard to form, it is the category of quality; if relatively, it is expressed by the category of relation. Finally, the predication can be related to and drawn from some extrinsic entity either as some cause or measure or possession: if the predication is related to some extrinsic entity as to something that is possessed, it denominates either the place itself and then we have the category of where, or the parts of place and then we have the category of position, or the time and then we have the category of when.[26]

Investigating the nature of being as it is expressed by essence and divided into the ten categories, St. Thomas establishes the metaphysical order of being according to greater and lesser proximity of particular accidents to substance. The reason for this is that substance is a being *in se*, and accident a being *in alio*. Consequently the very nature of being is primarily expressed by the essence of substance, and secondarily by that of accident. Having this in mind, we can establish the essential order of being according to a threefold *ratio* of any order, that is:

1. The order of priority and posteriority in being;
2. The order of distinction between substantial and accidental *esse*; and
3. The principle of the categorical order of being.

a. The Order of Priority and Posteriority

The order of priority and posteriority in being can be attributed to things inasmuch as the term 'prior' means something which can exist without other things, but not the reverse. This order can be attributed to things in three ways, namely:

1. Things are said to be prior in being because of community or dependence: "according to this those things are said to be prior which can exist without them."[27]
2. Things are said to be prior in being because of the relationship of substance to accidents: "for since the term being is used in many senses and not univocally, all senses of being must be reduced to one primary sense, according to which being is said to be the subject of other things and to subsist of itself. Hence the first subject is said to be prior; and thus substance is prior to accidents."[28]
3. Things are said to be prior in being because of the composition of actuality and potentiality: "for a thing is said to be prior in one way potentially and in another actually. A thing is said to be prior potentially in the sense that half a line is prior to an entire line, and any part to its whole, and matter 'to substance', that is, to form. For all of the first things mentioned in these instances are related to the others, to which they are said to be

prior, as something potential to something actual. However, from the viewpoint of actuality the first things mentioned are said to be subsequent, since they become actual only by the dissolution of some whole. For when a whole is dissolved into its parts, the parts then begin to exist actually."[29]

The main reason of the order of priority and posteriority is, therefore, a special relationship of dependence according to which prior things do not depend upon subsequent ones, but the reverse.[30] In view of the relation of priority and posteriority so understood, the essential order of being can be considered according to the following principle: that which is the first among the kinds of being, since it is being in an unqualified sense, and not being with some qualification, is the prior instance of being. Now, the question is, which of the ten categories is the first being? St. Thomas, following Aristotle, indicates that substance is the first kind of being.[31]

Commenting on the Aristotelian concept of being as substance, St. Thomas discusses the following two questions:

1. How substance is the first kind of being; and
2. In what way substance is said to be prior to accident.[32]

The term 'being' is used in many senses. But substance is said to be being in two ways: firstly, as the 'whatness of a thing', and, secondly, as 'this particular thing'.[33] But, since being is used in many senses, it is evident that being in the primary sense signifies substance.[34]

Proving that substance is the first kind of being, St. Thomas considers its priority to accidents. But, since something can be first in many different senses, the question is, in which respects is substance prior to accidents? Following Aristotle, Aquinas enumerates three instances by which substance is first to another being:

1. In the order of knowing;
2. In the order of definition; and
3. In the order of time.[35]

First of all, the priority of substance to accidents St. Thomas explains in terms of time. Any category which is able to exist apart from another necessarily is prior to that which is not capable of existing apart from the others. Substance, being a category which is *in se et non in alio*, can exist without accident, because accident is a category which consists in being *in alio*. In other words, substance can be found without any accident, but not the reverse. In concluding this argument, St.

Thomas says: "Thus it is clear that an accident does not exist whenever a substance does, but the reverse is true; and for this reason substance is prior in time."[36]

The priority of substance to accidents can be proved, secondly, in the order of definition. Substance can be understood without accident, but not the reverse. The reasons for this is that substance is not what is predicated of a subject, but that of which other things are predicated.[37] Substance, being that of which other things are predicated, must be necessarily prior to accidents, because in the definition of any accident it is necessary to include the definition of substance; for example, in the definition of man, animality is prior because the definition of animality is given in that of man.[38]

Substance, finally, is prior to accident in regard to the order of knowing. The general principle for this St. Thomas derives from the specific characteristics of knowing. In the order of knowing that which is better known and explains a thing better is prior to that which is less known.[39]

b. The Order of Distinction

The priority and posteriority which occurs in the essential order of being presupposes a real distinction between substance and accident. In searching for the principle of this distinction, St. Thomas analyzes the characteristics of substantial and accidental being as they are related to and separated from each other. In his *Commentary on the Metaphysics*,[40] Aquinas enumerates two characteristics for both substance and accident. On the one hand, substance is being which is capable of separate existence and as such constitutes a determinate particular thing. On the other hand, accident is being which in its existence depends upon substance and as such cannot constitute by itself any determinate particular thing. This twofold opposite characteristics of the essential order of being St. Thomas examines in view of his doctrine of the distinction between essence and being.

For St. Thomas, to have an essence means to be some definite thing, because the essence of a thing is what that thing is.[41] Consequently, those concepts which do not signify some definite thing do not have an essence.[42] But in signifying some definite thing essence can be taken in at least two senses, that is to say, absolute and relative sense. Now, in the absolute sense essence can be attributed to substance alone, because substance does not depend on anything else and as such constitutes a subject by itself. Accident, however, has an essence in a relative sense, because accident depends on its subject, which does not belong to the essence of the accident itself but to that of substance. To be more specific, St. Thomas considers this distinction between substance and accident as they are expressed in the order of definition.

The definition of a substance requires no other essence than that which substance has from itself.[43] The reason for this is that substance has its own quiddity which follows from the fact that substance is being *per se et non in alio*. In this sense St. Thomas can define substance as *res cui conveniat esse non in subiecto* [44] or *essentiam cui competit sic esse, id est per se esse*.[45] In contrast to substance, the definition of an accident needs an extrinsic essence-subject, at one time directly (when an accident is signified concretely as an accident fused with a subject) and at another indirectly (when an accident is signified in the abstract, after the manner of a substance). In the definition of an accident there must be given an extrinsic essence, because accident has being only by reason of the fact that it inheres in a subject which does not belong to its own essence but to that of substance. In this sense the essence of accident consists in being dependent on that of substance.[46]

The distinction between substance and accident can also be analyzed with reference to their being.[47] In the *De Ente et Essentia*, St. Thomas defines being as something having existence. But, again, things have existence in many different ways *secundum propriam rationem*.[48] Substance has being *simpliciter*, because it is substance alone that subsists. Accidents are called beings *secundum quid*, because by them something is; for example, whiteness is said to be because by it the subject is white. For this St. Thomas, following Aristotle,[49] describes accidents not as *simpliciter entia sed entis entia*.[50]

The being of accident is 'being in' and as such really distinct from that of substance.[51] In view of such a thesis/conclusion, it is clear that substance and accidents are really distinct as two different realities having their own being. In a word, substance has *esse subsistens*, but accident *esse inhaerens*.

The distinction which occurs between substance and accident reveals new aspects of the essential order of being, and as such can be considered in two ways:

1. As an order in which substance and accidents are separated from and opposed to each other; and
2. As an order in which substance is related to and united with particular accidents.

Substance as it is considered absolutely and in itself has *esse* which is immutable and independent of any kind of external determination. This doctrine St. Thomas proves from the structure of any substantial being as an *ens per se et non in alio*. Whatsoever is *ens per se* is in itself indivisible and does not have any composition of parts, for instance, the material substance considered absolutely and in itself. The only composition of material substance is that of matter and form. Yet this composition is not the same as that of parts. In fact, the material substance receives a disposition of parts from quantity or quality, that is, from accidents. As a matter of fact, substance is indivisible by negation of all kinds of quantitative characteristics. But being indivisible the material substance is indifferent from any accident and as such is immutable in itself.

Immutable and indivisible substance, however, being in union with particular accidents is diversified and multiplied in many ways.[52] For Aquinas, any determination does not come from a substance itself, but from a particular accident through which substance is determined to a definite operation. How to explain this relation between substantial and accidental being?[53]

Substance being a subject of mutation is disposed to receive some determination from accidents, although it remains in itself immutable and unchangeable. The principle of variation and mutation belong to the very essence of accidental being to such an extent that one accident can be alternated and diversified by another.[54]

To sum up, substance and accident are really distinct from each other by having a different kind of being. On the one hand, substance has being as something which is in itself immutable and indivisible and independent from any kind of external determination. On the other hand, accident has being which is changeable according to manifold variations and mutations. This different kind of being is a principle of distinction between substantial and accidental being.

c. The Principle of Order of Being

Substance and accidents are related to each other according to their being and essence. But, since substance being *essentiam cui competit per se esse et non in alio* and accident being *essentiam cui competit esse in alio*, the accidental being depends on the substantial one, and not the reverse.[55] This relation of dependence St. Thomas explains in terms of act and potency.[56] Now, the question is, what is the principle of the relation which occurs between substantial and accidental being? To solve this problem we have to examine the conditions under which accident depends on substance.

Accident being dependent on substance has *esse* only by participation. The reason for this is that accident can have its own being insofar as it inheres in a substance, and as such accident can never be found without a substance.[57] Now, the mode of being of substance can be participated in by all the accidents according to a certain proportional likeness. St. Thomas, referring to the distinction between qualified and unqualified sense of being, says that accidents have some whatness but in a qualified sense, that is to say, a whatness of a particular kind; for example, color has a whatness of whiteness, and number the whatness of double.[58]

In the structure of any real being St. Thomas distinguishes two kinds of form: substantial and accidental. The substantial form is related to the accidental as substance to accident, because the former belongs to the order of substantial being and the latter to the order of accidental being. But, since the accident is depended upon substance, the order of substantial and accidental form has to be considered in the same way.

In the essential order of being, the substantial form differs from that of accidental on the basis of origin of *esse*: a substantial form gives *esse simpliciter* and accidental form gives *esse tale*.[59]

In the order of substantial and accidental forms there is a specific relation according to actuality of their subjects. The substantial form being a principle of *esse simpliciter* is in regard to the actuality prior to its own subject to which it gives the actual existence. On the contrary, the accidental form being a principle of *esse tale* is in the order of actuality posterior to its subject from which it receives its actual existence.[60]

2. The Substantial Order of Being

Having established the essential order of being according to its threefold elements, it remains to consider the ways in which essence can be found in particular kinds of being. But, since the essence expresses being either in regard to substantial or accidental *esse*, the predicamental order of being can be established in two ways, namely:

1. As a substantial order of being; and
2. As an accidental order of being.

For being is predicated absolutely and primarily of substances and secondarily and in a qualified sense of accidents, we have to begin first to analyze the substantial order of being.

The substantial order of being can be established according to the essences as they are found in different kinds of substantial beings. St. Thomas distinguishes a twofold manner of having essence by a substantial being, namely:

1. Essence as found in the composite substance of a material being; and
2. Essence as found in the simple substance of an intellectual being.

The substantial order of being as it is found among the essences of simple and composite substances can be analyzed either in regard to their act of existing or in regard to the act of human understanding. The substantial order of being considered as it is related to the act of existing shows that the essence in simple substance is found in a truer and more noble way than in that of composite substance. The reason for this is based on the fact that simple substances have a more noble existence, and as such they are the cause of those which are composed. However, the substantial order of being considered in regard to the act of human understanding displays that the essences of simple substances are more hidden from our intellect, and for this they should be analyzed after considering the essence of composite substances.

The composite being is not only differentiated in its structure, but also in the mode of its composition. At least St. Thomas distinguishes three kinds of them: (a) aggregations; (b) ligaments; and (c) mixtures.[61] The different modes of composition depend upon the various kinds of proportion between them.

The general meaning of any proportion is a relation of the thing to another, as of matter to form, or of cause to effect.[62] In real beings there are two kinds of proportions: (a) the proportion of beings composed of various parts; and (b) the proportion of beings mixed from different opposites. These two kinds of proportions of beings St. Thomas calls a *harmonia*, in which the various parts of being or different functions coincide together in some unity.[63] Now, depending on the kind of proportion and the nature of components, we can distinguish different orders between all real beings. Hence, distinguishing between simple and composite substances, we can analyze the essential order of being in two ways, namely:

1. As an order of composite substances; and
2. As an order of simple substances.

a. The Order of Composite Substances

For St. Thomas to determine how essence is found in the very nature of composite substance means to give its definition. The reasons for this is that essence is what the definition of a thing is. However, definition of a thing comprises the specific principles of a thing and not the individual.[64] In order to determine the very essence of composite substance, then, we have to describe the specific principles which are included in a definition of a natural thing.

In the definition of a natural thing there is, according to Aristotle, a twofold principle, that is to say, matter and form.[65] To make clear why the essence of composite substance comprises both matter and form, St. Thomas analyzes the conditions under which a natural thing can be defined.[66]

Essence is something in virtue of which a thing can be grasped by the intellect, and something in virtue of which a thing can be categorized as one of ten predicaments. Now, essence so considered presupposes something that is actual because actuality can be the only principle of intelligibility. It is evident, then, that matter alone being a potentiality of itself cannot fulfill all the requirements of the definition of essence as such. In other words, matter alone cannot be the essence of a composite substance, because it cannot be a principle of intelligibility.[67]

Although the matter alone cannot constitute the whole essence of composite substance, neither can the form alone be said to be its essence. St. Thomas has recourse to Aristotle and says that according to the Stagirite natural things have sensible matter in their definition. This is evident from the meaning of essence as something expressing what a real being is. Now, since it cannot be said that natural substances are defined by something that does not pertain to their being, the sensible matter which is required by the definition of a natural thing must be an integral part of the essence of composite substance.[68] St. Thomas argues that sensible matter is required by the definition of natural things because, otherwise, there would not be any difference between them and the definition of mathematical objects. This argument Aquinas develops against the doctrine of Averroes according to which the whole essence of a species consists in the form alone.[69] If it would be so the definition of material and mathematical objects would have this in common that they are expressed by a form without matter.[70]

Granting, however, that the essence of composite substance includes both matter and form, Aquinas firmly states that essence so conceived cannot signify merely a relation between them or something added to them. The reason is that this would be an accident or something extraneous to the real thing, and the real thing would not be known through it. In other words, the composition of matter and form belongs not only to the definition of the essence of natural things, but also to their essences as they are found in reality.[71]

In the very structure of a composite substance, then, there is a specific order of matter and form. This order which occurs between matter and form can be analyzed in regard to both their being and operation. The order of matter and form analyzed in regard to their being does not admit that one element would be prior to another. Matter is not prior to form, because matter as something potential becomes an actual being through form.[72] Form also cannot be prior to matter, because as something which participates in matter it is posterior to it.[73] The order of matter and form considered in regard of their operations displays that form is a principle of operations, and matter the subject of operations. Form is a principle of operations, because it is an act *per se*.[74] Matter is a material principle of a subject of operations, because it is actualized by form.[75]

This order of composite substance results in the mutual determination of matter and form. Matter is determined by form, because matter before receiving a particular form is in potency to many different forms. But, as soon as matter receives a particular form it is determined by it.[76]

Matter and form being in mutual determination, they are subordinated to each other. Matter is subordinated to form,[77] because it can be an actual being only through form.[78] Form is subordinated to matter, because it is the act by which a composite substance receives an act of existing.[79]

The specific structure of a composite substance causes that material beings are some diversity because of matter,[80] and some unity because of form.[81] It is so because form as an act is a principle of unity, and matter as a potency is a principle of diversity. Thus material beings because of matter are in potency to different acts, and because of form they belong to a particular genus and species.[82]

The order which occurs in a composite substance between matter and form is of different kinds, and mainly depends upon the actualization of matter by form.[83] But, the different kind of composition and the special proportion of matter and form among natural beings constitutes a particular order of composite substances. In general, this order means a proportional descent from the highest things to the lowest,[84] and is based on the principle that the lowest in the higher genus touches the highest of the lower species.[85]

b. The Order of Simple Substances

Having recourse to Avencebrol and his medieval followers, St. Thomas firmly states that simple substances are completely and totally free from any kind of matter. The main argument Aquinas derives from the power of understanding which we can find in them. As a matter of fact, forms are not actually intelligible except insofar as they are separated from matter and from its conditions; nor are they made actually intelligible except by the power of a substance understanding them, insofar as they are received into, and are affected by, that substance.[86]

In refutation of the panhylomorphistic theory, St. Thomas refers to the principle that the activity of a being is in conformity with its nature. Since the activity of the soul is entirely immaterial, its intellect should be also immaterial; otherwise, the intellect would not comprehend the species of things in a spiritual way.[87]

The very essence of simple substance, then, is completely free from any kind of matter, and as such can be defined in terms of form alone. Yet, the essence of a simple substance defined in terms of form alone can be signified as a whole and as something undivided. To clear up the very manner of predication of formal one, St. Thomas makes a comparison between the essence of simple substance and that of composite substance. The essence of composite substance can be predicated as a whole or as a part, because of the designation of matter which is found in it. The essence of simple substance cannot be predicated except as a whole, because nothing is there besides the form as receiving the form. Moreover, the essence of composite substances, because they are received into designated matter, are multiplied according to its division. The essence of simple substance, however, since it is not received into matter, cannot be multiplied and as such there are among them as many species as there are individuals.[88] In a word, the essence of simple substance differs from that of composite substance on the basis of the absence of matter in the nature of simple substance. Thus the essence of a simple substance consists in being a subsisting form.

In the very essence of simple substance, however, there is a composition of form and existence. The main reason for this composition rests on the fact that in the very nature of any created being there is a distinction between essence and act of existing. In the second book of the *SCG*, chapter fifty-two, St. Thomas points out several arguments to prove that in the very nature of simple substance its essence does not imply the act of existence. In other words, actual existence does not enter into the definition of any created being. Proving this doctrine, St. Thomas has recourse to the fact that there can be only one being in which the act of existing would be included in its essence. In conclusion Aquinas says that since God is subsisting being, He alone can be His own being.

Some things have such a form that they are self-subsistent and self-complete, and as such they do not require any basis of matter. However, other forms require matter as a foundation, because they cannot subsist by themselves, and as such they have not simple form nor yet merely matter, but they are composed of both.[89] The things constituted from self-subsistent form are spiritual beings, and the things composed from matter and form are material beings.

Now, since forms differ because some are more perfect than others, there is a specific order between material and spiritual substances. Spiritual substances are superior to all material substances, as the immoveable and immaterial to the moveable and material.[90] This order of spiritual and material substances is diversified in many ways.[91]

The order of simple substances can be considered also as it is in itself. But, since there are two kinds of substances, united and separate from matter, we would have a twofold order of simple substances:
1. The order of separate substances, and
2. The order of united substances.

(1) The order of united substances

In the order of created beings man takes a special place among them. In relation to the spiritual beings, human souls hold the lowest rank in the order of the intellectual substances, but in regard to the material beings man is the highest being in the order of natural things. This cross position of the human being in the created world includes a special order of both its faculties and being.

In the order of human faculties there is an arrangement between intellectual, sensible, and bodily powers. The outline of this order is as follows: corporeal powers are subjected to sensible and intellectual powers, and the sensible powers are subjected to the intellectual ones. The interrelationship between these faculties is natural, and as such can be considered either in their nature or in their operation. Considering the human being in its nature, St. Thomas enumerates three kinds of soul, and in regard to its operation five different faculties and powers.

In the very nature of human being St. Thomas distinguishes three kinds of soul: the vegetative, the sensitive, and the intellectual.[92] Since each soul as a form is a principle of activity, there are five faculties and powers, namely: vegetative, sensitive, appetitive, local motion, and intellectual.[93] The vegetative soul is the principle of life and has three natural powers, that of generation, that of growth, and that of preservation. By generation a thing receives life, by growth size and strength, and by nourishment preservation.[94] The sensitive soul is the principle of sensation, and the intellectual soul is the principle of cognition.[95] Among these three kinds of souls and the five kinds of powers there is a specific order of perfection.

In conformity with the principle that multitude supposes a unity in some order, the souls and their operations are arranged gradually, according to the perfection of the forms. Generally speaking, the form of the intellectual soul is more perfect than the form of the sensitive soul, and the form of the sensitive soul is more perfect than the form of the vegetative soul.[96] Moreover, since the higher soul contains the perfections of the lower, the intellectual soul of man contains virtually the powers of sensitive and vegetative souls, and as such exercises their functions.[97] As a matter of fact, since the soul as a form is a principle of different kinds of perfection, a human being is a man, an animal, a living body, and an actual being.[98]

This order of perfection St. Thomas considers in three ways, that is, in regard to nature, time, and objects.[99] In the order of perfection considered in regard to the nature of particular faculties, the sensitive powers are prior to the vegetative, because perfect faculties are always prior to those less perfect in nature. But in the order considered in regard to time, the vegetative powers are prior to the sensitive, because the less perfect powers are prior to the more perfect faculties in time. Finally, in the order of perfection considered in regard to their objects, the sensitive powers are superior to the vegetative, because the more universal object requires the superior faculty.[100]

The order of perfection can be considered also in regard to the degree to which a particular soul arises above the powers of a corporeal being. The lowest rank of perfection occupies the vegetative faculty, because in its actuating there is a need to have a corporeal organ, and the help of corporeal qualities. The higher degree of perfection possesses the sensitive faculty, because its activity does not only regard its own corporeal organ, but all other things which strike the senses. Finally, above all these faculties there is an intellectual power with operation which is not limited only to sensible things, but to all intelligible objects.[101] With regard to these degrees of perfection, the higher being needs a multiplicity of powers and many operations.[102]

The order of perfection as it is considered in regard to the nature of the human being shows that man is the final destination of all material beings. St. Thomas, comparing the structure of the human body to that of the universe, says that the man is the end of the universe, *completio universi*.[103] In regard to this order the animals exist for man, the plants for the animals, and the inorganic beings for the plants. The principle of this order of being is based on the gradation of knowledge. Man is the end and completion of the universe, because he has the highest sort of knowledge, by which he is able to have all created perfections.[104]

(2) The order of separate substances

The universe is conceived by St. Thomas in a much wider way than it is in the modern sciences. In the diversity of beings there are beyond material substances also separate intellectual substances. In the philosophy of the ancient Greeks, Arabs, and Christian thinkers, the separate substances belong to the universe as one of its principal parts.[105] St. Thomas goes further and says: "each of the separate substances is a principal part of the universe, much more than the sun or the moon; since each of them has the nature of a species all its own, which is nobler than that of any corporeal things."[106]

In the acceptance of the statement that the separate substances belong to the universe as its principal parts, Aquinas goes so far that he rejects the teaching of the Greek Fathers that the angels had been created before the corporeal world. St.Thomas argues that if the separate substances are principal parts of the universe with a relation to the whole from which it receives its perfection, then the previous creation of them would not be in accord with the perfection of the universe.[107]

The order of the universe for the sake of its ultimate perfection and consummation requires the existence of intellectual substances: "as a result of the order established by God's assigning to creatures the optimum perfection consonant with their manner of being, certain creatures were endowed with an intellectual nature, thus being given the highest rank in the universe."[108] In the third book of the *SCG* St. Thomas explains how the universe achieves the ultimate perfection. And in book two of the *SCG* Aquinas has a treatise on intellectual substances[109] and points out a number of arguments in order to show that in the universe there exist also, beyond the intellectual substances of men, the separate substances of angels.[110]

The principal argument for the existence of the separate substances St. Thomas draws from the perfect structure of the universe, and says that for the sake of its perfection there can be some things in the genus of substance that are completely incorporeal. But all possible natures which are found in the order of things could be actualized, because otherwise the universe would be imperfect. According to this concept, a subsisting spiritual being is able to exist without animality, and from this possibility the actuality follows. Moreover, the same result can be achieved from the consideration of the proportional ascent of the universe.

The perfection of the universe requires a proportion between the number of created beings and the degree of their perfections, that is, the higher the perfection the greater the number of these beings in existence. But the abundance of created beings could be taken in a twofold sense: either in magnitude or in multitude. In the universe, in regard to magnitude, the most perfect beings are celestial bodies, but in regard to multitude the most perfect beings are separated intellectual substances. From this point of view St. Thomas concludes that the separate substances are not the same in number as the bodily substances, and the former are more numerous than the latter.[111]

Since the separate substances are compounded only from an act and form they should be immaterial.[112]

The immateriality of separate substances is the basis of their incorruptibility. The argument of incorruptibility of separate substances St. Thomas bases upon the different structure of their substance, as being composed only of act and potentiality.[113] The same result we can receive if we would consider the structure and the nature of the process of generation and corruption.[114]

The separate substances being incorruptible are also subsisting species,[115] and as such they result in a specific order of perfection. Since each individual which belongs to the species is superior to the individuating principle that lies outside the essence of the species, the universe is ennobled more by multiplication of species than by the multiplication of individuals of one species. Accordingly, it is more consonant with the perfection of the universe that separate substances constitute a plurality, each diverse in species from the other, rather than a numerical multiplicity within one and the same species. In this way, the universe achieves the highest degree of perfection.[116]

The order of perfection of separate substances as subsisting forms is dependent upon the degree of their potentiality. Generally speaking, one separate substance is superior to another insofar as it has less potentiality.[117] In the universe there are two separate substances which are equal to each other, because there are diverse species in separate substances according to the diverse grades allotted to them, and there are not several individuals in one species. Accordingly, in the whole multitude of separate substances there is a highest, middle, and lowest intelligence.[118]

3. The Accidental Order of Being

All accidents are beings by participation in substances. But, since particular accidents participate in substance in different ways, there is a determinate order of accidental beings. In the *De Ente et Essentia*, St. Thomas says:

> Whence, accidental words expressed in a concrete way, like 'the white' or 'the musical', are not placed in a category as species or genera, except by reduction. They belong to a category only when expressed in the abstract, like 'whiteness' and 'music'. Since accidents, moreover, are not composed of matter and form, we cannot take their genus from matter and their difference from form, as we do in composite substances. We must take their primary genus from their very manner of existing, according as being is predicated diversely, according to priority and posteriority, of the ten categories.[119]

In a word, the accidental order of being depends on the manner of existing according to a definite sequence of priority and posteriority. The Angelic Doctor describes this order as follows:

> Among these accidents a certain order is to be noted. Of all accidents, dimensive quantity adheres most closely to substance: afterwards, with quantity as a medium, the substance is affected with qualities: for instance with colour by means of the surface. Hence the division of the other accidents is incidental to the division of quantity. Further, qualities are the principles of actions and passions, as well as of certain relationships, for instance of father and son, master and servant, and so on; while some relationships are founded immediately on quantity, for instance greater and lesser, double and half, and the like.[120]

In view of this text we would like to consider the accidental order of being as it is found in quantity and quality.

a. Order in Quantity

The very nature of quantity St. Thomas defines as an order of parts.[121] Quantity so conceived consists in a disposition of parts by juxtaposition within the whole.[122] However, quantity is the category that presupposes matter, and as such is the first among the accidents to be predicated of substance. To establish the proper order in quantity,

then, one has to consider the relationship between substance and quantity. In regard to this St. Thomas states the following two theses, namely:
1. Quantity is really distinct from substance; and
2. Quantity consists in extension by which substance becomes a subject of some quantitative mutations.

Quantity as an accident must be really distinct from substance. In his *Metaphysics*, Aristotle, distributing substance and quantity among two different categories of beings, says:

> There are several senses in which a thing may be said to 'be', . . . ; for in one sense the 'being' meant is 'what a thing is', and in another sense it means a quality or quantity or one of the other things that are predicated as these are. . ."[123]

The real distinction between substance and quantity St. Thomas bases on the immutability of any substantial being. First of all, substance is prior to quantity,[124] and as such, it is also indifferent to any particular quantity, even though a material substance must be quantified.[125] Furthermore, even though substance is prior and indifferent to quantity, it is immutable and independent of all quantitative determinations. Consequently, substance as immutable and independent is also really distinct from quantity which, as an accident, is mutable and dependent.[126]

The relative immutability of substance and its independence in regard to quantity are very important in understanding properly the very essence of quantity as entailing an order of parts. The proper and formal element of quantity so considered consists in extension, that is, in a disposition of parts by which substance receives a definite position.[127] Defining quantity in terms of extension one may ask the question where this extension can be found--in quantity or in substance? But, because some modern Thomistic philosophers confused St. Thomas's doctrine of quantity with that of Suarez,[128] let us examine the theory of extension as explained by the *Doctor Eximius*.

In the very structure of extension, Suarez distinguishes a twofold aspect of matter: entitative and situated.[129] In view of this twofold material aspect Suarez distinguishes three kinds of extension: (1) *extensio entitativa*, (2) *extensio aptitudinis*, and (3) *extensio situalis actualis*.[130] Applying this threefold division of extension to the order of substance and accidents, the *Doctor Eximius* states that (1) *extensio entitativa* can be attributed both to substance and quality; (2) *extensio aptitudinis* cannot be separated from the very structure of the material substance; and (3) *extensio situalis actualis* could be separated from the corporeal substance but only by means of miracle.[131] So, according to the Suarezian theory of extension, the corporeal substance, even before receiving quantitative determinations, "contains some parts." However, Suarez adds that the contrary theory is among the majority of St. Thomas's Commentators "valde vulgaris."[132]

John of St. Thomas was one of the first who accepted Suarez's theory of extension and tried to apply it to St. Thomas's doctrine of quantity as an order of parts. In his *Cursus Philosophicus*, John of St. Thomas accepts the view that in material substance there is an entitative composition of some integral parts which does not come from quantity as such but from substance itself.[133]

In the very structure of any substance there is, according to the Suarezian theory of extension, some entitative composition of parts. This conclusion, however, can be hardly reconciled with another Suarezian doctrine, according to which there is no real distinction between essence and existence. If, as Suarez held, there is no real distinction between the essence and the existence of quantified substance, then it seems inescapable that there would be no real distinction between the essence and the existence of quantity itself. This, however, seems to entail a certain confusion of substance and accident, for indeed, on what ground would a quantified substance be distinct from the accident of quantity that inhered in it? If the very essence of extension is an 'entitative composition of parts', then is not an extended substance identical in the order of essence with its own accident of quantity? And, since a real distinction between essence and existence has been precluded, the ground for distinguishing between substance and quantity cannot be found in their existence, for in that case the existence of substance and that of quantity would be the same, and, accordingly, the distinction between substance and accident of quantity would be a modal one. Suarez, however, holds that there is a real distinction between substance and any accident.[134] The foundation of the real distinction between substance and quantity, therefore, cannot be made either in regard to their existence. The Suarezian view is that the essence and existence of a substance are really the same and only virtually distinct; hence, if a quantity were '*res distincta a substantia*' it would possess its own existence, only virtually distinct from its essence, and thus a quantified substance would be two things.

The real distinction between substance and accident, then, demands and can ground only on the real distinction between essence and existence. This conclusion, however, cannot be adjusted to the Suarezian doctrine of being and extension. Furthermore, according to St. Thomas, composition of parts does not consist in the being of substance, but in the entitative structure of quantity itself.[135] In a word, the very structure of quantity consists in an essential composition of integral parts, by which substance receives extension, that is, a definite position.

Quantity, since it is an order of parts within the whole and thus possesses a certain unity in diversity, is the foundation of multiplication: "any quantity consists of multiplication of parts."[136] The reason for this is that quantity is a principle of individuation.[137]

Quantity, by its union with substance, communicates to substance the composition of parts by which it becomes a whole that is susceptible of division. Yet this does not mean that quantity causes the integral parts in substance, because quantity as an accident cannot produce anything in substance.[138] In other words, the immutable and indivisible substance becomes by quantity a whole and a potentially multiplied thing which can be broken up into some integral parts. In this sense quantity is a measure of substance.[139] Quantity so conceived is a principle of divisibility and measurability, of impenetrability and integrity, of unity and plurality, that is, the first properties of material being.[140]

Quantity, conceived as a disposition of parts, constitutes a specific order of equality and inequality.[141] This order St. Thomas defines in terms of proportion.[142] But quantity is not an order of equality according to the essence but only in respect to commensuration (*secundum essentiam sed solummodo secundum commensurationem*), because quantity does not determine substance in respect to being but quiddity of whatever genera (*per respectum ad esse sed quidditatem alicuius generis*).[143]

One can consider the order in quantity in two ways: there is the order among a plurality of discrete things and there is the order within single, continuous quantity. If the arrangement takes place among discrete things, the principle consists in some one determinate being to which all other things are related differently, depending on their nearness to it, for example, as one who stands second and one who stands third--the one who stands second being prior to the one who stands third. But in the case of continuous things, what one takes as principle depends on place or time or motion. So, as to the order in quantity St. Thomas discusses the continuous thing in three ways in which they are prior, namely, with the reference to place, time, and motion.[144]

The first order in quantity is that of place. In this order a thing is said to be prior in place inasmuch as it is nearer to some determinate place, whether that place be the middle point in some continuous quantity or an extreme; for example, as the principle of elements we can take the center of the world or the outermost sphere. But nearness to a principle of place can be considered in two ways, that is, with reference to an order naturally determined, and with reference to an order that depends on chance, for example, in the case of stones which lie on top of one another in a heap. The general criterion is as follows: what is nearest to a principle is prior, and what is further away from a principle is subsequent.[145]

The second order in quantity St. Thomas considers in regard to time. Things are said to be prior in time in two ways, namely:
1. Some things are prior because they are further away from the present, as occurs in the case of things which have taken place, that is, past events; and
2. Some things are prior because they are closer or nearer to the present.

So, the principle in the order of the continuous things in time is the present, because we say that something is prior or subsequent on the ground that it is nearer to, or further away from, the present. Even in the position that holds that time to be eternal we have to recognize the present as the principle, because the only starting point of time which can be taken is one that relates to some present moment, which is the middle point between the past and the future, inasmuch as time might, by hypothesis, proceed to infinity in both directions.[146]

The order in quantity, finally, can be considered with reference to the order in motion, both the natural and the voluntary motion. Things with reference to natural motion constitute a special order of activity, and things with reference to voluntary motion are based on the order of power.

In the order of activity things with natural motion are said to be prior in the order found in motion, because what is nearer to a first cause of motion is prior and what is further away from it is subsequent.

However, this order of motion is two-sided, because the nearness to some principle can be considered here either in regard to the mover or to the moved thing; for example, a boy is prior to a man because he is nearer to his primary mover, that is, the one begetting him; but the latter is also said to be prior because he is a principle of begetting or moving. So, the order of mover and the moved is taken here in an absolute sense and as it is found in nature of the thing itself.[147]

In the order of power, things with voluntary motion are said to be prior in the order found in motion because that which is nearer to a more powerful thing is prior to that which is less powerful; for example, man who surpasses another in power is said to be prior to that which is surpassed. The principle of this order, therefore, consists in the intention of the one who moves and commands others by his will; for example, a king in his kingdom moves his subjects by his authority. So, the position of someone in a particular society depends on an approximation to the ruler: the ones through whom his commands are made known to his subjects are prior to those subjects.[148]

In the order of priority and posteriority that is found in quantity there is a natural interdependence between the order of place, motion, and time. The general outline of it St. Thomas formulates as follows: "insofar as there is priority and posteriority in continuous quantity, there is priority and posteriority in motion; and insofar as there is priority in motion, there is priority and posteriority in time."[149]

b. Order in Quality

Aristotle describes quality as "that on account of which we are said to be such and such."[150] This description, however, reveals only the etymological meaning of quality. In his *Metaphysics* Aristotle explains more precisely the meaning of quality and says:

> Thus there are, roughly speaking, two meanings which the term 'quality' can bear, and of these one is more fundamental than the other. Quality in the primary sense is the differentia of the essence; and quality in numbers falls under this sense, because it is a kind of differentia of essences, but of things either not in motion or not *qua* in motion. Secondly, there are the affections of things in motion *qua* in motion, and the differentiae of motions. Goodness and badness fall under these affections, because they denote differentiae of the motion or functioning in respect of which things in motion act or are acted upon well or badly. For that which can

function or be moved in such-and-such a way is good, and that which can function in such-and-such a way in the contrary way is bad. Quality refers especially to 'good' and 'bad' in the case of living things, and of these especially in the case of such which possess choice.[151]

In the division of quality the Stagirite posits four pairs of species: habitus and disposition, capacity and incapacity, passion and passive quality, form and figure. Simplicius was one of the first who tried to set up an order among the various types of quality. In general his division of quality is based upon the distinction between the natural qualities and those which are added on from without or produced by an external cause. In view of this principle Simplicius establishes the following order in quality:

1. The order of habits and dispositions which is based on those qualities which are produced by an external cause;
2. The order of capacities and incapacities that is found among the natural qualities which express a potency of a thing;
3. The order of passion and passive quality that is included within the natural qualities which express something actual but deeply rooted in the thing;
4. The order of form and figure that is attributed to the natural qualities which expresses something actual but superficially rooted in the thing.[152]

St. Thomas rejects Simplicius's systematization of quality and shows its insufficiency. First of all, there are many forms and sensible qualities which are not natural, but something from without. Secondly, there are also many dispositions which are not from without but natural, for example, beauty and health. In conclusion Aquinas says: "Whatever is natural, it is always prior."[153]

In describing the essence of quality, St. Thomas has recourse to the Augustinian definition of *modus* which the Angelic Doctor defines as "some determination according to a specific measure."[154] The notion of 'measure,' however, as it is found in Aristotle St. Thomas extends from the order of quantity on all kinds of created beings.[155] In the *Summa theologiae* Aquinas, discussing the threefold aspect of any being, that is, *esse*, *species* and *ordo*, refers the notion of measure to substance and says: "for measure relates to substance of a thing limited according to its own principles."[156] Consequently, in applying the notions of *modus* and *mensura* to the doctrine of quality, one has to consider quality as it is related to the substance according to some particular principles by which a specific subject is limited and determined intrinsically, St. Thomas defines the very essence of quality as a mode of substance. In a word, quality conveys a certain determination of substance according to some measure, that is, a disposition of parts among which there exists a certain order.[157]

Having established the very nature of quality, St. Thomas tries to propose his own systematization of all kind of qualities. Rejecting Simplicius's principle of distinction of qualities, Aquinas bases his own proposition on the mode of substance according to the perfections of accidental *esse*. Quality as a mode of substance can determine it in the following three ways, namely:

1. The order according to the proper nature of a particular substance;
2. The order according to the actions and passions resulting from particular principle of nature, that is, matter and form; and
3. The order according to quantity.

This threefold order of quality is congruent with the order according to place, potency, and species.

The Thomistic definition of quality as a mode of substance became the target of criticism for Francis Suarez. In his *Disputationes metaphysicae*, Suarez reproaches St. Thomas's definition of quality as a mode of substance according to accidental *esse* with two alternative difficulties, namely:

1. In the definition of quality as a mode of substance, if the term 'modus' is taken strictly and exactly, that is, as something by which substance is distinct from any accidental entity, then such an assumption would be false, because many, if not all, qualities are proper entities affecting the substance; and
2. In the definition of quality as a mode of substance, if the term '*modus*' is taken in its broad sense, that is, as some form determining the capacity of subject, then such a definition can be applied to any kind of accident.

Moreover, Suarez, referring to Cajetan's *Commentary on Summa Theologiae*, I-II,q.49, a.2c, says that, according to the definition of quality as a mode of substance, the *definiendum* is not substance but quality, and as such the term *modus* should not be understood as a determination in its absolute sense, but with some qualification, that is, in regard to this kind of determination which is proper to a particular accident. However, this is the question to be solved: what is the proper essence and kind of determination of substance accomplished by quality? The *Doctor Eximius* does not think that the Thomistic doctrine of quality gives any definite answer to this problem.[158]

To propound his own theory, Suarez commences with a proposition that the very structure of any accident consists in being an affection of substance by which the subject is relieved of some imperfection: *ad supplendum aliquem defectum eius*. The Suarezian theory of accident, then, accepts the assumption according to which any created substance is so limited in its entity that *per seipsum* it cannot have *complementum perfectionis*. Particular accidents perfect the substance in different ways. Among all other accidents quality is the most perfect instance of accidental being, because it affects the substance in its existence and operations. In other words, quality is an ornamentation of substance both in regard to its existence and operations. Quality so considered is an absolute accident to the created substance *ad complementum perfectionis eius tam in existendo quam in agendo*.[159]

To what extent are the Suarezian objections against St. Thomas's doctrine of quality as a mode of substance justified? In answering this question we must recall the Thomistic solution of the relationship which takes place between quality and quantity. But, since quality is a determination of substance *ex ratione formae* and quantity *ex ratione materiae*, the question is how substance is determined by quality and quantity.

Quality belongs to the order of accidental form and as such consists in being an accidental mode of substance. Quality so considered is a special kind of determination of substance, that is, a disposition of subject according to the perfections of accidental *esse*. However, the disposition that is accomplished by quality can be considered both in regard to the actuality and to the potentiality of the subject. Quality, if considered in regard to the actuality of its subject, is caused by, and depends upon it. Yet the subject, considered in regard to its potentiality, can be perfected by a quality which gives to the actually existing subject an accidental *esse* by increasing or diminishing its natural perfections. In a word, quality is a kind of determination of substance which disposes it in respect to its natural perfections, according to accidental *esse*.

However, quantity is also a kind of determination of substance and belongs to the order of accidental *esse*. Moreover, St. Thomas defines both quality and quantity as an order of parts. So, the very important question arises here as to what is the principle of distinction which takes place between the mode of determination of a substance realized by quality and that which is realized by quantity. In general, the difference between quantity and quality is based on the relationship they have to matter and form: quantity corresponds to matter and quality to form.[160] Quantity and quality are dispositions of parts by which they determine a substance, but they do so in different ways. In other words, quantity and quality have the same function of setting parts in order, but the orderings they effect are different. Quantity is a determination of substance in the order of extension by which one part is placed outside another in relation to itself or to some place. Quality, on the other hand, is a determination of substance in the order of perfections and as such it disposes the material parts in a range of intensity, whether in relation to nature itself and the termination of its quantity, or in relation to action and the term of action, or even in relation to the intensity of quality and the extension of *habitus*.[161]

To sum up, the difference between the order of quantity and that of quality depends upon the different effects which they cause in a substance. Quantity, since it is related to the order of matter, affects a substance extrinsically by extending it into some material parts. Quality, since it is related to the order of form, affects a substance intrinsically by rendering substance such and such. Moreover, quantity, because it is related to matter, affects substance in its potentiality, and quality, because it is related to form, affects substance in its actuality. Since there is an order between matter and form within the composite, there must be an order between quantity and quality also. This order St. Thomas considers both in regard to their *esse* and to their function. In general, since substance has *esse* of itself, the determination of substance, which is accomplished by quality and quantity, is necessarily related to an actual and formed subject. Accordingly, quantity and quality affecting substance in its *esse* render the subject more perfect, not in its substantial being, but in its accidental being.

Thus the Suarezian objections against the Thomistic doctrine of quality do not seem to invalidate St. Thomas's teaching on the nature of accidental being.[162]

As a matter of fact Suarezian *esse*, only virtually distinct from essence, is a principle which cannot be differentiated lest the thing itself be fragmented. In one thing (*res*), there is only one *esse*, that of a substance which is in a state of ontological imperfection, to be removed only by the accident of quality. In fact, the accidental *esse* of quality is intrinsically, and absolutely, and *per se*, related *ad complementum perfectionis formalis ipsius substantiae*. The being of quality so considered would belong to the order of substance. In this case the Suarezian objections against the Thomistic doctrine of accidents are somehow beside the point.

* * * *

In his *Quodlibetum* Aquinas writes:
> Being is not found in the definition of the created thing, because it is neither a genus nor a differentia; consequently, whether something *is* and *what it is* are two different questions. Whence everything which is beyond essence, it is said to be accident; *esse* [therefore] which pertains to the question whether it is, is an accident; and in this way the Commentator says in V Metaph., that such a proposition 'Socrates is' is accidentally predicated, according what it brings upon the being of thing or the true proposition. But, truth is that what the name *ens* signifies in regard to the essence of thing and which is divided into ten genera.[163]

In this text St. Thomas summarizes his metaphysical doctrine on the categorical order of being by saying that since *esse* is found in both essence and existence, the very being of natural the essence alone. The reason for this is that being as expressing the being of natural things in respect to its act of existence is neither a genus nor a differentia. Moreover, the act of existing of being can only be grasped by our intellect as something through which we can realize that what is contained in the essence of natural thing, is present and real in reality as something positively existing.

The challenge to the metaphysical explanation of the being of natural things in their composition of essence and existence came from Rene Descartes.The existential approach to explain being of natural things, Descartes tries to overcome by explaining the being of natural things by finding in their structure various attributes, thus discovering in natural things different essential properties, especially, two principal attributes of all beings, that is, that of thinking (*res cogitans*) and that of extension (*res extensa*). This Cartesian dualism will end in a dichotomy of man between his mind and his body, because their principal attributes which are radically opposed to each other will remain inexplicable in respect to their mutual interaction. Moreover, defining substance as being which does not require anything else for its existence, the Cartesian philosophy of being will lead either to extreme monism (for example, Spinoza's pantheism) or to radical pluralism (for example, Leibniz's monadology). Furthermore, the pseudo transparency of the *cogito* enforces Descartes, according to Marcel, to remove the ego from its existence, because the Cartesian 'I' can be intelligible apart from its act of 'to-be',[164] and as such it could be treated as if it were a mental substance endowed with all the spiritual qualities, that is, those of thinking.[165] In other words, Descartes failed to understand the act of existing, because he did not grasp the primacy of existence over the distinction between the subject and object.[166]

Although Descartes in his *cogito ergo sum* was trying to bridge the gap between subject and object, nevertheless he separated them from each other, thus opening up a chasm between thinking and being, spirit and matter, mind and body, that is, a chasm between knowledge and existence. As a result of the opposition of knowledge and existence, Descartes not only separates the knower from the thing known, but made any objective knowledge of external world questionable. As a matter of fact, if *cogito* precedes existence, then our ideas and concepts cannot come from external reality but from the thinking thought. Consequently, *cogito* reveals much more about the very structure of the knower and the way it knows rather than the things themselves.

The separation of knowledge from existence started to alienate the human intellect from the external reality, and to isolate more and more the human mind from real things. In this situation Kant saw a desperate need for critical reexamination of the possibility of human reason, and to find an unshakable foundation for the certainty of man's intellect of his power of knowing. But, starting with the critique of the pure reason, Kant could not transcend the world of phenomena of things and to get to the world of noumena. Kant's attempt, then, to save the objectivity of human knowledge ends in the ambiguity of man's reason. On the one hand, in the very structure of human reason Kant realizes that there is a natural inclination for metaphysical questions, and as such a natural need to satisfy the intellectual curiosity of finding the unity of all empirical findings, namely by establishing the proper order of things represented in the mind by appropriate Ideas. However, on the other hand, Kant realizes that these Ideas are neither abstracted from experience nor are they innate in our mind, but they belong simply to the very nature and structure of human reason itself. Metaphysics, therefore, as a natural disposition of human mind to discover the order of natural things must be in vain, because the transcendental Ideas which are sought by our reason are unattainable, and as such are not related to any real objects. In the end, metaphysics fails not only to be a scientific knowledge but it becomes absurd, and the Cartesian demon Kant relocates from the transcendental to the immanent order of human reason.

The separation of knowledge and existence introduced by Descartes and deepened by Kant becomes very destructive for any human knowledge, because it undermines the confidence of human mind to know anything whatsoever. Human knowledge becomes a process of pure abstractions in which concrete things are lost, and metaphysics changes itself into some sort of epistemology, "a battlefield of endless controversies," thus giving "way to complete anarchy."[167]

In order to overcome the dangers of separation of knowledge and existence is only possible, according to Marcel, if we will reject "the temptations of a neo-gnosticism and a new-manicheism, temptations which, it must be recognized are, in such a world as ours, in danger of becoming irresistible for an increasing number of persons."[168] To do this we have to establish the confidence in intelligibility of being and to reject absurdity of reality.[169]

IV: TELEOLOGICAL ORDER OF BEING AND BECOMING

From the time of the pre-Socratics, the basic question in philosophy is: how to explain reality in its unity and plurality? Unity calls for conjunction, and plurality for disjunction of all things. Although both Heraclitus and Parmenides proclaim the priority of unity over diversity of things, the former explains the oneness of things by a tension of opposites, and the latter by likeness and similarity. Consequently, the question on *hen panta* can be formulated in two ways, namely, in Heraclitean manner: "how the things are steered through all,"[1] or in Parmenidean manner: "how the things that seem, as they all pass through everything, must gain the semblance of being."[2] In other words, the problem of unity and plurality of things can be resolved either in terms of the differentiation of being[3] or the unification of becoming.[4]

But the issue of *hen panta* of the pre-Socratics posed to the Greek philosophers a very serious problem: how can one become the other? Aristotle was one of the first to undertake a systematic analysis of the process of becoming[5] by his doctrine on nature (*physis*) and on change (*metabole*), a doctrine which has been later developed by the scholastics and which received its acme in St. Thomas Aquinas. From the times of John Locke and David Hume, however, the Aristotelian philosophy of nature has been challenged, especially by contemporary process philosophers.

Bergson charges Aristotle with making metaphysics a simplistic "systematization of science,"[6] presenting thus a static view on reality with a "more or less clumsy interpretation of the physical in terms of the vital."[7] Whitehead accuses the Stagirite for introducing the logical category of substance into metaphysics, making it thus "rarely relevant to metaphysical description.... The evil produced by the Aristotelian 'primary substance' is exactly this habit of metaphysical emphasis upon the 'subject-predicate' form of proposition."[8] Metaphysics understood only in terms of substance which has been conceived "as always a subject and never a predicate"[9] exerts a negative influence on the whole development of Western philosophy.[10] Echoing his master, Charles Hartshorne blames the classical philosophers for deprecating the process of becoming and of overemphasizing being as such. Admitting that process philosophy is "siding with becoming," Hartshorne states that it does not however "reject(s) being"; it only "defines 'being' or permanent reality in terms of becoming" by viewing 'nature' through creativity and finality."[11]

In this chapter we will make an attempt to negate the charges made by the process philosophers against classical philosophy of neglecting 'becoming' and, on the basis of St. Thomas's works, to demonstrate how creativity and finality of natural things can be treated equally in the order of both being and becoming.

A: Nature and Becoming

In his explanation of the concept of nature, Whitehead distinguishes between philosophical and metaphysical interpretations of nature. In the philosophical interpretation of nature we consider nature in itself, namely, what is given in sense-perception. In the metaphysical interpretation of nature we analyze nature in its relation to the mind, that is, as a synthesis of the knower and the thing known. In his book *The Concept of Nature* Whitehead is concerned with the philosophical interpretation of nature: "We are endeavoring in these lectures to limit ourselves to nature itself and not to travel beyond entities which are disclosed in sense-awareness."[12]

Whitehead distinguishes two ways of thinking about nature, namely, homogeneous and heterogeneous. In the former we think about nature without thinking about thought, and in the latter we think about "nature in conjunction with thought about the fact that nature is thought about."[13] In view of this distinction Whitehead says that "natural science is exclusively concerned with homogeneous thoughts about nature."[14] Whitehead is convinced that it is possible to think about nature without thinking about thought, and also without "any reference to moral or aesthetic values."[15] In homogeneous thinking nature reveals itself stripped of all reference to any other values, and as such it is "the terminus of the sense-awareness."[16]

In homogeneous thinking about nature, percipient is taken for granted and concern should not be given to the percipient nor to the process of perception as such, but to the perceived thing itself. What is perceived in sense-perception Whitehead calls nature: "nature is that which we observe in perception through the senses." [17] In sense-perception we are aware of something which is self-contained for thought. This self-containedness of something of which we are aware in sense-perception is just what we call nature.

Nature, as that which is disclosed in sense-perception, and as that which is self-contained for thought, is something which excludes thought. Nature is self-contained for thought both in regard to the sense-awareness and to the mind. This self-containedness of nature Whitehead expresses by saying that "nature as disclosed in sense-perception is self-contained as against sense-awareness, in addition to being self-contained as against thought. I will also express this self-containedness of nature by saying that nature is closed to mind."[18]

This closure of nature to mind, however, Whitehead does not understand in a sense that we cannot know nature. On the contrary, the closure of nature to thought guarantees us that we can think about nature as it is in itself:

> This closure of nature does not carry with it any metaphysical doctrine of the disjunction of nature and mind. It means that in sense-perception nature is disclosed as a complex of entities whose mutual relations are expressible in thought without reference to mind.[19]

In other words, nature is grasped in the sense-perception as something which is independent from any thought about, because "we can think about nature without thinking about thought."[20]

But, in the knowledge of nature we can distinguish three elements, namely, fact, factors, and entities. These elements Whitehead describes as follows: "Fact is the undifferentiated terminus of self-awareness; factors are termini of sense-awareness, differentiated as elements of act; entities are factors in their function as the termini of thought."[21] In view of this distinction, our knowledge of nature consists of the consideration of entities and their relations as disclosed in sense-perception.[22]

Nature, then, means a complexity of related entities. All entities are the same as natural things, and as such they can be classified into two groups, namely, events and objects. Events are the constituents of becoming, and objects are the ingredient characteristics of things. In view of this distinction Whitehead says: "The continuity of nature is to be found in events, the atomic properties of nature reside in objects."[23]

Events are what actually happen in nature: "An actual event is thus divested of all possibility. It is what does become in nature. It can never happen again; for essentially it is just itself, there and then. An event is just what it is, and is just how it is related and it is nothing else."[24] Events are unique and concrete with a definite "where" and "when," that is, they can never happen again. So considered, events are the subjects of passage from one state to another, that is, they always pass into larger events. In other words, every event is a part of a larger group of events.[25] As such, events can be described in terms of extension: "Events are the things related by the relation of extension."[26] Events are extended in space and time, and as such they constitute the four-dimensional manifold of nature.

Events, however, require "a certain structure in their mutual relations and certain characteristics of their own."[27] Whitehead calls the characters of events objects. In general, objects are the ingredient properties of things by which nature is permanent and can be subject to change. Objects do change, but they do not pass: "Objects are elements in nature which do not pass."[28] Objects are of different kinds and can be classified in many distinct groups. All objects can be classified in five groups:
1. Sense-objects, for example, blue;
2. Perceptual objects, for example, a chair either in delusion or fact;
3. Physical objects, for example, a chair in fact;
4. Scientific objects, for example, a molecule;
5. Figures, for example, a geometrical shape.

Nature, as a complexity of related entities, displays some activity: "Nature is a theatre for the interrelations of activities. All things change, the activities and their interrelations."[29] Whitehead describes this activity in terms of life:

> The doctrine that I am maintaining is that neither physical nature nor life can be understood unless we fuse them together as essential factors in the composition of 'really real' things whose

interconnections and individual characters constitute the universe.[30]

Life, however, is understood in the wide sense of the word, and can be defined as "the enjoyment of emotion, derived from the past and aimed at the future. It is the enjoyment of emotion which was then, which is now, and which will be then."[31]

Within the notion of life three aspects are distinguished by Whitehead, namely, self-enjoyment, creative activity, and aim. Self-enjoyment is the organic unity and self-identity of the individual "arising out of this process of appropriation."[32] Creative activity is "the transformation of the potential into the actual, and the fact of such transformation includes the immediacy of self-enjoyment."[33] Aim, the final aspect, means "the exclusion of the boundless wealth of alternative potentiality, and the inclusion of that definite factor of novelty which constitutes the selected way of entertaining those data in that process of unification."[34]

Nature, then, is the principle of creativity and finality by which reality is in a constant process of becoming. And if this is the case, nature itself then is but a function of becoming and not of being. As a matter of fact, being is becoming: "it belongs to the nature of every 'being' that it is a potential for every 'becoming'."[35] But, if being is becoming, then nature as such is itself a "principle of process."[36] Consequently, natural things are not substantial entities, but actual ones or occasions whose nature is to become what they are to be, that is, what their potentialities can realize.

B: Finality and Activity of Nature

The existence of nature is known *per se*, insofar as natural things are manifest to the senses. But what the nature of each thing is, and what the principle of its motion is, is not so evident. In regard to the Aristotelian doctrine of nature we have two classical texts: the fourth chapter of the fifth book of the *Metaphysics*,[37] and the first chapter of the second book of the *Physics*.[38] The fifth book of the *Metaphysics*

contains the philosophical lexicon of Aristotelian terms; the term 'nature' occupies the fourth place, and is described after the terms of 'beginning', 'cause', and 'element'; Aristotle enumerates there six different meanings of the term 'nature'. But in the first chapter of the second book of the *Physics* Aristotle examines more precisely the definition of nature as a principle of motion and rest. The outline of the problem of 'nature' in the *Physics* is brought up by Aristotle in order to establish how things exist. Following Aristotle we have to ask how we are using the terms. We can consider the following two problems:
1. What nature is by explaining the meaning of the terms 'by nature' and 'according to nature';
2. How the nature of natural things is conceived.

As a matter of fact, the distinction of things into natural and artificial implies that nature is a principle of motion and rests in those things in which it is primarily and *per se* and not *per accidens*. In this sense things which have a principle of motion and rest in themselves, 'have a nature'. But things 'having a nature' are substances, because nature always implies a subject in which it inheres. Furthermore, being a substance, a thing with all its attributes and something 'having a nature' is not only 'by nature', but also 'according to nature'. [39]

After establishing what nature is, Aristotle considers how the nature of natural things is conceived. In the fifth book of the *Metaphysics* the Stagirite says:

> From what has been said, then, it is plain that nature in the primarily and strict sense is the essence of things which have in themselves, as such, a source of movement; for the matter is called the nature because it is qualified to receive this, and processes of becoming and growing are called nature because they are movements proceeding from this. And nature from this sense is the source of the movement of natural objects, being present in them somehow, either potentially or in complete reality.[40]

By reducing all these different meanings of the term 'nature' to matter and form, the question may arise concerning which of these two meanings deserve the name of nature in a higher and fuller sense of the word. Aristotle is in favor of form, and says: "The form indeed is 'nature' rather than the matter."[41] The main argument of the superiority of form over matter is based upon the superiority of actuality over potentiality. Form is nature more than matter because a thing is said to be greater insofar as it is in act rather than in potency. Also in the process of generation the form of natural things is nature more than the matter because the process of generation, which is the process towards nature, is not that from which nature is derived, but that to which it tends, namely, the form. In this sense nature denotes the *genesis* of form or the *genesis* of the formed object.[42]

Having shown that 'nature' in the fuller and greater sense means 'genesis of form' Aristotle states that nature is teleological: "nature is a purpose cause."[43] Nature has to become teleological, because the essence of that which is coming to be, that is, the form, is the end of 'that for the sake of which' it is accomplished.[44] In the eighth chapter of the second book of the *Physics* Aristotle demonstrates that nature acts for an end. In his conclusive argument the Stagirite writes: "Since 'nature' means two things, the matter and the form, of which the latter is the end, and since all the rest is for the sake of the end, the form must be the cause in the sense of 'that for the sake of which'."[45]

'Nature' conceived as a 'genesis of form' tends to an end as to its own good, because 'that for the sake of which' means what is best and the end of the things that lead up to it.[46] But nature does not wholly express its own form, until it reaches its own good completely and perfectly. All things, however, tend by their nature to ends which are their full realization and perfection of their forms. So, the end is the completed nature, and is called *'telos'*, because it is the completion of the thing or completed thing. Having reached this completion nature is *'teleion'*, that is, perfect. In other words, each thing tends naturally towards its own completion and perfection, and as such it is not only *from its nature*, but also it is *towards its whole nature and essence*.[47]

The direction of nature's actions is towards its own completion and fulfillment, and as such is not in vain. Moreover, Aristotle holds that nature tends towards the best: "Nature produces nothing in vain, but with a view to that which is better."[48] In other words, not only nature, but also its direction of actions is teleological.

Nature as a principle of motion can be understood in two ways: as an act of *the mover* and as an act of *the moved*. This distinction is made on the basis of the definition of motion as the actualization of an existing thing in potency precisely as such.[49] Nature is an act of *the mover* insofar as it is a cause by which the natural thing is in motion. But nature is an act of *the moved* insofar as it is an act of the subject in which the motion has taken place. Aristotle adds, however, that the act of *the mover* and of *the moved* is the same, because a natural thing is called *a mover* insofar as it does something and *the moved* insofar as it is acted upon.[50]

Now the question is: can nature be the self-sufficient source of all natural motions? Aristotle, making a distinction between moving by itself and being moved by something else,[51] states that a natural thing having movement by itself still is unable to actualize itself its own motion without some impulse from an external mover, namely, an animal being in sleep can wake up and start moving, because the food which enters into it nourishes and this causes its motion.[52] In this sense we have to understand that whatever is moved is moved by another.[53] But, since it is impossible for a thing to be moved by another indefinitely, it is necessary to accept a first unmoved mover.[54]

Adapting the Aristotelian definition of nature as a principle of movement and rest in those things to which it belongs *per se* and not *per accidens*,[55] St. Thomas indicates that nature should be understood both as a passive and as an active principle of motion.[56] These two senses of nature, as an active and as a passive principle of motion, Aquinas following Aristotle derives from the meaning of nature as form and matter. Nature as a passive principle of motion is associated with matter or what is material (*principium passivum et materiale*). But nature as an active principle of motion is combined with form or what is formal (*principium activum et formale*).[57] However, nature as a passive and material principle of motion does not signify only the pure potentiality of prime matter, but also all other possibilities of things which require a natural agent to actualize it. Nature as an active and formal principle of motion includes the actuality of the substantial form which it realizes through all its active qualities. Thus, nature is an active principle of motion insofar as *it moves* spontaneously, and nature is a passive principle of motion insofar as it must be *moved* by external force.[58]

Establishing the twofold meaning of nature as a passive and as an active principle of motion, we might ask the question how does Aquinas adapt the Aristotelian concept of nature to his doctrine of finality? There is no doubt that Aquinas develops the Aristotelian doctrine of the teleological structure of nature, and goes far beyond the Stagirite's teaching, especially in the theory of divine direction of nature.[59]

St. Thomas agrees with Aristotle that nature *exists*, and conceives it as *nature-end*. But for Aristotle this *nature-end* is not brought out as clearly as the function of nature in an efficient causality; A. Mansion says: "Aristotle insists more on the tending of nature to an end than on the role which nature enjoys in being an end itself."[60] St. Thomas, however, makes more explicit the meaning of *nature-end*, and emphasizes much more the internal actuality of the natural things than Aristotle does. In order to see this difference between Aristotle and St. Thomas we must explain more precisely Aquinas's doctrine of finality.

In his doctrine of finality St. Thomas distinguishes two orders of ends:
1. Intrinsic order of finality (*ordo in finem*); and
2. Extrinsic order of finality (*ordo finium*).

This distinction coincides with the distinction of nature as an individual and as a plurality. The intrinsic order of the end corresponds to the concept of nature in the individual in both senses of active and passive principles. The intrinsic order of the end corresponds to the concept of nature in the individual in the passive sense of having to be actualized by an agent: "whatever is moved is moved by something else." The intrinsic order of the end more significantly corresponds to the concept of nature in an active sense of being ordered to a definite end: "nature is directed to a determined end." In a word, the intrinsic order of nature intends perfection and good. The order of extrinsic ends involves subordination and hierarchy of good contributing to the *bonum totius universi*. In other words, the good of individuals and species is subordinated to the good of the whole.

In every agent there is a natural inclination towards an end.[61] In chapter two of the third book of *SCG* St. Thomas shows how every agent tends towards something definite.[62] If an agent would not incline towards some definite effect, then all happenings would be a matter of chance and as such it would be impossible to produce anything at all.[63] In other words, the agent must tend to an end as to its ultimate and determined goal beyond which it does not seek anything else, otherwise, the actions of the agent would tend to infinity, which is impossible according to Aristotle:[64] "it is impossible to proceed to infinity."[65]

The agent by its very nature acts for an end, and as such it tends to something definite. But the agent, by acting for an end, tends to it as for its own completion and perfection, for example, for its own goodness.[66] Now St. Thomas posits a new general principle: "every agent acts for a good." In proving this, St. Thomas argues: if the agent tends to a definite end, then it has to be appropriated to it, because, otherwise, the agent would not be inclined to something that does not agree with it; but whatsoever is appropriated to something is good for it; so, every agent acts for a good.[67] Moreover, St. Thomas, confronting the principle that every agent acts for an end with the principle that being and goodness are convertible, says that since every action is ordered towards being, the agent in its activity has to act for the sake of the good.[68]

For the fact that every agent acts for the sake of the good, St. Thomas concludes that the end of every agent is good. In this sense *'propter finem'* and *'propter bonum'* are the same.

The principle that the end of everything is good St. Thomas extends to every created being. The differentiation is based on the difference of the agents and the objects. The things that know their ends are moved towards them through themselves. The things that do not know their ends incline to them as directed by another being, for example, the archer directs the arrow to the target. The things that know their ends are always ordered to the good as an end through desires which are the appetite drives toward the known ends. Similarly, the things which do not know their end are ordered to a good as an end. Therefore, the end of all things is a good.

So, in the universe there is an intrinsic order of all created beings on the basis of the principle that the nature and agents act for an end as for their own good. But a very important question arises here, namely, the problem of causality of the end on nature and agent. Causality supposes an existential influence on the thing caused: "this term 'cause' carries the meaning of a certain influx to the being of something which has been caused."[69] However, a new question arises here: what is the difference between the causal influence of the end on nature and on agent?

St. Thomas, comparing the causal influence of the efficient and final cause, says: "just as the influx of an efficient cause is to act, so the influx of a final cause is to seek and desire."[70] In other words, to understand the causal influence of the nature as an agent-end is to understand the meanings of the terms *agere* and *appetere*.

For St. Thomas *'agere'* is synonymous with *'facere'*, and means to make something actual.[71] But, since the form is a principle of being, the agent makes something actual through its form.[72] However, on the other hand, since that in which act is present is a potentiality, the act of the agent must also be referred to potentiality.[73] In this sense, the causal influence of the agent means a making something actual from its potentiality through the proper form.[74]

In the universe among the acts pertaining to forms there is a certain gradation according to the principle that the more posterior and more perfect an act is, the more fundamental the inclination of being towards it. But, since a thing is perfect insofar as it is actualized, the intention of everything existing in potency has to tend through motion towards actuality.[75] The causality of the agent, therefore, consists in the natural inclination of its nature and inner motion to its own being and the completion of its being.

Having a natural inclination to an end as to its own perfection and good, the agent is able *to act*. But in order *to act* the agent must be *moved* by that *towards which* it tends, that is, by the end. In other words, the agent *acts*, but it must be *moved* by its end. So, the causality of the end is *to move* the agent *to act*. In this sense the final cause is called *'causa causarum'* and St. Thomas explaining its causal influence on the agent in terms of *'appetere'* and *'desiderare'*, says that the end is a cause insofar as it is being wanted or desired by the agent.[76]

C: *Creativity and Perfectibility of Nature*

The Aristotelian universe is an unoriginated, eternal, and everchanging sensible world. The universe so conceived exists of necessity, and everything in it can be explained by the world itself, except the beginning of the movement, that is, the process of coming to be. In the first book of the *Physics* Aristotle considering the relationship between unity and plurality, asks: "in what sense is it asserted that all things *are* one."[77] In order to answer this question the Stagirite started with the plurality and tried to reduce it to some kind of unity. The question arises: what kind of principles there are in the process of becoming by which there is in the universe a unity of diversity?

Aristotle examining his predecessors assumes that the principles of becoming a unity out of plurality consists in the contraries:

> [E]verything that comes to be or passes away comes from, or passes into, its contrary or an intermediate state. But the intermediates are derived from the contraries — colors, for instance, black and white. Everything, therefore, that comes to be by a natural process is either a contrary or a product of contraries.[78]

Having established that principles of becoming consist in contraries, Aristotle says that the contraries need a substratum.[79] Generally speaking, a substratum is a subject of any kind of coming to be.[80] But, things which come to be, come to be in different ways. The Stagirite enumerates five ways in which the process of becoming takes place, namely:

1. By change of shape, as a statue;
2. By addition, as things which grow;
3. By taking away, as the Hermes from the stone;
4. By putting together, as a house; and
5. By alteration, as things which 'turn' in respect of their material substance.[81]

In the process of *genesis* there are two senses in which something comes to be, namely, something which comes into existence, and something which becomes that.[82] *Genesis*, then, is always a complex which includes three factors: substratum-form-privation, and as such is a change of substratum from 'privation' to 'form', for example, from not-white to white. But, since 'privation' in its own nature is 'non-being'[83] then we can say that in *genesis* something comes to be out of "not-being."[84]

Aristotle, distinguishing between 'being' and 'being something,'[85] states that *genesis* should be understood as becoming something rather than as becoming being in its absolute sense. *Genesis* is not a process of becoming out of a pure and simple 'not-being', because from nothing comes only nothing. In a word, *genesis* is only a change, *metabole*, from something to something. *Genesis* so conceived is a principle of becoming both simple and composite being:

Anything that is in harmony must arise out of what is not in harmony and pass away into....And it makes no difference whether we speak of harmony or of order or of combination; for the rule is clearly the same. Indeed, a house or a statue or anything else comes to be in a similar way. For a house comes into being out of things that are not put together but separated in such and such a fashion and a statue out of things that have not received shape but are shapeless.... And all these things represent either an ordering or a combining. [86]

In this way, then, plurality is reduced to unity.

The Aristotelian doctrine of *genesis* St. Thomas explains in terms of universal causality and extends its meaning also on the notion of creation. But, the idea of creation is not limited only to the process of becoming something, and as such denotes the production of things in the fullness of their being by the first cause: *emanatio totius entis a causa universali*.[87] In this sense, *creatio* can mean *emanatio*.

God alone has being by nature, and, therefore, He is the proper source of all created being.[88] Creatures exist only when God causes them to be. In this sense creatures are absolutely dependent upon God.[89] God brings things into being from nothing, and in His creative action God does not require any pre-existing matter, because the proper mode of His action is to produce the whole subsisting thing.[90] Consequently, creation is not a motion nor a change, because both of these require a substratum existing in potency. Moreover, motion involves succession and creation is instantaneous.[91] A thing is being simultaneously created, but something in motion comes to be in time before it is made.[92] Creative action of God produces not only existence but also essence. So, in contrast to a finite agent that causes being in a certain way, God produces being as such. His effect presupposes nothing, because nothing pre-exists outside of being.[93]

Since creation is not a movement, then it is not a duration. At this point Aquinas is against two positions, namely, the position of the philosophers who argued that the world is necessarily eternal, and the position of the theologians who tried to demonstrate that creation had beginning in time. First of all, from the fact that the first agent is eternal, it does not follow that His effect is eternal, because God acts voluntarily and absolutely freely.[94] Secondly, creatures themselves cannot claim eternity in virtue of their necessity, because this necessity is consequent to substance.[95] Finally, since creation is not a motion, it is not necessary that creatures always be in order that nothing precede their being.[96] Similarly, Aquinas rejects the argument for the temporal character of creation in time, and says:

> ...that the agent necessarily precedes the effect resulting from its operation, is true of things which produce something by way of motion, because the effect does not exist until the motion is ended, but the agent must exist even when the motion begins. No such necessity obtains, however, in the case of things that act instantaneously.[97]

Although it is in fact more fitting that things had a beginning in time, because this most readily manifests the divine goodness and distance separating God from creatures, the attempts to prove a beginning of duration lack conclusiveness.[98]

Reason can demonstrate two essential characteristics of a creature. First, nothing is presupposed in the thing said to be created, because the causality of God extends to all that the creature is. Second, the creature possesses within itself a priority of non-being over being, not according to time but to nature. We cannot prove the temporal existence of the created beings by reason, but only by faith.[99]

The order of creation contains all grades of goodness, because all grades of goodness were required for the kind of universe that God intended to create. In his *Commentary to the Sentences* St. Thomas lists eight kinds of goodness of created things, namely, the good of:

1. A multiplicity of species;
2. Their accidental perfections;
3. Their essential perfections;
4. The fact of a thing's being ordered to other things;
5. The order following accidental perfections;
6. The order following essential perfections;
7. The end to which things are ordered, that is, God; and
8. The order to the end which follows from the goodness of the parts and their order to one another.[100]

Having established that creation contains all grades of goodness, St. Thomas says that the perfection of the created universe consists of a twofold goodness:

1. In the goodness of its being, and
2. In the goodness of the divine nature.

But, since the goodness of the universe consists in its order,[101] the perfection of the universe would be finally included in the goodness of the order of created beings to one another and to God: "the good of the universe is twofold in a way a separated good which is precisely God, and in another way in things themselves; and these goods are the order of the parts of the universe."[102]

This twofold goodness of the order of the universe is the principle of the unity and the plurality of all created beings. The goodness of the order of all created beings to one another is the principle of plurality, because the perfection can be better shown by a variety of species.[103] The goodness of the order of all created beings to God is the principle of unity, because the perfection of the universe can be achieved by an ordering of things to the most simple being, namely, God.[104] But, since the goodness of the order of all created beings to God is said to be the chief goodness, and since the goodness of the order of all created beings to one another exists on account of the former, then there is in the universe a specific order between the diversity and the unity.

Before commenting upon a detailed explanation of this twofold order of goodness we have to ask how St. Thomas is using terms. First of all, Aquinas considers the order of goodness of created beings either from the matter or from the form or from both of them. Form is a good *secundum se*, matter is a good *secundum quod est in potentia ad formam*, and composite is a good *prout actu habet formam*. In a word, everything is good insofar as it is a being. In this sense St. Thomas says: "being is spoken of absolutely, and good consists in order."[105] The order of goodness of created beings so conceived is different from that of the divine goodness. God has a perfect and entire goodness, because His goodness is *secundum suum simplex esse*. But the created beings do not have a perfect and entire goodness, because their goodness is not *per solum suum esse sed per plura*, that is, they have the participate goodness. Consequently, creatures have to be ordered to God as to the ultimate end in a way of participation. St. Thomas says:

> It is obvious, then, that things are ordered to God as an end, not merely according to their substantial act of being, but also according to those items which are added as pertinent to perfection, and even according to the proper operation, which also belongs to the thing's perfection.[106]

In the universe, since there is a diversity of beings, the final subordination of all perfections to an end must include some gradation in which St. Thomas distinguishes two kinds of the highest goodness, that is, the highest goodness to which all other beings are subordinated as to their end, namely, the highest goodness of the universe as a whole and the highest goodness of the intellectual nature. The first highest goodness is the whole, because "a whole does not exist for the sake of its parts, but, rather, the parts for the whole."[107] The second highest goodness of the universe is the intellectual nature, because "intellectual natures have a closer relationship to a whole than do other natures."[108] In a word, the highest goodness and perfection of the universe in its whole is the intellectual nature.

The final subordination of the perfection to one another is ordered to the intellectual nature, because the intellectual nature is the summit of all created beings, and as such the ultimate consummation of the perfections given by God in creation. St. Thomas says: "as a result of the order established by God's assigning to creatures the optimum perfection consonant with their manner of being, certain creatures were endowed with an intellectual nature, thus being given the highest rank in the universe."[109] This issue Aquinas proves in two ways, namely, in a way of the characteristics of the divine creation, and in a way of the nature of the structure of the universe as a whole.

First of all, the finality of divine creation required that in the universe there should be some beings endowed with the intellectual nature. The argument for this statement is based on two principles, that is, on the principle that an effect is most perfect when it can return to and bears the likeness of its source, and on the presupposition that the source of all created beings is God's intellect. So, if God's intellect is the source of bringing all created beings into existence, then there should be in the universe some beings which could reflect themselves the resemblance of divine perfections by bearing the divine likeness and by possessing the ability to return to God. But, this could be given by the mere existence of an intellectual nature, because the form of the divine intellect can be represented only by intelligible being. The greatest perfection of the universe requires the existence of some intellectual natures.[110]

Secondly, the need of existence of intellectual nature in the universe St. Thomas shows also from the final subordination of all parts of the universe to the perfection of the whole. Aquinas agrees:

> Whenever things are ordered to an end, and some of these things cannot attain the end through their own efforts, they must be subordinated to things which do achieve the end and which are ordered to the end for their own sake. Thus, for instance, the end of an army is victory, and this the soldiers may achieve through their own act of fighting; that is why only soldiers are needed for their own sake in an army. All others, who are assigned to different tasks — for instance, caring for the horses and supplying the weapons — are needed for the sake of the soldiers in the army. Now..., it is established that God is the ultimate end of the whole of things; that an intellectual nature alone attains to Him in Himself, that is, by knowing and loving Him.... Therefore, the intellectual nature is the only one that is required in the universe, for its own sake, while all others are for its sake.[111]

Having established that the intelligibility is the end of creation and all other beings are created in view of intellectual nature, we can search for the next problem how creatures are tending to their ultimate and their transcendent goodness and end, that is, to God. But, since all created beings of the universe are divided into intellectual and non-intellectual beings, then final subordination of all perfections of the universe to God should be considered differently, according to their different nature.[112]

Generally speaking, the transcendent goodness and the ultimate end of the order of the universe is that which is *propinquissimum* in creatures to the divine goodness.[113] The created beings of the universe participate in the divine goodness if they have a likeness to it,[114] and if they are able to attain the divine goodness as its ultimate end by imitating God's perfection.[115]

The created beings naturally tend to become like God by helping causes of other things: "a thing tends to the divine likeness by tending to be the cause of other things."[116] This is the highest way of becoming like God, because this way belongs only to the most superior among beings: "and since a cause as such, is superior to the thing caused, it is evident that to tend towards the divine likeness in the manner of something that causes others is appropriate to higher types of beings."[117]

All created beings, from the lowest to the highest, imitate God's perfections by their activity. Since in the universe there is a diversity of things, the created beings imitate God's perfections by many various proper actions, in virtue of those they are able to be and to become the causes for other things. In the universe there has to be diversity of things, and, accordingly, many various proper actions, because that "what could not be perfectly represented by one thing might be, in more perfect fashion, represented by a variety of things in different ways."[118] The created beings imitate God's perfections because they desire the divine goodness as their ultimate end. Every being tends to the divine likeness according to its proper nature. But, since all created beings tend to the divine likeness by their proper operations, intellectual creatures will become like God by knowing and understanding Him.[119] In chapter twenty-five of the third book of *SCG* St. Thomas gives the reasons why understanding God or intellectual contemplation of God is an ultimate end of human intellect. [120]

* * * * *

Whitehead attributed to Aristotle the introducing to contemporary philosophy the concept of nature as a principle of creativity and finality and praises him for "a masterly analysis of the notion of 'generation'."[121] But he reproaches the Stagirite for being "the apostle of 'substance and attribute' and of classificatory logic which this notion suggests."[122] By introducing 'substance and attribute' from logical to philosophical realm, Aristotle made metaphysical description highly abstract, and consequently was unable to explain the process of becoming. "Both for Plato and Aristotle the process of the actual world has been conceived as a real incoming of forms into real potentiality, issuing into that real togetherness which is an active thing."[123] And again, referring to the question of order of natural things Whitehead writes:

> This [Aristotle's] philosophy led to a wild overstressing of the notion of final causes during the Christian middle ages; and thence

by a reaction to the correlative overstressing of the notion of 'efficient causes' during the modern scientific period.[124]

Reading such accusations one might wonder whether Whitehead understood Aristotle's doctrine on substance at all. First of all, it is a well-known fact that Aristotle charges Plato for hypostatizing *eide* as having existence *a parte rei*.[125] Secondly, Aristotle's *ousia* has not only a predicational meaning but it is considered as an immanent element of composite beings:

> We are in habit of recognizing, as one determinate kind of what is, substance, and that in several senses, (a) in the sense of matter or that which in itself is not 'a this' and (b) in the sense of form or 'essence' which is that precisely in virtue of which a thing is called 'a this', and thirdly (c) in the sense of that which is compounded of both (a) and (b)."[126]

The reason that *ousia* is compounded of form and matter is the fact that both together are fulfilling the prerequisites of any substance, namely, separateness (*choriston*) and individualness (*tode ti*):[127] "for both separability and 'thisness' are thought to belong chiefly to substance."[128] Finally, for Aristotle *ousia* is not a category but a principle both in the order of being and becoming: "substance is a principle and a cause."[129]

In the order of being *ousia* is the formal[130] and material cause,[131] and the intelligible essence and an existent.[132] In the order of becoming Aristotle enumerates three principles which are involved in the process of substantial change, namely, the immanent form (*eidos*), the privation (*steresis*) of the form of the thing which is on the way to become, and substratum (*hypokeimenon*) which remains intact during the change that takes place during the process of becoming.[133]

Although agreeing with Whitehead that Aristotle is "the apostle of substance and attribute," it is however difficult to accept that the Stagirite's concept of *ousia* leads us to a "classificatory logic which this notion suggests." Furthermore, Aristotle's *ousia* is best expressed by *eidos*, but understood only as an actualization of things (*energeia, entelecheia*).[134] Moreover, Aristotle's understanding of substance as principle of being and becoming cannot be understood in term's of Plato's "incoming of forms into real potentiality," for Aristotelian *ousia* is not only a predicational entity (that is, species) but a real formal cause which makes a thing what it is in reality, namely, a real being. In a word, Whitehead in his critique of Aristotle's notion of 'substance' does not distinguish between primary and secondary substances.

The dynamic interpretation of substance has been inherited from him by some followers of Aristotle, especially by St. Thomas. For the Angelic Doctor, substance is "that whose nature is to exist in its own right and not in another" (*id cui competit existere in se et non in alio*). Substance so conceived is an active principle according to which "the operation of a thing follows its being" (*operatio sequitur esse*). *Esse*, therefore, is not only an active principle of being, but of becoming as well. Whitehead's fallacious reasoning consists in a misunderstanding and an incomplete presentation of the Aristotelian concept of substance.

In addition, Whitehead's critique of the ancient and medieval views on nature seems to be inconsistent with his own attempt to work out a dynamic interpretation of reality. In his book, *Alfred North Whitehead*, while discussing the modern subjectivistic evolution of the experience of the structure of nature, Paul G. Kuntz observes:

> Whitehead has in *Symbolism* worked his way back from modern subjectivism that makes problematic...our knowledge of the external world. Not only did Whitehead revert to pre-Kantian realism but to a position that justifies the use of Plato, Aristotle, and the medievals in his realism.[135]

In view of this fact, one may reexamine — as did also Paul Kuntz — Whitehead's critique of Aristotle's and St. Thomas's views on nature.

Trying to overcome the Aristotelian subject-predicate logic, Whitehead not only could not avoid categorical scheme in explanation of reality, but made it even more complex.[136] But beneath this terminological complexity there are more resemblances to Aristotle than he ever admitted. One can hardly resist quoting again Paul Kuntz:

> Just as Aristotle, taking his predecessors into account, came upon a doctrine of four causes, so Whitehead has four classes or groups of categories.... Although he is busy telling us how Aristotle both created and prevented the tradition, he does not point out that his four kinds of categories have a resemblance to Aristotle's four causes. Is not creativity likened to prime matter, the out of which? Are not eternal objects very close to Aristotle's forms? Are not explanations frequently appeals to efficient causes? And the like-

ness between Aristotle's prime mover and Whitehead's God is not providing a lure and drawing power toward ideal ends.[137]

CONCLUSIONS

CONCLUSION

The aim of this study was to discover the order as it is included in the very structure of being *qua* being. But, since the notion of order contains a threefold element, namely, *ratio prioris et posterioris, distinctio*, and *ratio ordinis*, being can reveal itself only in its inner disposition of essential and existential characteristics as something in which essence and existence are related to each other mutually and reciprocally. Consequently, to discover the order as it is included in the very structure of being, we have to examine the concept of being itself.

On the basis of essential and existential characteristics of being we can distinguish a twofold mode of predication, namely, the predicamental and the transcendental mode of predication. In the predicamental mode of predication a predicate is considered as something that is added to a thing as its determining principle. In the transcendental mode of predication, however, nothing can be added to the being as an extraneous nature in the manner in which a difference is added to a genus or an accident to a subject, because every nature is essentially being.

In view of this distinction we can formulate two kinds of concepts, namely, the predicamental and transcendental. The predicamental concepts describe the diverse grades of entities which correspond to diverse modes of existing (*modi essendi*) and by which the diverse genera of being are obtained. The transcendental concepts describe being in its universality by expressing more clearly what is already contained in the very nature of being as such. The predication by predicamental concepts describes a being by the essential characteristics, and establishes a predicamental order of being. The predication of being by transcendental concepts describes being as expressed by the existential characteristics of *esse*, and establishes a transcendental order of being.

The order of being, then, consists in a disposition of essential and existential characteristics. The order of being considered in its essential characteristics establishes a predicamental order, and analyzed in its existential characteristics it constitutes a transcendental order of being. In the predicamental order the stress is placed on the essential aspects and as such it displays the disposition of being as it is expressed in itself and divided in terms of the ten categories. But in the transcendental order of being the emphasis lies on the existential aspect of being and as such it shows the manifestation of being in aspect which surpasses all individual particularities of things, that is, to the most common properties of any kind of entity.

The predicamental order can be established according to the essences as they are found in different kinds of substantial accidental beings. The *ratio* of the predicamental order so considered consists in a relation of dependence which occurs between substance and accidents. In this order accident is dependent on substance, and not vice versa. The reason for this is that accident can have its own being insofar as it inheres in a substance, and as such accident can never be found without a substance. Now the distinction between substance and accident St. Thomas bases on the different kind of *esse*: a substance gives *esse simpliciter*, and an accident gives *esse tale*. But, since an accident is dependent on a substance, substance has *esse* in its own self, and accident according to the mode in which it is participated in substance.

The transcendental order of being can be established according to some general modes of existing by which being *qua* being is described under certain intelligible aspects. These intelligible aspects, known as transcendental concepts of being, are common to all being, and are related to being in respect of its existential characteristics. Now the *ratio* of the transcendental order of being consists in the very notion of being itself. But, since being as conceived by human intellect bespeaks essence with relation to existence, and since *esse* signifies existential act, the *ratio* of the transcendental order of being can be considered in its *ordo ad esse* either absolutely or relatively. The *esse* of the transcendental characteristics of being is related to *esse* absolutely as when they express some entitative properties which follow upon being as something which is expressed through essence, because essence is that by which a being is a subject possessing the act of existing. The *ratio* of the transcendental characteristics of being is related to *esse* relatively as when they express some entitative properties which follow upon being as something which is participated, because in the very structure of any created being the existential act is something which is received as a principle of the whole being and as something which is required by its very essence. In a word, the *ratio* of the transcendental characteristics of being is described in its relation to *esse*, since they follow upon existential act whether expressing the very nature of being *per essentiam* or *per participationem*. The *ratio* of the transcendental order of being so considered can be attained by our intellect in a judgement on the basis of which being is conceived in its general modes of existing as *unum, verum,* and *bonum*.

Ens, then, is totally related to *esse*, and has to be understood *cum ordine ad esse*. This relation between *ens* and *esse* can be analyzed both as it is expressed in its essential and existential characteristics. In view of this order St. Thomas elaborates the notion of being as something by which the relation of essence to a distinct existence is expressed. Now, this order of essence and existence can be considered according to the various relations of potency to act according to a mutual and reciprocal proportion of actuality and potentiality.

On the account of the proportion between actuality and potentiality we can distinguish a twofold order of being, namely, the intrinsic and the extrinsic order of being. The intrinsic order of being occurs within all particular concrete beings and takes place by manifold modes of composition in view of the nature possessed by a particular thing, for example, this concrete stone is not a simple being, but composed in many ways. The extrinsic order of being happens between particular things and can be obtained according to the different modes of dependency in view of which one being is related to another, for example, this stone is multiple related to all other things. But both the intrinsic and extrinsic order of being are principles of unity and plurality of things. In this way St. Thomas can express the very nature of being as some unity and plurality, namely, diversity and community.

Thus the task of our investigation is accomplished by indication that the order is an attribute of being and can be found in the very structure of *esse*. The metaphysical foundation of the order of being, then, is the same as the entitative elements of being, namely, essence and existence. In a word, being is an order of essence and existence by which *esse* is constituted in reality as some unity and plurality.

REFERENCES

REFERENCES

Introduction

1   *Cf.* Hermann Krings, "Das Sein und die Ordnung. Eine Skizze zur Ontologie des Mittelalters, " *DVLG* 18 (1940): 236: "Das Sein ist der *ordo* und der *ordo* ist das Sein. Die Begriffe sind also vertauschbar? Man muss sagen ja; denn es ist kein Sein das nicht *ordo* wären; nicht *ordo* zu sein, ist neben das Charakteristikum des Nicht-Seins: 'ordinatio esse cogit, inordinatio vero non esse' (Aug., de mor. manich., II, 8). *Ordo* und *esse* sind als Begriffe vertauschbar und in sich identisch:' haec vero qui tendunt in esse, ad ordinem tendunt: quem cum fuerint consecuta, ipsum esse consequuntur, quantum id creatura consequi potest' (*Ibid.*)..."*Cf.* also Juan Jose Sanguinetti, "El concepto de Orden, " *Sap* 35 (1980): 559-572. On the relation of the order and philosophy, see Paul G.Kuntz, "Philosophy as the Discovery of Orders, " *TP* 3 (1979): 65-81.

2   Hans Meyer, *The Philosophy of St.Thomas* (St.Louis-London: B.Herder Book Co., 1944), 137. *Cf.* Jean Theu, "L'ordre du connaître et l'ordre de l'être ou l'ordre des choses et celui de la pensée, " *Dia* 23 (1984):571-596.

3   *ST* 1a. 42, 3c:"...ubicumque est pluralitas sine ordine, ibi est confusio." On the teaching of order in St.Thomas, see Brian Coffey, "The Notion of Order According to St.Thomas, " *MS* 27 (1949): 97-107; Giorgio Giannini, "S.Tommaso d'Aquino, Genio dell'Ordine, " *GM* 29 (1974): 441-460; Frank J. Yartz, "Virtue as an *Ordo* in Aquinas, " *MS* 47 (1970):305-319; *idem*, "Order and Right Reason in Aquinas' Ethics, " *MSt* 37 (1975): 407-418. On unity and plurality in St.Thomas, see John F. Wippel, "Thomas Aquinas on the Distinction and Derivation of the Many from the One: A Dialectic between Being and Nonbeing," *RM* 38 (1985): 563-569.

4   *Cf.* Arthur Adkins, "Cosmogony and Order in Ancient Greece," in *Cosmogony and Ethical Order*, ed. by Lovin and Robin (Chicago: University of Chicago Press, 1985), 39-66; Guy Davenport, *Herakleitos and Diogenes*

(Bolinas: Grey Fox Press, 1976); Herman Krings, *Ordo* (Haale-Saale: M.Niemeyer, 1941); Paul L. Landsberg, *Die Welt des Mittelalters und Wir* (Bonn: F.Cohen, 1922).

5   *Cf.* Plutarch, *Epitomes* II, Prooemium I, 1-3, in Hermanus Diels, *Doxographi Graeci* (Berolini et Lipsiae: Walter de Gruyter, 1929), 327. For the pre-Pythagorean development of the idea of *kosmos*, see Walther Kranz, *Kosmos*, 2, 1 *Archiv für Begriffsgeschichte* (Bonn: H. Bouvier u.Co. Verlag, 1955), 7ff. *Cf.* also Jacob Needleman, *The Heart of Philosophy* (Cambridge: Harper and Row, 1986); James A. Philip, *Pythagoras and Early Pythagoreanism* (Toronto: University of Toronto Press, 1966).

6   *Cf.* Alan C. Bowen, "The Foundations of Early Pythagorean Harmonic Science: Archytas, Fragment I, " *AP* 2 (1982): 79-104.

7   *Metaphysics* I, 5.986a2-3. Some neo-Platonic philosophers attributed also to Pythagoras the mathematical theory of proportion, *cf.* Iamblichus, *In Nicomachi Geraseni arithmeticam introductionem*, ed. a Samuele Tennulio (Arnhemiae: J.F. Hagium, 1668), 171; Proclus, *In Euclidis Elementorum librum commentarii*, ed. a G. Friedlein (Lipsiae: B.G.Teubneri, 1873), 65.

8   *Metaphysics* I, 5. 985b23-26.

9   *Cf.* Philolaos B, 10, in Hermann Diels and Walter Kranz, *Die Fragmente der Vorsokratiker*, 1 (Dublin-Zürich: Weidmann, 1968), 410; *ibid*. B, 6, 408-410. A similar theory of harmony can be found in Herakleitos, B, 51; 54; *ibid*., 162; *cf.* also Aristotle, *Ethics* VIII, 1.1155b4.

10   *Cf.* Aristotle, *De Coelo* II 9. 290b12.

11   *Cf.* Aristotle, *Metaphysics* I, 5. 986a2-3.

12   *Cf.* Friedrich Überweg and Max Heinze, *Grundriss der Geschichte der Philosophie* (Basel-Stuttgart: Benno Schwabe and Co. Verlag, 1957), 1:61ff.

13   *Gorgias*, 503-504.

14   *Cf.* Philo, *De opificio mundi* 3, in *Philonis Alexandrini opera quae supersunt*, vol. 1 (Berlin: Georgii Reimari, 1896), 4.

15   *De Officiis* I, 40, in *M. Tullii Ciceronis opera, ex recensione Christ Godofr.Schützii additis comentariis*, vol.15 (Augustae Taurinorum ex typis Josephi Pomba et soc., 1835), 141: "Nam ordinem sic definiunt, compositionem rerum aptis et accomodatis locis."

16   *De Civitate Dei* XIX, 13, *PL* 41, 640. On St.Augustine's teaching on order, *cf.* also: *De Civitate Dei* XII, 5, *PL* 41, 352-353; XI, 18, *PL* 41, 332; XI, 22, *PL* 41, 335-336; XII, 4, *PL* 41, 351-352; *Epistulae* 138, 5, *PL* 33, 527; 166, 13, *PL* 33, 726; *Contra Faustum Manichaeum* 16, 21, *PL* 42, 329; *De ordine* I, 6, 15-16, *PL* 32, 985; II, 4, 11-13, *PL* 32, 999-1001; *De libero arbitrio* III, 9, 26, *PL* 32, 1283-1284; 11, 33, *PL*

32, 1287; *De natura boni* 8, *PL* 42, 554; *Contra Secundinum Manichaeum* 15, *PL* 42, 590-591.

17   Proclus, *Elementa theologiae* 18, ed. Dodds (Oxford: The Clarendon Press, 1933), 21.

18   *Ibid.*

19   *Ibid.*

20   *In Parmenidem*, ed. V. Cousin (Paris: A. Durand, 1864), 704.

21   *Enneades* I, 6, 2-3, in *Ennéades*, texte établi et traduit par Émile Bréhier, vol. 1 (Paris: Société d'édition "Les belles lettres", 1924), 97-99.

22   *Ibid.* VI, 3, 1, vol. 6 (1936), 125-126.

23   *Ibid.* IV, 8, 3, vol. 4 (1927), 220.

24   *Ibid.* V, 2, 2, vol.5 (1931), 34-35.

25   *Ibid.* 1, 7, 23-25.

26   On the origin and the authorship of Pseudo-Dionysius Areopagita, cf. U. Riedinger, "Der Verfasser der pseudo-dionysischen Schriften, " *ZK* 75 (1964): 146-152.

27   *De coelesti hierarchia* III, 1, *PG* 3, 163.

28   *De divinis nominibus* I, 1, *PG* 3, 588; *De coelesti hierarchia* IX, 2, *PG* 3, 257.

29   *De ecclesiastica hierarchia* I, 2, *PG* 3, 372.

30   *In de Anima* I, lect. 9.

31   *In De Coelo* II, lect. 14.

32   *Ibid.*

33   *Cf. In de Anima* I, lect. 9.

34   *In De Coelo* III, lect. 4. *Cf.* also *ibid.* III, lect. 3; 4.

35   *CG* II, 64: "Harmonia dicitur dupliciter: uno modo, ipsa compositio; alio modo, ratio compositionis."

36   *Ibid.* II, 68.

37   *Ibid.*

38   *Ibid.* I, 20.

39   *Ibid.* III, 78.

40   *Ibid.* II, 68.

41   *Ibid.*

42   *De Potentia* X, 3c.

43   *CG* II, 39. *Cf. ibid.* II, 42; *ST* 1a. 44, 3c.

44   *Ibid.* 1a. 108, 2c.

45   *II Sent* . 9, 1, 1.

46   *In Phys* . VIII, lect. 3.

47   *De Veritate* I, 1 ad 3. In view of this text one must wonder at F.A. Cunningham statement that "St.Thomas never said 'Essence is distinct from *esse*'," see "Distinction According to St.Thomas," *NS* 36 (1962): 279.

48   In understanding being, essence and existence are necessary and complementary elements, *cf.* André Marc, *L'idée de l'être chez Saint Thomas et dans la scolastique postérieure* (Paris: E. Beauchesne et ses fils, 1933), 85: "L'essence et l'existence sont ainsi les éléments complémentaires de l'affirmation qui apprécie la proportion des essences à l'esse, les jauge dans l'être. Tel est l'être du jugement, expression de l'être des choses. Et c'est pour quoi des idées éparses et diverses que l'apprehension lui offre, une unité d'ensemble."

Part A: Unity and Plurality of Being

1   *De Veritate* II, 2c.

I. The Notion of Order

1   *Metaphysics* V, 19. 1022b1.
2   *Physics* VIII, 1. 252a13.
3   *Metaphysics* V, 19. 1022b1.
4   *In Meta,* V, lect. 20.
5   *ST* 1a. 22, 1c.
6   *Physics* VIII, 1. 252a12.
7   *In Phys* .VIII, lect. 3.
8   *Ibid.*
9   *ST* 1a. 6, 1; 1a2ae. 102, 1c; 2a2ae. 45, 5, 2; *CG* I, 1; II, 24; III, 77; etc.
10 *Categoriae* 7. 8a12-b24.
11 *Ibid.* 7. 6b6-14. Aristotle has some doubts whether or not his definition can be applied to prove that no substance is relative; *cf. Categoriae* 7. 8a28-35. Some medieval philosophers would recognize in this text a proposition of

second intention, cf. St. Albert, Summa Theologiae, Liber II, tractatus 1, quaestio 2, in Opera Omnia, ed. Augusti Borgnet, vol. 32 (Parisiis: apud Ludovicum Vivès, 1895-1899), 106; Alexander of Hales, Summa Theologica, Liber I, parts II, inquisitio 2, tractatus 1, quaestio 5, articulus 1 ad 1, ed. Quaracchi, vol. 1 (Ad Claras Aquas prope Florentiam: ex typographia Collegii s. Bonaventurae, 1924), 554; Anicius Manilius Severinus Boethius, In Categorias Aristotelis II, PL 64, 235.

12   Metaphysics V, 15. 1020b26-30.
13   Categoriae 7. 7a22-8a11.
14   De Veritate XXI, 6; CG IV, 14; ST 1a. 28, 1c; Quodl. I, 2; Compendium theol. I, 212.
15   ST 1a2ae. 110, 3 ad 3; De Potentia VII, 8; In Phys . II, lect. 5.
16   De Potentia III, 4; ST Suppl. , 92, 1 ad 6; De Veritate VIII, 1 ad 6; In Ethic. V, lect. 5; I Sent . 19, 1, 1 ad 4; ST 1a. 12, 1 ad 4; De Potentia VI, 7 ad 6.
17   In de Trinitate IV, 3c.
18   De Potentia VII, 1 ad 9; CG II, 18.
19   De Veritate I, 1; ST 1a. 16, 8c.
20   De Veritate I, 1 ad 5; I Sent . 39, 2, 1.
21   ST 1a. 60, 1c; II Sent . 39, 3, 1 ad 5.
22   I Sent . 34, 3, 1 ad 2.
23   ST 1a. 4, 3c.
24   De Veritate I, 5.
25   I Sent . 2, 2.
26   CG IV, 14.
27   Compendium theol. I, 54.
28   III Sent . 4, 1, 2, 1.
29   De Potentia VII, 9.
30   Ibid. X, 3, 2.
31   I Sent . 14, 2, 1, 2 ad 4.
32   De Potentia III, 3, 7.
33   De Virtutibus Cardinalibus 3c.
34   I Sent . 20, 1, 3.
35   ST 2a2ae. 26, 2c.
36   In Phys . I, lect. 10.
37   Quodl. V, 10.
38   In Meta, V, lect. 1; ST 2a2ae. 26, 1c.
39   Ibid. 1a. 33, 1 ad 1; 2a2ae. 26, 6c.
40   Ibid. 1a. 33, 1c.

41 Ibid.
42 In Meta, V, lect.1.
43 In Phys . I, lect. 10.
44 Ibid. I, lect.1.
45 In Meta, V, lect. 1.
46 Ibid.
47 Ibid.
48 Ibid.
49 Ibid.
50 Ibid.
51 Ibid. V, lect. 13.
52 ST 1a. 42, 3c; I Sent ., 20, 3.
53 De Potentia X, 3. Cf. St.Bonaventure, In Sententiarum, Liber I, distinctio 20, articulus 2, quaestio 1, ed. Quaracchi, vol. 1 (Ad Claras Aquas prope Florentiam: ex typographica Collegii St. Bonaventurae, 1882), 372: "ubi ordo ibi distinctio."
54 ST 1a. 42, 3.
55 Ibid. 1a2ae. 104, 4.
56 CG I, 7.
57 De Potentia IX, 7.
58 ST 1a. 39, 2, 1; In Phys . I, lect. 10.
59 De Potentia IV, 2 ad 29.
60 ST 1a. 5, 2 ad 1; 4c; 105, 5c, 1a2ae. 1, 2c; CG III, 17.
61 CG I, 25.
62 Ibid. I, 26.
63 ST 1a. 47, 2c; 59, 2 ad 2; 80, 1 ad 2; 2a2ae. 24, 5c.
64 Ibid. 1a. 30, 3c.
65 Ibid. 1a. 47, 2c.
66 CG I, 54.
67 Ibid.
68 ST 1a. 47, 2c.
69 In Meta, XII, lect. 12.
70 ST 1a. 40, 2c.
71 Ibid., 29, 3 ad 4.
72 Ibid.; De Potentia IX, 2 ad 10; In Post. Anal. I, lect. 44.
73 I Sent . 2, 1, 3; 33, 1, 1 ad 3.
74 ST 1a. 26, 2c; ad 1.
75 Ibid.

76   In Post. Anal. I, lect. 13.
77   I Sent . 2, 1, 5 ad 1.
78   Ibid. 20, 1, 3.
79   ST 1a. 32, 3c.
80   I Sent . 20, 3.
81   ST 1a. 93, 5c.
82   CG IV, 24.
83   ST 1a. 40, 2c.
84   CG IV, 24.
85   ST 1a. 40, 2c.
86   Ibid. 1a. 42, 3c.
87   Ibid. 1a. 33, 1c.
88   Ibid. 1a. 13, 7c; De Potentia VII, 11; De Veritate I, 5 ad 16.

II. Order of Natural Things

1   Quotation from Ruth Nanda Anshen, *Alfred North Whitehead; His Reflections on Man and Nature* (New York: Harper, 1961), 3.
2   *Science and the Modern World* (New York: The Macmillan Comp., 1948). On the role of the notion of order in the Western culture and sciences, see Paul G. Kuntz (ed.), *The Concept of Order* (Seatle-London:The University of Washington Press, 1968); Marion L. Kuntz and Paul G. Kuntz [eds], *Jacob's Ladder and the Tree of Life. Concepts of Hierarchy and the Great Chain of Being..* (New York: Peter Lang Publishing, 1987.) G.C. Waterston, *Une étude sémantique du mot 'Ordre'* (Geneva: Librairie Droz, 1965); idem, *Order and Counter-Order* (New York: Philosophical Library, 1966).
3   ST 1a. 42, 3.
4   *Beiträge zur Geschichte der Philosophie des Mittelalters*, I, 2-4 (Münster, 1892-1895). *Cf.* also Michael Wittman, *Die Stellung des Hl.Thomas von Aquin zu Avencebrol*, in *Beiträge zur Geschichte der Philosophie des Mittelalters*, III, 2 (Münster, 1900).
5   *Summa Theologica*, I-II, 2, 2, q. unica, c. 106, ed. Quaracchi, vol.2 (1928), 135.
6   *II Sententiarum* 3, 1, 1, 1, ed. Quaracchi, vol. 2 (1885), 91.

7   *Liber primus communium naturalium,* pars 4, distinctio 3, c. 4, in *Opera* (Oxonii: e typographeo Clarendoniano, 1911), fasc. III, 291.

8   *Cf.* Odon Lottin, "La composition hylémorphique des substances spirituelles, " *RNP* 34 (1932): 21-41.

9   In his treatise *De Substantiis Separatis* 3; 15; 16; St.Thomas enumerates three errors regarding the nature of spiritual substance, namely, *conditio, modus existendi* and *gubernatio rerum;* for a detailed discussion of this subject, see John O. Rield, "The nature of Angels," in *Essays in Thomism,* ed. by Robert E. Brennan (New York: Sheed and Ward, 1942), 123-142.

10   *De Anima* 6.

11   For the historical background and discussion about the universality of matter, see Aimé Forest, *La structure métaphysique du concret selon saint Thomas d'Aquin* (Paris: J. Vrin, 1931), 98-127; James Collins, *The Thomistic Philosophy of the Angels* (Washington: The Catholic University of America Press, 1947), 42-74.

12   *De Anima* 6.

13   St.Thomas's doctrine of the unicity of substantial form in any created being caused a controversy which led to the condemnation of his doctrine by Robert Kilwardby on March 18, 1277; *cf.* Henricus Denifle, *Chartularium Universitatis Parisiensis,* vol. 1, n.474 (Parisiis: ex typis Fratrum Delalain, 1889), 558-560. On application of the Aristotelian hylomorphism to the human composition, see J. E. Bolzan, "Hilemorfismo y corporalidad, " *Sap* 40 (1985): 25-32.

14   *CG* III, 97.
15   *Ibid.*
16   *In Phys* . VIII, lect. 3.
17   *I Sent* . 20, 1, 3.
18   *Cf. CG* II, 54.
19   *Ibid.* I, 18.
20   *Ibid.*
21   *Ibid.*
22   *Ibid.*
23   *Ibid.*
24   *Ibid.*
25   *ST* 1a. 45, 7c. *Cf. CG* III, 97. For St.Augustine's teaching on the order of natural things, see W.J. Roche, "Measure, Number and Weight in St.Augustine, " *NS* 15 (1941): 350-376.

26   Cf. Gaston Isaye, *La théorie de la mesure et l'existence d'un maximum selon saint Thomas* (Paris: Beauchesne, 1940), 4: "La théorie de la mesure, telle que saint Thomas la trouve dans Aristote, se développe par extensions successives. La mesure de definit d'abord dans l'ordre de la quantité. On decouvre ensuite une mesure dans les austres genu et notamment dans celui de la qualité ... "

27   *I Sent* . 8, 4, 2 ad 3.

28   *CG* III, 97.

29   *De Genesi ad litteram* 4, 3, *PL* 34, 299.

30   *ST* 1a. 5, 5c; 1a2ae. 49, 2c.

31   *ST* 1a2ae. 85, 4c. *Cf.* Herman Krings, *Ordo*, 92.

32   *ST* 1a2ae. 49, 2c.

33   *Cf. ST* 1a. 10, 5c.

34   *ST* 1a. 82, 3 ad 2: "Ad secundum dicendum quod illud quod est prius generatione et tempore, est imperfectus: quia in uno et eodem potentia tempore praecedit actum, et imperfectio perfectionem. Sed illud quod est prius simpliciter et secundum naturae ordinem, est perfectius: sic enim actus est prior potentia."

35   *In Meta*, V, lect. 1; *In Phys* . IV, lect. 17.

36   *ST* 2a2ae. 183, 1 ad 3. *Cf.* Remigius Kwant, *De gradibus entis* (Amsterdam: H.J. Paris, 1946), 74: "Gradus entis seu ens limitatum non potest haberi, nisi essentia ab esse realiter distinguatur; " grade of being contains "plura adesse entia, sed ita, ut hoc ipsum quod est esse, in eis modo inferiore et superiore verificetur."

37   *ST* 1a. 23, 5 ad 3.

38   *De Veritate* IX, 5, 6; *ST* 2a2ae. 183, 3c.

39   *II Sent* . 9, 1, 1 ad 2.

40   *I Sent* . 2, 1, 3 ad 2. For metaphysical foundation of the ontic gradation of things, see Gonsalv Mainberger, *Die Seinsstufung als Methode und Metaphysik* (Amsterdam: B.G.Gruener, 1959), 137-140.

41   *CG* III, 97.

42   *Ibid.*, 71.

43   *Ibid.* II, 45.

44   *Ibid.* III, 94.

45   *Ibid.*, 72.

46   *Ibid.*, 71.

47   *Ibid.* I, 70.

48   *Ibid.*, III, 74.

49 Ibid., 97.
50 Ibid.
51 Ibid.
52 Ibid., II, 68.
53 Ibid., III, 22.
54 Ibid.
55 Ibid., 69.
56 Ibid., II, 88.
57 Ibid., III, 22.
58 Ibid.
59 ST 1a. 30, 2, 5.
60 Ibid., 3c.
61 Ibid., 7, 4c; 85, 8, 2. Cf. also Aristotle, Metaphysics I, 1.1053a30; 6. 1057a 2-4.
62 CG III, 97.
63 ST 2a2ae. 17, 6c.
64 Ibid., 1a2ae., 91, 5c; 2a2ae. 8, 6.
65 De Potentia IX, 7c.
66 ST 1a2ae. 91, 5c.
67 Ibid., 1a. 12, 1 ad 4.
68 In De div. nom. 4, lect. 21; 22.
69 ST 1a. 5, 5c; 1a1ae. 85, 4c; I Sent . 20, 3; De Potentia VII, 11c.
70 CG III, 97.
71 Cf. Gustaf Joseph Gustafson, *The Theory of Natural Appetency in the Philosophy of St.Thomas* (Washington: The Catholic University of America Press, 1944).
72 ST 1a. 60, 1c.
73 Cf. Patrick K. Bastable, *Desire for God* (London-Dublin: Burns, Oates and Washbourne, 1947), 21-30.
74 CG II, 47.
75 ST 1a. 59, 2c; 2 ad 1; 1a2ae. 36, 2c; 49, 2c.
76 Ibid., 8, 1c.
77 Ibid., 1a. 78, 1 ad 3.
78 In Phys ., I, lect. 15.
79 CG III, 3: "Finis est in quo quiescit appetitus agentis vel moventis, et eius quod movetur."
80 ST 1a2ae. 27, 2c. For St.Thomas "amor naturalis" is integral to"appetitus naturalis; " Ibid., 29, 1c.

81 CG I, 75.
82 ST 1a2ae. 8, 2c.
83 CG III, 17. Cf. James E. O'Mahony, *The Desire of God in the Philosophy of St.Thomas Aquinas* (Dublin-Cork: Cork University Press, 1929), 78-89. On the contrary, Duns Scotus emphasizes the efficient causality over the final causality, see Francois-Xavier Putallaz, "Efficience et finalité dans le 'Traité du Premier Principe'," *RTP* 116 (1984): 131-146.

III. Being in Its Singularity and Universality

1 *Parmenides* , 128b.
2 As against the pre-Socratics Plato argues that the meaning of *arche* of our knowledge should be taken not in cosmological but in epistemological order.
3 *Republic* , 532a-b; *Timaeus* , 51d.
4 *Republic* , 476a-480a.
5 *Ibid.*, 509d-511e.
6 *Ibid.*, 514a-521b.
7 *Ibid.*, 534e.
8 *Phaedo* , 101d; *Republic* , 511e.
9 *Ibid.*, 532.
10 *Phaedrus* , 265d; *Sophist* , 253d.
11 *Republic* , 533.
12 *Ibid.*
13 *Ibid.*
14 *Timaeus* , 51d.
15 *Ibid.*, 51e.
16 *Parmenides* , 131a. Plato criticizes a simplistic way of understanding his doctrine of participation, and agrees that not any name of singular things must be referred to some particular universal forms, e.g., "hair, mud, dirt" (*Ibid.*, 130d).
17 *Sophist* , 248.
18 *Republic* , 509b.
19 *Parmenides* , 130b.
20 *Republic* , 509d.

21 Ibid.
22 Phaedo, 100d.
23 Sophist, 252a.
24 Ibid., 100c. Cf. Zofia J. Zdybicka, Partycypacja bytu (Lublin:Towarzystwo Naukowe KUL, 1972), 25f.
25 Metaphysics I, 6. 987b13. On the attitude of Aristotle to the concept of participation, see Cornelio Fabro, La nozione metafisica di partecipazione secondo S. Tommaso d'Aquino (Torino: Società Editrice Internazionale, 1963), 54-74.
26 Metaphysics I, 6. 988a3.
27 Ibid., VII, 13. 1038b7-14. His critical remarks of Plato's participation, Aristotle presents on various occasions; cf. Metaphysics VII, 16. 1040b29-30; IX, 8. 1050b35; XII, 1. 1069a25-30; I, 9. 991a20-23.
28 Ibid., VII, 13. 1038b5-15. For the comparision between Aristotle and Plato, cf. L.-B. Geiger, La participation dans la philosophie de S.Thomas d'Aquin (Paris: J. Vrin, 1953), 118.
29 Metaphysics VII, 13. 1038b15.
30 Ibid., 15-35.
31 Categoriae 5. 2a.
32 Metaphysics III, 6. 1003a.
33 De interpretatione 7. 17a39.
34 Cf. Metaphysics IX, 8. 1049b; VII, 13. 1038b-1039.
35 Posterior Analytics I, 29-31. 87b-88a; De Anima II, 5. 417b.
36 Metaphysics VI, 2. 1026a33-b2; Cf. Ibid. V, 7-8.
37 Ibid., IV, 2. 1003b5-9.
38 Ibid., VII, 3. 1028b33-36.
39 Ibid., V, 8. 1017b25; I, 3. 983a27-28.
40 Ibid., VIII, 1. 1042a12-13.
41 Ibid., VII, 8. 1033b22-26; 11. 1037a5-8.
42 Ibid., VII, 10. 1036a5-6.
43 Ibid., XIII, 10. 1087a15-19.
44 Ibid., VII, 8. 1033b24-26; 11. 1037a5-8.
45 Ibid., VII, 10. 1035b27-31.
46 Ibid., V, 8. 1017b25; VIII, 1. 1042a29.
47 Distinguishing between essential and existential possibility, Etienne Gilson, Being and Some Philosphers (Toronto: Pontifical Institute of Mediaeval Studies, 1952), writes:"For, indeed, they belong in two distinct metaphysical orders, so much that there is no way for us to reach the second one through the

first one. An essence is possible, *qua* essence, when all its determining predicates are compossible. If they are, the existence of the corresponding being is possible; if they are not, it is not. And this is true only in the order of essential possibility, not at all in the order of existential possibility" (p. 182).

48   From the logical point of view it is possible to have knowledge of an object which actually does not exist; William Ockham bases such a possibility on the fact that God can produce this kind of knowledge in our intellect, *cf. Quaestiones in librum quartum sententiarum (Reportatio), IV,* 7, in *Opera philosophica et theologica,* vol. 7 (St.Bonaventure, N.Y.: St.Bonaventure University, 1984), 118f. However, it is difficult to understand, as some contemporary phenomenologists try to claim, how the very nature of non-being can be grasped by our intellect, e.g., Roman Ingarden, *Spór o istnienie swiata* (Warsaw: Panstwowe Wydawnictwo Naukowe, 1960).

49   For the textual study on this topic, see William Walton, "Being, Essence and Existence for St.Thomas Aquinas, " *RM* 3 (1950): 339-365.

50   Joseph Owens, "A Note on the Approach to Thomistic Metaphysics," *NS* 28 (1954): 464: "Being, of course, can never be known apart from quiddity, and quiddity can never be known apart from being." On the mutual relation of essence and *esse,* see André Marc, *L'idée de l'être chez Saint Thomas.* Some notion of the act of being can be found in Aristotle, see John R. Catan, "Aristotele e San Tommaso intorno all' *actus essendi,* " *RFNS* 73 (1981): 639-955.

51   The relation of existence and a subject Maritain explains in view of the axiom *causae ad invicem sunt causae,* see "On the Notion of Subsistence, " in *Progress in Philosophy,* ed. James A. McWilliams (Milwaukee: Bruce Publ., 1955), 37.

52   *ST* 2a2ae. 1, 2 ad 2.

53   Jacques Maritain, *Court traité de l'existence et de l'existant* (Paris: P. Hartmann, 1947), 24-25.

54   Gerald B.Phelan, "A Note on the Formal Object of Metaphysics, " *NS* 18 (1944): 199.

55   *I Sent* . 38, 1, 3.

56   *Ibid.,* 19, 5, 1 ad 7.

57   *In Perihermeneias* I, lect. 5.

58   Etienne Gilson, "Limites existentielles de la philosophie," in *L'existence,* essais par Albert Camus (Paris: Gallimard, 1945), 80.

59   Donald O'Grady, "Esse and Metaphysics, " *NS* 39 (1965): 284.

60   Joseph Owens, *St.Thomas and the Future of Metaphysics* (Milwaukee:Marquette University Press, 1957), 32.

61   *III Sent* . 6, 2, 2.c

62   Jacques Maritain, *Sept leçons sur l'être les premiers principes de la raison spéculative* (Paris: P. Tequi, 1934), 103-104.

63   On the problem of understanding of being as a predicate, subject and copula 'is', *cf.* Joseph Owens, "A Note on the approach to Thomistic Metaphysics, " *NS* 28 (1954): 475.

64   *De Veritate* XXVII, 1 ad 8.

65   *De ente et essentia* V, 5. Accepting Boethius's terminology of *quo est* and *quod est*, St.Thomas gives an entirely new meaning to these terms. For Boethius *quo est* designates a form of thing, and *quod est* means a whole thing composed of matter and form. But, since in God there is no distinction between *quo est* and *quod est*, His being is simple, i.e., not having any composition; *cf. De Trinitate* , 2, *PL* 64, 1250, and *De Hebdomadibus, PL* 64, 1311. For St.Thomas, however, *quo est* is being's existence, and *quod est* its essence. In view of this doctrine not only is physical composition denied of God, but also metaphysical composition. As a matter of fact, Boethius's pure form does not exclude from itself some potentiality which is not the case with the Thomistic solution; *cf.* Marie Dominique Roland-Gosselin, *Le " De ente et essentia "de s.Thomas d'Aquin* (Paris: Librairie Philosophique J. Vrin, 1948), 142-145; Louis B. Geiger, *La participation*, 36.

66   *Cf.* Etienne Gilson, *Le Thomisme* (Paris: J. Vrin, 1947), 216, n. 2.

67   Leo Sweeney in his article "Existence/Essence in Thomas Aquinas' Early Writings, " *PACPA* 37 (1963): 105, says: "According to Aquinas *esse* is not the mere composition of other components but a unique component over and above all other components and with its own function to perform." This position, however, seems to conceive *esse* only as something which is common being. Joseph Owens in his article, "Diversity and Community of Being in St.Thomas Aquinas, " *MSt* 22 (1960): 257-302, analyzes St.Thomas's doctrine of *esse* as it is considered both in its community and diversity. Now community and diversity of *esse* are required by the analogical predication of being, and as such consists in a composition of essence and existence. Scott MacDonald, in his paper "The Esse/Essentia Argument in Aquinas's *De ente et essentia* , " *JHP* 22 (1984):157-172, argues against Owens that St.Thomas accepts the real distinction between essence and existence.

68   *Cf.* Etienne Gilson, *Being and Some Philosophers*, 172.

69   *CG* II, 52.

70   *ST* 1a. 54, 3c.

71   According to Cornelio Fabro, *La nozione metafisica*, 243, the real distinction between essence and existence was first thought out by St.Thomas in terms of participation. *Cf.* also remarks of André Hayen, *L'intentionnel selon Saint Thomas* (Paris: Desclée de Brouwer, 1954), 251.

72   Henri Renard, "Essence and Existence, " *PACPA* 21 (1946): 57-66.

73   *Cf.* L.-B. Geiger, *La participation*, 122-124. On the relation of essence and existence, see W. Norris Clarke, "What cannot be said in St.Thomas Essence-Existence Doctrine, " *NS* 48 (1974):19-39.

74   *CG* I, 22; *ST* 1a. 44, 1c. *Cf.* Octavio N. Derisi, "El ser y los entes, " *Sapz* 39 (1984): 91-100.

75   *CG* II, 52. *Cf.* Augustin Basave, "La doctrina metafisica de la participacion en S.Tomas de Aquino, " *GM* 30 (1979): 257-266; John F.Wippel, "Metaphysics and Separation According to Thomas Aquinas, " *RM* 31 (1978): 431-470.

76   *Quodl.* II, 3c.

77   *In De hebdomadibus* , lect. 1. According to Keith A. Buersmeyer, "Predication and Participation, " *NS* 66 (1981): 35-51, participation and judgement have for St.Thomas a mutual dependence.

78   In *De Coelo* II, lect. 18.

79   Participation requires a composition of participating subject and participated perfection, *cf.* Cornelio Fabro, "Un itineraire de St.Thomas, " *RP* 39 (1939): 297-298.

80   *ST* 1a. 75, 5 ad 4.

81   For the development of the notion of participation, see M. Anice, "Historical Sketch of the Theory of Participation, " *NS* 26 (1952): 49-79. St.Thomas's use of participation is discussed by W. Norris Clarke, "The Meaning of Participation in St.Thomas, " *PACPA* 26 (1952): 147-157.

82   *De Anima* 6 ad 2.

83   *CG* II, 53.

84   *Ibid.*, III, 65. *Cf.* Octavio N. Derisi, "Participación, acto y potencia y analogia en Santo Tomás, " *RFNS* 66 (1974): 415-435; Cornelio Fabro, "The Intensive Hermeneutics of Thomistic Philosophy. The Notion of Participation, " *RM* 27 (1973-1974): 449-491.

85   *ST* 1a. 7, 2c.; *De Potentia* VII, 2 ad 5; *De Veritate* II, 11c; *Compendium theol.* 14.

86   *CG* III, 7; *In Phys* . I, lect. 15; III, lect. 2.

87   *Ibid.*

88 *In Meta,* IX, lect. 5. *Cf.* Nicolas J. Balthasar, *Mon moi dans l'être* (Louvain: Editions de l'Institut Supérieure de Philosophie, 1946), 96: "C'est une dichotomie de puissance et d'acte dans l'ordre même de l'existence; il y a limite réelle d'être (*ut quo*); il y a acte ultime d'être (*ut quo*). Les composants sont corrélatifs; leur causalité respective et réciproque; leur simultaneité même logique est requise de soi. Un composant est par l'autre et l'autre composant est par l'un; l'un est connu par l'autre, et l'autre est connue par l'un. Il n'y a pas de 'disessentiation' ou de 'desexistentiation' possible. Il y a conconnaissance de ces deux principes incomplets formant un compose qui n'est que 'cum his', puisque l'existence n'ajoute rien a l'essence comme contenu d'essence."

89 *ST* 1a. 77, 3c.
90 *In Meta,* XI, lect. 9.
91 *Ibid.,* IX, lect. 10.
92 *Metaphysics* IX, 9. 1051a21-33.
93 *ST* 1a. 84, 2c.
94 *Ibid.,* 5, 1 ad 1.
95 *CG* II, 83; *Cf. ST* 1a. 54, 3c.
96 *CG* II, 83.
97 *ST* 1a. 77, 3c:"oportet rationem potentiae accipi ex actu ad quem ordinatur: et per consequens oportet quod ratio potentiae diversificetur, ut diversificatur ratio actus. Ratio autem actus diversificatur secundum diversam rationem obiecti." *Cf. In Meta,* XI, lect. 6; *De Potentia* II, 6, 2; *De Veritate* XV, 2 ad 12; *I Sent* . 7, 1, 2, 2; ad 2.
98 *Ibid.,* Prol., 2 ad 2.
99 *Metaphysics* IX, 8. 1049b10.
100 *In Meta,* IX, lect. 7.
101 *Metaphysics* VII, 10 and 11.
102 *Cf. Metaphysics* IX, 8. 1050a7-10; *In Meta,* IX, lect. 7.
103 *CG* II, 78.
104 *Ibid.,* 16.
105 *In Meta,* VII, lect. 2; IX, lect. 7.
106 *Metaphysics* IX, 8. 1050a4-b6; 1050b6-34.
107 *Ibid.,* 1050a3-b2.
108 *Ibid.,* I, 3. 983a26-32.
109 *In Meta,* IX, lect. 8. Léon Robin, *Aristote* (Paris: Presses Universitaires de France, 1944), 90-98, correctly observed that Aristotle was conscious of the role of form in individuation. In this sense the principle of limitation of act by

potency can already be found in Aristotle. Réginald Garrigou-Lagrange, *Reality: A Synthesis of Thomistic Thought* (St.Louis: Herder, 1950), 43-44: "Aristotle already taught this doctrine. In the first two books of his *Physics* he shows with admirable clearness the truth, at least in the sense world, of this principle. Act, he says, is limited and multiplied by potency. Act determines potency, actualizes potency, but is limited by that same potency...Aristotle studied this principle in the sense world. St.Thomas extends the principle, elevates it, sees its consequences, not only in the sense world, but universally in all orders of being, spiritual as well as corporeal, even in the infinity of God." However, against this well established view, W. Norris Clarke, "The Limitation of Act by Potency," *NS* 26 (1952): 171, denies that "Aristotle himself ever held the doctrine that potency plays the role of limiting principle with respect to act."

Part B: The Transcendental Order of Being

I. Intelligible Order of Investigation

1. *CG* II, 24.
2. *In Meta*, Proem.
3. *Ibid.*
4. *In Post.Anal.* II, lect. 20.
5. *ST* 1a2ae. 57, 2. *Cf.* Aristotle, *Ethics* VI, 7. 1141a19.
6. *CG* I, 77.
7. *ST* 1a2ae. 55, 3c.
8. *Ibid.*, 57, 2c.
9. *CG* I, 61. *Cf.* Aristotle, *Ethics* II, 5. 1106a23-24.
10. *ST* 1a. 79, 8c.
11. *CG* I, 1; II, 24.
12. *ST* 1a1ae. 57, 2c. *Cf.* Aristotle, *Metaphysics* I, 2. 981b28-29; *In Meta*, I, lect. 1.

13 *CG* II, 83.
14 *ST* 1a2ae. 57, 2c.
15 *In Post.Anal.* I, lect. 7 and 44.
16 *ST* 2a2ae. 9, 1 ad 1; *cf.* *CG* III, 39.
17 *Ibid.*, I, 57.
18 *ST* 2a2ae. 9, 2c.
19 *In De Trinitate* 5, 4 ad 6.
20 *In Ethic*, VI, lect. 5. *Cf.* Thomas A. Fay, "The Problem of Intellectual Intuition in the Metaphysics of Thomas Aquinas," *Sapz* 27 (1974): 352-359; Gerald B.Phelan, "Being and the Metaphysicians," in *From an Abundant Spring* (New York: Kennedy and Sons, 1952), 423-447.
21 *CG* I, 3.
22 *Ibid.*
23 *ST* 1a. 55, 2c.
24 *CG* I, 65. For the differences of knowledge between human, angelic and divine intellects, see J. Durantel, *Le retour á Dieu par l'intelligence et la volonté dans la philosophie de S.Thomas* (Paris: Felix Alcan, 1918), 49-177.
25 *CG* III, 25. The relation between being and God can be expressed as a reference which takes place between the parts and the whole, *cf.* Joseph Legrand, *L'universe et l'homme dans la philosophie de Saint Thomas* (Bruxelles-Paris: Desclée de Brouwer, 1946), 1:38: "Tout ce que nous avons avancé en exposant la théorie de la partie et du tout, il faudra donc le redire à propos du rapport de la créature à Dieu. Ce rapport de participation implique donc une identité très réelle, quoique imparfaite, entre la créature et Dieu..."
26 *Ibid.*, 50.
27 *Ibid.*, 25.
28 *Ibid.*, I, 4. The order of assimilation among intellectual substances is described by John H. Wright, *The Order of the Universe in the Theology of St.Thomas Aquinas* (Romae: apud aedes Universitatis Gregorianae, 1957), 46-51.
29 *Ibid.*, 5.
30 *Ibid.*, IV, 1.
31 *Ibid.*, III, 25.
32 *Ibid.*, IV, 1.
33 *Ibid.*
34 *Ibid.*
35 *Ibid.*
36 *Ibid.*

37   Ibid.
38   Ibid.
39   Ibid.
40   Ibid., III, 54.
41   *Dzieje filozofii europejskiej w XV wieku* (Warsaw: Akademia Teologii Katolickiej, 1978), 3:352.
42   *Prior Analytics* II, 23. 68b13-14. *Cf.* Wayne Noel Thompson, *Aristotle's Deduction and Induction. Introductory Analysis and Synthesis* (Amsterdam: Rodopi, 1975).
43   For the contemporary evaluation of the Aristotelian and Thomistic understanding of reasoning by both induction and deduction, see Innocenty M. Bochenski, Jan Fr. Drewnowski and Jan Salamucha, *Rola logistyki w filozofii chrzescijanskiej* (Warsaw: Verbum, 1936). On the relationship between classical philosophy and contemporary logic, see Desmond P. Henry, *Medieval Logic and Metaphysics* (London: Hutchinson, 1972); Howard Kahane, *Logic and Philosophy* (Belmont: Wadsworth Pub.Co., 1969), 330; D. Prawitz, "Meaning and Proofs: On the Conflict between Classical and Intuitionistic Logic," *Theoria*, 48 (1977):2-40.
44   *Odczyty filozoficzne* (Torun: Panstwowe Wydawnictwa Naukowe, 1958), 76.
45   *Cf.* Louis Bourgey, *Observation et expérience chez Aristote* (Paris:J.Vrin, 1955); Emil Simard, *La nature et la portée de la méthode scientifique* (Quebec: Presses Universitaires Laval, 1956), 261-287; S. Vanni-Rovighi, "Concezione aristotelico-tomistica e concezioni moderne del l'induzione, " *RFNS* 23 (1934): 578-593.
46   *Cf.* J. Sikora, "The Problem of Induction, " *T* 22 (1959): 25f.
47   *Topics* I, 12. 105a13-19.
48   *Prior Analytics* II, 21. 67a22-25.
49   *Phaedrus* , 265d; *Sophist* , 253d.
50   *Topics* VIII. 156a6.
51   *In Post.Anal.* I, lect. 1.
52   Mieczyslaw A. Krapiec, "Induction and Philosophy, " in *Saint Thomas Aquinas 700th Anniversary of His Death: Modern Interpretation of His Philosophy* (Lublin: Towarzystwo Naukowe KUL, 1976), 45.
53   Ibid.
54   Ibid., 46.
55   *Phaedo* , 100b101c.
56   *Sophist* , 251d-e.

57 *Parmenides* , 130c-131a.
58 *Metaphysics* XIII, 9. 1086a-1087a.
59 *De interpretatione* 7. 17a39.
60 "Induction and Philosophy, " 50.
61 *Ibid.*, 49.
62 *Ibid.*, 52.
63 *Ibid.*, 54.
64 *ST* 1a. 2, 1c.
65 Mieczyslaw A. Krapiec, "Induction and Philosophy, " 56.
66 *Ibid.*, 63f.
67 *Ibid.*, 67.
68 "Indukcja i metafizyka, " *Tygodnik Powszechny* 35 (1951): 7.
69 *Posterior Analytics* I, 18. 81a38-b9.
70 *Ibid.*, 2. 71b17: "apódeixin dé légo sillogismòn epistemonikón." *Cf. ST* 1a2ae. 54, 2 ad 2.
71 *In Post.Anal.* I, lect. 4. *Cf.* Aristotle, *Posterior Analytics* I, 2.71b19-22.
72 "Induction and Philosophy, " 95.
73 *Ibid.*, 96.
74 *In Post.Anal.* I, lect. 23.
75 Mieczyslaw A. Krapiec, "Induction and Philosophy," 96, writes: "Explanatory demonstration through knowledge of the particular causes of a thing - *demonstratio ex causis rei procedit et primis et immediatis* - is called *demonstratio propter quid*. According to John of St.Thomas, in this type of reasoning-demonstration we know not only that something is, that something exists in such a way, but also why something is such and no other; in other words, we know the peculiar real source of a given state, revealed in a true assertion. To indicate the proper cause of some effects is to reason apriori in relation to the knowledge both of the existential fact and of the nature of the given effects, and that is why all explanatory reasoning *propter quid* is apriori reasoning."
76 *Ibid.*, 97.
77 *Ibid.*
78 *Cf.* James Anderson, "On Demonstration in Thomistic Metaphysics, " *NS* 32 (1958): 476-494.
79 On the mutuality of demonstration *quia* and *propter quid*, *cf.* "Induction and Philosophy, " 100.
80 *Ibid.*, 123.
81 In *De Coelo* I, Proem.

82   De Veritate II, 2c.
83   ST 2a2ae. 31, 3c.
84   IV Sent . 31, 1, 3c.Cf. ibid. 5, 1, 3, 1c.
85   ST 1a. 62, 3 ad 1.
86   IV Sent . 47, 2, 2, 1c.
87   Cf. ST 1a. 1, 6 ad 3.
88   Cf. Jacque Maritain, *The Degree of Knowledge* (London: G. Bles, 1959), 253.

II. Rational Order of Created Things

1   CG II, 15.
2   ST 1a. 5, 5. Cf. also Ibid. 6, 3; 16, 3; 4; 1a1ae. 52, 1; CG I, 40.
3   For discussion on the interconnection between plurality of beings and analogy, see Mieczyslaw A. Krapiec, *Teoria analogii bytu* (Lublin:Towarzystwo Naukowe KUL, 1959), 175-185. Seeing the ontological foundation of interdependency of analogy and plurality of beings in the very composition of things, Krapiec argues: "If, then, monism is associated inseparably with the homogenous nature of beings, pluralism demands that beings be composed of some heterogenous elements" (177).
4   ST 1a. 13, 7. Cf. Robert Blanch., "Notes sur les relations d'ordre, " *RPFE* 165 (1975): 431-433; Clifford G. Kossel, "Orders and Relations, " *PACPA* 39 (1965): 140-144.
5   *Summa Theologiae* , I, 13, 52, ed. Borgnet, vol. 31 (1895), 535. Cf. *Enciclopedia Italiana* (Rome: Instituto della Enciclopedia Italiana, 1948), 29:24: "(La relazione) - è uno dei concetti filosofici più problematici e più ricchi di storia."
6   On the metaphysical foundations of relation, see Mieczyslaw A. Krapiec, *Metafizyka* (Lublin: Redakcja Wydawnictw KUL, 1985), 329-337.
7   Friedrich A. Trendelenburg, *Geschichte der Kategorienlehre. Zwei Abhandlungen* (Berlin: Gust.Bethge, 1846), 120, states that Aristotle borrowed the concept of relation from Plato; see also Alexander Horvath, *Metaphysik der Relationen* (Graz: U. Mosers Buchhandlung, 1914), 14. However, modern historical investigations indicate that the doctrine of relation was first given by Aristotle, *cf.* A. Krempel, *La doctrine de la relation chez Saint Thomas* (Paris: J.

Vrin, 1952), 1: "Au vrai dire, dans ses cinq catégories, Platon ne fait aucune place au relatif, tout préoccupe qu'il est de la notion parenté d'intermédiaire qui réapparaitra dans la philosophie de Hegel." *Cf.* also Joseph Souilh., *La notion platonicienne d'intermédiaire dans la philosophie des dialogues* (Paris: F. Alcan, 1919).

8   The classical texts of the Aristotelian doctrine of relation are: *Categoriae* 7.6a36-8b24; *Metaphysics* V, 15. 1021b26-1022a3; *Topics* 6.146a36-146b19.

9   *Categoriae* 7. 6a36.

10   *Ibid.*, 6b1-14.

11   Originally the term *tò prós ti* is taken from the Pythagorean philosophy, *cf.* A. Krempel, *La doctrine de la relation*, 1.

12   *Categoriae* 7. 6b15-31.

13   Creation and conservation St.Thomas defines in terms of relation, *cf. De Potentia* III, 3 ad 3; *ST* 1a. 45, 3c; ad 3; *Compendium theol.* I, 99; *Quodl.* VII, 10 ad 4; *II Sent* . 1, 1, 2 ad 4; *CG* II, 18; etc. Distinguishing two kinds of creation, namely, active and passive, Aquinas in both cases defines them by relation, *cf. De Potentia* III, 3 ad 2; *ST* 1a. 45, 3 ad 1; *II Sent* . 1, 1, 2 ad 4.

14   Among the categories St.Thomas attributes to God only two, namely, substance and relation, *cf. De Potentia* X, 5; *ST* 1a. 28, 2 ad 1; *I Sent* .2, 1, 3; 22, 1, 3 ad 2; 33, 1, 1 ad 5. The category of relation is in the nature of God as a principle of distinction of the three Divine Persons, *cf. ST* 1a. 29, 4c; 36, 2c; *De Potentia* IX, 5 ad 3; *I Sent* . 33, 1, 2 ad 1; ad 5; 26, 2, 1; 8, 4, 1 ad 4. In the nature of Divine Persons there are two kinds of relations, namely, logical and real relations, *De Potentia* I, 1 ad 1.

15   The unity of the divine and human nature of Christ, St.Thomas explains by recalling to the theory of relation: *ST* 3a. 2, 7c; ad 2; 8c; 16, 6 ad 2; *I Sent* . 30, 1, 2 ad 4; III, 5, 1, 1, 1.

16   *Cf.* Hans Meyer, *The Philosophy of St.Thomas Aquinas*, 114.

17   *I Sent* . 26, 2, 1. *Cf. ibid.*, 33, 1, 1; *De Potentia* VII, 9 ad 7; *ST* 1a. 28, 2c. *Cf.* also Clifford G. Kossel, "Principles of St.Thomas' Distinction between the *Esse* and *ratio* of Relation, " *MS* 24 (1946): 19-36; 25 (1947): 93-107.

18   *I Sent* . 2, 1, 5.

19   *Commentaria in Porphyrii Isagogen ad praedicamenta Aristotelis*, ed.P. Isnardus M. Marega (Romae: apud Institutum "Angelicum," 1934), 31:"Essentia enim propria relativi, ut sic, in ipso ad consistit." *Cf.* also *idem*, *In Summa Theologicae*, I, 28, 1c, vols. 3 (Lugduni: apud G.Rouillium, 1588), 1:149: "quandocunque de ad aliud seu relatione secundum propriam rationem

loquimur de ad est sermo." Thomas Pègues, *Commentaire français littéral de la Somme Théologique de Saint Thomas d'Aquin* (Toulouse: E. Privat, 1907-1912), 2:88: "La relation elle, ne signifie, selon sa raison propre, qu'un rapport à quelque chose; on peut la définir par une simple préposition, selon l'expressive remarque de Cajetan, par la préposition ad, en français verse La relation, c'est le ad, le vers. Elle est essentiellement un rapport."

20   *ST* 1a. 45, 3 ad 2: "Relationes, cum hoc ipsum quod sunt, ad-aliquid dicantur." John of St.Thomas attributes the preposition *ad-aliquid* only to predicamental relation, while expression for transcendental relationis *ab alio*; see *Cursus Philosophicus*, Log. II, 17, 2, ed. Beato Reiser (Taurini: Marietti, 1930), 1:583. *Cf.* also Alexander Horvath, *Metaphysik der Relationen*, 81; A. Krempel, *La doctrine de la relation*, 645ff.

21   In St.Thomas Aquinas the analogical character of relation is expressed by such relative terms as: *respectus, De Veritate* XXI, 6; *CG* IV, 14; *ST* 1a. 28, 1c; *Quodl.* I, 2; *Compendium theol.* I, 212; *habitudo, ST* 1a2ae. 110, 3 ad 3; *De Potentia* VII, 8; *In Phys* . II, 5; *proportio, De Potentia* III, 4; *De Veritate* VIII, 1 ad 6; *In Ethic,* V, 5; *I Sent* .19, 1, 1 ad 4; St 1a. 12, 1 ad 4; *De Potentia* VI, 7 ad 6; *comparatio, DeTrinitate* IV, 3 for relation in general, but for particular type of relation the relative terms are: *dependentia, De Potentia* Vii, 1 ad 9; *CG* II, 18; *adequatio, De Veritate* I, 1; *ST* 1a. 16, 8c; *dispositio, De Veritate* I, 1 ad 5; *I Sent* . 39, 2, 1; *inclinatio, ST* 1a. 60, 1c; *II Sent* .39, 3, 1 ad 5; *assimilatio, I Sent* . 34, 3, 1 ad 2; *communicatio ST* 1a. 4, 3c; *commensuratio, De Veritate* I, 5; etc.

22   *IV Sent* . 27, 1, 1, 1 ad 3. Relation so considered Aquinas expresses by such words as: *fundari, Ibid.,* I, 2, 2; *causari, CG* IV, 14; *sequi, Compendium theol.* I, 54; *consequi, III Sent* . 4, 1, 2, 1; *ordinari secundum, De Potentia* VII, 9; *nasci, Ibid.,* X, 3, 2; *innasci, I Sent* . 14, 2, 1, 2 ad 4; *acquiri, De Potentia* III, 3, 7; etc.

23   *De Potentia* VII, 9.

24   *CG* IV, 14; *De Potentia* VII, 8 ad 2.

25   *Ibid.,* 9.

26   *Ibid.; CG* IV, 14.

27   *Ibid*.

28   *In Meta,* V, lect. 8; X, lect. 2; lect. 3.

29   *De Potentia* VII, 11.

30   Similarly St.Thomas set down the concept of order with others, e.g., *ordo et proportio, ST* 1a. 13, 5c; *ordo vel proportio, CG* II, 16; *ordo et habitus, ST* 1a.13, 7c; *ordo et distinctio, CG* II, 42; *ordo vel relatio, In Phys* . V, lect.3; etc.

31   *Cf. ST* 1a. 13, 7c; *Quodl.* IX, 4.

32 *De Potentia* VII, 9.
33 *Ibid.*, ad 7.
34 *ST* 1a. 28, 2c.
35 *De Potentia* VII, 9 ad 7.
36 *ST* 1a. 36, 2c; *In Meta,* V, lect. 1.
37 *Ibid.*, lect. 17. *Cf. De Potentia* VII, 10; , 9 ad 7.
38 *In Meta,* V, lect. 17; *De Potentia* VII, 9 ad 7; 10.
39 *Ad Anibaldum.* On the metaphysical foundation of relation, see Michele Malatesta, "Logika e ontologia delle relazioni nel pensiero di Tommaso d'Aquino," *RSF* 26 (1973): 273-303.
40 *De Veritate* II, 3 ad 3.
41 *De Potentia* VII, 11.
42 *Ibid.*, I, 1 ad 10; VII, 6; 9.
43 *I Sent* . 23, 1, 3; 26, 1, 1 ad 3.
44 *Cf. De Relatione,* 1.
45 *De Potentia* VII, 11.
46 *In Phys* . III, lect. 1.
47 *IV Sent* . 12, 1, 1.
48 *De Potentia* Vii, 9 ad 7.
49 *ST* 1a. 13, 7.
50 *De Potentia* VIII, 1c; *ST* 1a. 28, 3c.
51 *Ibid.*, 13,7c.
52 *Cf.* George P. Klubertanz, *Introduction to the Philosophy of Being* (New York: Appleton-Century-Crofts, 1955), 252.
53 Antoine Goudin, *Philosophia juxta inconcussa tutissimaque D.Thomae dogmata,* vol. 1 (Urbeveteri: prelis Speraindeo Pompei, 1859), Logica Maior, pars I, d. 2, q. 4, a. 1. *Cf.* also John of St.Thomas, *Cursus Philosophicus,* Logica, II, 17, 2, 578.
54 *De Veritate* II, 3 qd 4; VIII, 1 ad 6; *ST* 1a. 31, 1 ad 3; *In Meta* .V, lect. 17; *CG* III, 54.
55 *Cf. ST* 1a. 85, 3, 1; 1a2ae. 62, 4c; 83, 3, 2; etc.
56 *CG* I, 30. *Cf.* F. M. Sladeczek, "Die Verschiedenen Bedeutung des Seins nach dem Hl. Thomas von Aquin," *Sch* 5 (1930): 192-209; 523-550.
57 *De Veritate* I, 1c.
58 *Teoria analogii bytu,* 163.
59 *CG* I, 25. For the historical development of the terminology of *ens* and *esse,* see Etienne Gilson, "Notes sur le vocabulaire de l'être," *MSt* 8 (1946):150-158.

60   Cf. I Sent . 2, 1 2; 8, 1, 1; 25, 1, 4; 33, 1, 2; II, 71, 1; De Veritate I, 1; VII, 5 ad 3; CG I, 25; 30.

61   Ibid.

62   Cf. Mieczyslaw A. Krapiec, Struktura bytu (Lublin: Towarzystwo Naukowe KUL, 1962).

63   Idem,Teoria analogii bytu 164. Cf. Frederik D. Wilhelmsen, "The Concept of Existence and the Structure of Judgement: A Thomistic Paradox," T 41 (1977): 317-349.

64   On the historical development of this distinction, see Etienne Gilson, Being and Some Philosophers, 77-107.

65   Teoria analogii bytu, 162.

66   Ibid.

67   Ibid.

68   Ibid., 163.

69   Ibid.

70   Ibid., 178.

71   Ibid., 165.

72   Ibid. Cf. also William R. Darós, "La analogia en el concepto de ciencia Aristotélico-Tomista," Sap 39 (1984): 19-36.

73   Teoria analogii bytu, 173.

74   Ibid., 193. The analogical structure of real being consists, according to Krapiec, in "a synthesis of transcendental relation," because "it is impossible for the same essence and existence to occur more than once (the possibility arising out of the supernatural order are not taken into account here), since the identity of essence and existence depends on the identity of all constituent elements, of both the substantial and accidential orders. For this reason the same essence and existence cannot be repeated in another being. Hence, the essence as well as the proportional to it existence are always concrete,unique, nonrepeatable, subordinated to each other and linked together so closely that it would be impossible to separate them without destruction of the whole being" (185).

75   Ibid., 194. In view of the existential aspect of being, one can see why the Lublin School is charging Cajetan and his followers with narrowing the analogy of proportionality to an order of pure essential characteristics of being entirely based on predicamental relation, and consequently treating the whole metaphysical knowledge of being qua being " in the same way as in other non-metaphysical investigations" (188). The proper understanding of analogy of proper proportionality of being requires that the metaphysical knowledge of

being *qua* being be based on transcendental relation, because otherwise one could mentally separate "the analogical proportion from the analogates ... and hence destroy the structure of analogy" in being as such (191). Moreover, the predicamental relations are "pure correspondence" and the transcendental ones "contains in itself the ontological element which, at the same time, relates one thing to another" (192). In conclusion Krapiec says:"Wherever there is a proportionality between pairs of analogical proportion based on the categorical, nontranscendental relations, this is the result of our cognition and is not realized in beings themselves existent independently of our knowledge. What does take place is a projection of our mentality but not a cognitive reception" (197).

76   *Ibid.*, 180.
77   *Ibid.*, 181.
78   *Ibid.*, 201.
79   *Ibid.*, 202.
80   *Ibid.*, 187-189.
81   *Ibid.*, 210.
82   *Ibid.*, 211.
83   *CG* I, 43.
84   *Teoria analogii bytu*, 211. On the question of *analogia graduum entis*, see Joseph de Finance, "Le degrès de l'être chez Saint Thomas d'Aquin," in *Analecta Husserliana* (Dordrecht: Reidel, 1981), 51-57; Paul G. Kuntz, "The Analogy of Degrees of Being: A Critique of Cajetan's Analogy of Names", *NS* 56 (1982): 51-79.
85   *Teoria analogii bytu*, 215.
86   *Ibid.*
87   *Ibid.*, 216.
88   *Ibid.*, 217.
89   *Ibid.*, 218. Cf. Thomas A. Fay, "Analogy: The Key to Man's Knowledge of God in the Metaphysics of Thomas Aquinas," *DTP* 76 (1973): 343-364.
90   *CG* II, 15.

III. The Existential Order of Being

1   *De ente et essentia* VI. Cf. *ST* 1a. 3, 5c.

2   *CG* I, 25.
3   *I Sent*. 19, 5, 2.
4   *CG* I, 26.
5   *Ibid.*, 25.
6   *ST* 1a. 3, 5c.
7   *Cf.* Francisco L. Peccorini, "Knowledge of the Singular: Aquinas, Suarez and Recent Interpreters," *T* 38 (1974): 606-655.
8   *Cf.* Ralph W. Clark, "Saint Thomas Aquinas' Theory of Universals," *M* 58 (1974): 163-172.
9   *CG* I, 26.
10 *De Potentia* IX, 7.
11 *De Veritate* I, 1c.
12 *In De Trinitate* VI, 1, 3c.
13 *I Sent*. 8, 1, 3.
14 *Ibid.*, 24, 1, 3.
15 *ST* 1a. 11, 2c.
16 *I Sent*. 24, 1, 3.
17 *De Potentia* IX, 7c.
18 *I Sent*. 24, 1, 3.
19 *ST* 1a. 30, 3 ad 3.
20 *De Potentia* IX, 7.
21 *ST* 1a, 11, 1 ad 2.
22 *I Sent*. 24, 1, 3.
23 *ST* 1a. 11, 2 ad 4.
24 *De Potentia* IX, 7 ad 5.
25 *ST* 1a. 11, 1 ad 2; *cf. I Sent*. 2, 1, 1.
26 *ST* 1a. 11, 4 ad 1. The unity and plurality of created beings is discussed by Leonard J. Eslick, "The Thomistic Doctrine of the Unity of Creation," *NS* 13 (1939): 49-70.
27 *ST* 1a. 11, 1c.
28 *CG* III, 97. On the analogical predication of being in regard to the unity, see Rudolf Allers, "Ens et Unum Convertuntur," in *Philosophical Studies in Honor of I. Smith*, 65-75.
29 For the Thomistic doctrine of *esse commune*, see Joseph de Vries, "Das 'esse commune' bei Thomas von Aquin," *Sch* 39 (1964): 167-177.
30 The origin of the transcendentals in St.Thomas's doctrine of being is studied by Stanislas Breton, "L'idée de transcendental et la genèse des transcendentaux chez Saint Thomas d'Aquin," *Saint Thomas Aujourd'hui*,

Recherches de Philosophie 6 (1963): 45-74. On transcendentals as expressions of *esse*, see Marc D. Jordan, "The Grammar of Esse: Re-Reading Thomas on the Transcendentals," *T* 44 (1980): 1-26; H. Pouillon, "Le premier traité des propriétés transcendentales," *RNP* 42 (1939): 40-77; Louis Marie Regis, *L'Odyssée de la metaphysique* (Montreal-Paris: 1949), 39.

    31   Henri Renard, "What is St.Thomas' approach to Metaphysics," *NS* 30 (1956): 81-83, proposes a distinction between *esse commune* and *esse transcendentale* on the basis that *esse commune* is predicated but only of created beings. For discussion with this statement, see Joseph Owens, "Diversity and Community of Being in St.Thomas Aquinas," *MSt* 22 (1960): 264.

    32   *De ente et essentia* VI. *Cf.* also *I Sent* . 8, 4, 1 ad 1; *De Potentia* VII, 2 ad 6; *CG* I, 26; *ST* 1a. 3, 4 ad 1.

    33   *I Sent* . 8, 1, 3.

    34   *In Meta* , X, lect. 3.

    35   *De Veritate* XXI, 3c.

    36   The transcendental characteristics of being, Edgar de Bruyne, *S.Thomas d'Aquin* (Paris: G. Beauchesne, 1928), 114, describes as follows:"Tous les genres, au contraire, sont des modes d'être et l'être lui-même n'est pas un genre suprême. Dans le genre, en effet, se distinguent les espèces gràce à des différences qui s'ajoutent à la détermination générique et qui, par conséquent, sont autres qu'elle; dans l'être les différences, sont encore de l'être: à l'être rien ne peut être ajouté qui ne soit de l'être. C'est porquoi l'être ne s'appliquant pas à telle ou telle catégorie des choses, mais absolument à tout ce qui est, est appelé transcendental; il est ce qui embrasse et contient tout, l'infinité qui attire l'intelligence." *Cf.* also Antonin D. Sertillanges, *S.Thomas d'Aquin*,1:27-32; August Brunner, *Der Stuffenbau der Welt* (München und Kempten:Kösel Verlag, 1950), 431-451.

    37   *De Veritate* I, 1 ad 3.

    38   *Ibid.*, XXI, 5 ad 8.

    39   *ST* 1a. 11, 1 ad 3; *In Meta* , IV, lect. 2; XI, lect 3; *De Veritate* XXI, 5 ad 7; *De Potentia* IX, 7c; *I Sent* ., 24, 1, 3 ad 1.

    40   St.Thomas's evaluation of the Avicennian doctrine on the nature of *one* has been discussed and traced to its textual sources by Thomas O'Shaughnessy, "St.Thomas and Avicenna on the Nature of the One," *Greg* 41 (1960):665-679. The author tries to prove that St.Thomas's objections against Avicenna cannot be verified in his whole philosophy of being (p. 671). In his criticism Aquinas followed Averroes and was using Avicenna's name "as a convenient label to designate a class of doctrines that made one univocal" (p.

678). O'Shaughnessy expresses also an opinion that St.Thomas admitted in the beginning of his philosophical career that Avicenna distinguishes between the transcendental and predicamental unity. Recalling the text from the *Commentary to the Sentences* I, 24, 1, 1 ad 2, the author writes: "This might favor the view that he was opposing a tendency rather than an individual. Still it is true that his practice in earlier works of citing Avicenna with approval is gradually relinquished for a less benevolent interpretation in his latter years. This change of attitude on St.Thomas' part seems to have been prompted by the wider reaction in the Church against the heterodox Aristotelianism inspired by Arabian philosophy which occurred in the last decade of his life" (p. 678).

41 *ST* 1a. 11, 1c. *Cf. ibid.*, 3 ad 2; 30, 3c; *I Sent* . 24, 1, 1 ad 4; De Veritate XXI, 5 ad 7; *De Potentia* IX, 7c; *In Meta* , III, lect. 12; IV, lect. 2; XI, lect. 3.

42 *ST* 1a. 11, 1c. In his *Quodlibetum*, IX, 2, 2 ad 2, St.Thomas discussing the unity of *esse* in Christ points out that being is that on which unity of the subject is based, and so manifold *esse* prejudices the unity of being: "esse est id quo fundatur unitas suppositi: unde esse multiplex praeiudicat unitati essendi."

43 *ST* 1a. 11, 1c.

44 *De Veritate* XXI, 5 ad 8.

45 *I Sent* . 19, 1, 1.

46 The question of unity as expressed through essence and as related to its existential act of being is discussed at length by Joseph Owens,"Unity and Essence in St.Thomas Aquinas," *MSt* 23 (1961):240-259.

47 *De Potentia* IX, 7c. *Cf. In Meta* , XI, lect.3: "Tam manifestum est quod ad invicem convertuntur; quia omne unum est aliqualiter ens, et omne ens est aliqualiter unum. Et sicut substantia est proprie et per se ens, ita proprie et per se unum; " *ibid.*, X, lect. 3.

48 *ST* 1a. 30, 3 ad 1.

49 *Ibid.*, 16, 1c.

50 *Ibid.*, 3c.

51 *Ibid.*, 4c.

52 *De Veritate* XXI, 3c.

53 *ST* 1a. 16, 4c.

54 *Ibid*.

55 *De Veritate* XXI, 3c.

56 *CG* I, 30.

57   *De Veritate* I, 1c. *Cf.* Charles A. Hart, *Metaphysics for the Many: A Thomistic Inquiry Into the Act of Existence* (Washington: The CatholicUniversity of America, 1957), 280.

58   'Property' is defined by Aristotle as "a predicate which does not indicate the essence of a thing, but yet belongs to that thing alone, and is predicated convertibly of it," *Topics* I, 5. 102a18. Transcendentals cannot be properties of being in a strict sense, because property belongs to the qualitative order; *cf.* Joseph Owens, *An Elementary Christian Metaphysics* (Milwaukee: The Bruce Publishing Com., 1963), 117.

59   *I Sent* . 25, 1, 4.

60   Some commentators of St.Thomas try to prove that the transcendental *aliquid* expresses a separate property of being on the ground that it designates division from non-being; *cf.* F.-X. Maquart, *Elementa philosophiae*, vol. 3, 2 (Paris: Andreas Blot, 1938), 106-107. This interpretation of *aliquid*, however, is difficult to reconcile with St.Thomas's definition of *aliquid* as "divisionem illius ab alio," *De Veritate*, I, 1c.

61   *Cf.* James B. Sullivan, *An Examination of First Principles in Thought and Being in the Light of Aristotle and Aquinas* (Washington: The Catholic University of America Press, 1939).

62   *In Meta* , X, lect.3.

63   *ST* 1a. 6, 11c.

64   Ralph Masiello, *Intuition of Being According to the Metaphysics of Saint Thomas Aquinas* (Washington: The Catholic University of America Press, 1955), 17-22; John E. Twomey, *The General Notion of the Transcendentals in the Metaphysics of Saint Thomas Aquinas* (Washington: The Catholic University of America Press, 1958), 15-16.

IV. Metaphysical Order of Being and Truth

1   *Summa Theologiae* , I, 6, 28, ed. Borgnet, vol. 31 (1895), 287-290.

2   *In De Coelo* I, lect. 2.

3   *An Introduction to Metaphysics*, trans. by T.E. Hulme (New York-London: G. P. Putnam's Sons, 1912), 7.

4   *An Introduction to Metaphysics*, trans. by Ralph Manheim (New York:Doubleday and Company Inc., 1961), 25.

5   Ibid., 53.
6   Ibid., 72.
7   Ibid.
8   Ibid., 65.
9   CG I, 25.
10 CG I, 30. Cf. Carlo Giacon, "La distinzione tra l'esistenza in Avicenna e in Tommaso," DC 28 (1974): 30-45.
11 *What is Philosophy?*, trans. by William Kluback and Jean T. Wilde (New York: Twayne Publishers Inc., 1958), 55. For comparision of St.Thomas's and Heidegger's notion of being, see John D. Caputo, "The Problem of Being in Heidegger and Aquinas," T 41 (1977): 62-91; Joseph Stellmach, "Seinsdenken bei Thomas von Aquin und Heidegger," H 60 (1967-1968): 1-13.
12 *I Sent*. 8, 4, 2 ad 2.
13 *The Essence of Reasons*, trans. by Terrence Malick (Evanston:Nortwestern University Press, 1969), 3. Cf. Johannes B. Lotz, "A diferenca ontologica em Kant, Hegel, Heidegger e Tomas de Aquino," RPF 33 (1977): 21-38.
14 *De Natura Gen.* . 1.
15 *Quodl.* II, 3.
16 *In Meta* , XII, lect. 1.
17 *What is Philosophy*, 49. On the immediate presentation of beigness, see Thomas Sheehan, "Heidegger's Topic: Excess, Recess, Access," TF 41 (1979): 615-635.
18 *Nietzsche* (Pfullingen: Neske, 1961) 402. Cf. John Caputo, "Heidegger's 'Difference' and the Distinction between Esse and Ens," IPQ 20 (1980): 161-182; *idem*, "Heidegger and Aquinas: The Thought of Being and the Metaphysics of Esse," PT 26 (1982): 194-203.
19 William J. Richardson, *Heidegger: Through Phenomenology to Thought* (The Hague: Martinus Nijhoff, 1967), 13. On the ambiguity of *ens* and *esse* in St.Thomas and Heidegger, see William R. Daròs, "Nota sobre el concepto de 'ente' en Tomas de Aquino," Sap 33 (1978): 285-296.
20 *Nietzsche*.
21 *Sein und Zeit* (Tübingen: Max Niemeyer, 1963), 226.
22 *I Sent* . 19, 5, 1c. Cf. Jakob Fellermeir, "Wahrheit und Existenz bei Heidegger und Thomas von Aquin," SJP 15-16 (1971-1972): 39-70; M. E.Sacchi, "Santo Tomas de Aquino interpretado por Heidegger," A 19 (1976):64-87.
23 *De Veritate* I, 1 ad 4.

24   *Ibid.*, 1c. The connection between being and truth is discussed by Gerald B. Phelan, "Verum Sequitur Esse Rerum," *MSt* 1 (1939): 11-22. *Cf.* also Rudolf Allers, "The Problem of Truth," in *Essays in Thomism*, 67-79.
25   J. A. Chollet, *De la notion d'ordre. Parallélisme des trois ordres de l'être, du vrai, du bien* (Paris: P. Léthielleux, 1898), 91-92.
26   *ST* 1a. 16, 3 ad 1.
27   *I Sent* . 3, 1, 2, 3.
28   *ST* 1a. 12, 11c.
29   *Ibid.*, 77, 7c.
30   *Cf.* Joseph de Tonquédec, *La critique de la connaissance* (Paris:Gabriel Beauchesne, 1929); André Marc, *Psychologie Réflexive*, vol. 1 (Paris: Desclée de Brouwer, 1948).
31   *In Meta* , V, 13.
32   *Ibid.*
33   *Ibid.*
34   *Ibid.*
35   *ST* 1a. 79, 1c.
36   *Ibid.*
37   *Ibid.*, 77, 3c.
38   *CG* II, 72.
39   *ST* 1a. 77, 3 ad 4.
40   *De Anima* 13c.
41   *CG* IV, 11.
42   *ST* 1a. 105, 3c.
43   Joseph Gredt, "De unione omnium maxima inter subiectum cognoscens et obiectum cognitum, *Xenia Thomistica*, ed. by Sadoc Szabó (Romae: Typis Polyglotis Vaticanis, 1925), 1:303-318. *Cf.* J. Brinkmann, "Zur Rationalen Begründung der Philosophischen Grundgewissenheiten," *PJ* 3 (1927), 252; Antoine de Coninck, *L'unité de la connaissance humaine et le fondement de sa valeur* (Louvain: Editions de l'Institut Supérieure de Philosophie, 1947), 132-138.
44   *CG* II, 60. *Cf. I Sent* . 36, 1, 2, 3.
45   *De Veritate* XI, 1.
46   The relation between the knower and the thing known is discussed by Antonin D. Sertillanges, "L'être et la connaissance dans la philosophie de S.Thomas d'Aquin," *Mélanges Thomiste* (Kain: Le Saulchoir, 1923),1:182,187.
47   *CG* I, 56.

48   The foundation of the order of knowledge is being, *cf.* Réginald Garrigou-Lagrange, "Le prémiere donné de l'intelligence," *Mélanges Thomiste* (Kain: Le Saulchoir, 1923), 3:201: "Cette question de la premiére donné de notre intelligence est manifestment le noend problèmes métaphysique; c'est à elle que se rattachent celui de l'être et du devenir, celui de la valeur ontologique du principe de contradiction ou d'identité, celui des universaux, celui de la distinction de Dieu et du monde, celui de la distinction dans les creatures de l'essence et de l'existence, problémes fondamentaux dont la portée est incalculable."

49   Against Marechal's view of the psychological apriority of intelligible species, see F.-X. Maquart, "L'espèce intelligble," *RP* 35 (1928): 603.

50   *De Veritate* XX, 2. *Cf.* also *Ibid.*, X, 2c : "Species intelligibiles in intellectu possibili remanet post actualem considerationem, et harum ordinatio est habitus, nihil aliud videtur esse quam generatio specierum intelligibilium."

51   *De Veritate* XX, 2c.

52   Jacque Maritain, *Distinguer pour unir. Les degrés du savoir* (Paris:Desclée de Brouwer, s.d.), 235: "Dans le concept nous avons distingué deux choses: une fonction entitative, par laquelle il est une modification ou un accident de l'âme, et une fonction intentionelle, par laquelle il est signe formel de la chose, dans lequel l'object est aisi par l'esprit."

53   *CG* I, 48.

54   *In De Anima* II, lect. 5.

55   *De Veritate* II, 2c. *Cf.* John of St.Thomas, *Cursus Theologicus*, 16,1, vol. 2 (Parisiis-Tornaci-Romae: Desclée et Sociorum, 1934), 328ff. The problem of immateriality is discussed at length by Jacques Maritain, *Distinguir pour unir*, 217ff.

56   Immateriality as a principle of cognition result in that intelligible species constitute an order of intentionality, *cf.*Jacques Maritain, *Réflections sur l'intelligence et sa vie propre* (Paris: Desclée de Brouwer,1938), 58-63. For the existential interpretation of the order of intentionality, see Mieczyslaw A. Krapiec, *Realizm ludzkiego poznania* (Poznan: Pallotinum, 1959), 449-480.

57   *De Veritate* I, 9c. For the textual study of the role of reflection in the philosophy of St.Thomas, see Jordanus Wébert, "Reflexio. Étude sur le opérations réflexives dans la psychologie de St.Thomas," *Mélanges Thomiste* (Kain: Le Saulchoir, 1930), 1:285-325.

58   *De Potentia* VII, 11c.

59   *ST* 1a. 14, 2c.

60 *Sein und Zeit*, 226. For further discussion, see Charles B. Guignon, *Heidegger and the Problem of Knowledge* (Indianopolis: Hackett Publishing Company, 1983), 198-201, 247-252; in regard to St.Thomas, *cf.*John D. Caputo, *Heidegger and Aquinas: An Essay on Overcoming Metaphysics* (New York: Fordham University Press, 1982), 201-203, 222-229.

61 *An Introduction to Metaphysics*, 116.

62 *Ibid.*, 117.

63 *The Essence of Reasons*, 3.

64 *Ibid.* On Heidegger's understanding of nothinness, see James F. Anderson,"Bergson, Aquinas, and Heidegger on the Notion of Nothingness," *PACPA* 41 (1967): 143-148.

65 "The Onto-Theo-Logical Constitution of Metaphysics," in *Identity and Difference*, trans. by Joan Staumbaugh (New York: Harper and Row,1974), 50-51.

66 *Ibid.*, 57.

67 *Ibid.*, 67.

68 *The Essence of Reasons*, 3-10.

69 *Ibid.*, 35.

70 *Ibid.*, 37-39.

71 *Ibid.*, 35-37.

72 *Being and Time* (London: SCM Ltd., 1962), 62.

73 *Ibid*.

74 *Ibid.*, 67.

75 Cf. *Was ist Metaphysik ?* (Frankfurt a.M.: V. Klostermann, 1949).

76 *Being and Time*, 67-68.

77 *The Essence of Reasons*, 39.

78 *Ibid.*, 41.

79 *Ibid.*, 101.

80 *Ibid.*, 103.

81 *Ibid.*, 105.

82 *Ibid.*, 111.

83 *Ibid.*, 113-117.

84 *Ibid.*, 123. On Heideggerian concept of foundation, see Johannes B.Lotz, "Die Frage nach dem Fundament bei Heidegger und in der Scholastik," *Sapz* 26 (1973): 280-331.

85 "On the Essence of Truth" (trans. by R.F.C. Hull and Alan Crick), in *Existence and Being*, introduction and analysis by Werner Brock (Chicago: H. Regnery Company, 1968), 303.

86   *Being and Time*, 262ff.
87   *Ibid.*, 263.
88   *Ibid.*
89   *Ibid.*
90   *ST* 1a. 14, 1c.
91   *What is Philosophy*, 49. *Cf.* Ambrose McNicholl, "Heidegger: Problema e precomprensione," *A* 20 (1977): 180-206.
92   *Vom Wesen der Wahrheit* (Frankfurt a.M.: V. Klostermann, 1949).
93   *Metaphysics* IV, 6. 1011b26-29.
94   *ST* 1a. 17, 1c.
95   *De Veritate* I, 4c.
96   *Identity and Difference*, 55. On the difference between St.Thomas's and Heidegger's teachings on truth, see Olinto Pigorard, "Note sur la vérité chez Saint Thomas et M. Heidegger," *RPL* 74 (1976): 45-55.
97   *Identity and Difference*, 71. On the relationship between Heideggerian and Aquinas's understanding of metaphysics, see John D.Caputo, *Heidegger and Aquinas*; Cornelio Fabro, "Il retorno al fondamento di Heidegger e la metafisica di S.Tommaso d'Aquino," *Sapz* 26 (1974): 265-278; G. Perini, "Rapporti tra pensiero heideggeriano e metafisica tomistica," *DTP* 76 (1973): 139-174; Thomas J. Sheehan, "Notes on a 'Lovers' Quarrel:' Heidegger and Aquinas," *L* 9 (1974): 137-143.

Part C: The Immanent Order of Being

I. Order of Being as Harmony and Hierarchy

1   *I Sent* . 20, 1, 3.
2   *ST* 1a. 7, 1c.

3   Ibid., 8, 1c. Cf. Joseph de Finance,*Être et agir dans la philosophie de Saint Thomas* (Paris: Beauchesne, 1945), 111-118; Aimé Forest, *La structure métaphysique*, 37-39.

4   *ST* Ia. 4, 1 ad 3.

5   *I Sent* . 17, 1, 2 ad 3. For St.Thomas's teaching on *esse*, see Eudaldo F. Giralt, "El 'esse' en Santo Tomás," *E* 31 (1982): 95-99; J. Christopher Maloney, "Esse in the Metaphysics of Thomas Aquinas," *NS* 55 (1981): 159-177; Ernst Rüppel, "Das Sein bei Thomas von Aquin," *FZPT* 20 (1973): 198-223; Emmanuel Trépanier, "De diverses implications du nom'ens' en Saint Thomas," *LTP* 30 (1974): 407-422.

6   *In Meta* , II, 1. On the priority of *esse*, see Frederick D. Wilhelmsen, "Existence and Esse," *NS* 50 (1976): 20-45.

7   *De Potentia* , VII, 2 ad 9.

8   *In De Trinitate*, V, 3c.

9   *Ibid.*: "Quando hoc per quod constituitur naturae, et hoc per quod natura intelligitur habet ordinem et dependentiam ad aliquid aliud, tunc constat quod natura illa sine alio intelligi non potest."

10   *In Meta* , IV, lect. 2. *Cf. De Veritate* I, 1c; *I Sent* . 19, 5, 1; 25,1, 4; II, 37, 1, 1.

11   *Ibid.*, I, 8, 4 2 ad 2.

12   *De Natura Gen.* . 1.

13   *Quodl.* II, 3.

14   *Cf.* Jacques Maritain, *Court traité de l'existence*, 45: "Mais ce concept, le concept de l'existence ou de l'exister (*esse*), n'est pas et ne peut pas être (*ens*, ce-qui est, ce-qui a pour acte d'exister), précisément parce que l'affirmation d'existence, ou le jugement, qui lui fournit son continu, est de soi la 'compositio' d'un sujet avec l'existence, l'affirmation que *quelque chose* (actuellement ou possiblement, simplement ou avec tel ou tel prédicat)."

15   *Cf.* Etienne Gilson, *Being and Some Philosophers*, 175.

16   *De Potentia* III, 4c.

17   *De Anima* , 6c.

18   *Oxoniensis* , II, 16, 10, in *Opera Omnia*, ed. Wadding, vols. 26 (Parisiis: apud Ludovicum Vivès, 1891-1895), 13:33.

19   *Met.* IX, 2, 7, 7:535.

20   *Ox.* I, 3, 3, 8, 9:108.

21   *Ibid. Cf.* Simo Knuuttila, "Being qua Being in Thomas Aquinas and John Duns Scotus," in *The Logic of Being*, ed. by Simo Knuuttila (Dordrecht: Reidel, 1986), 201-222.

22 *Met.* VI, 3, 4, 7:336. *Cf. Ox.*, II, 3, 11, 4, 12:272; *ibid.* I, 3, 3,5, 9:98.

23 *Ibid.*, I, 3, 3, 3, 9:89-90. *Cf.* Etienne Gilson, "Avicenne et le point de départ de Duns Scot," *AHDLMA* 2 (1927): 102-103; André Marc,"L'idée de l'être chez St.Thomas et dans la scolastique postérieure," *AP* 10 (1930): 32-33.

24 Robert P. Prentice, *The Basic Quidditative Metaphysics of Duns Scotus as Seen in His De Primo Principio* (Rome: Antonianum, 1970), 50.

25 *Ox.*, I, 3, 2, 24, 9:30; 9, 9:20; *De An.* 16, 5, 3:569.

26 *Quodl.* VI, 7, 25:243. *Cf. Ox.* II, 3, 9, 6 12:212.

27 *Ibid.*, I, 3, 2, 22, 9:48.

28 *Ibid.*, I, 3, 3, 3, 9:89.

29 *Ox.*, IV, 43, 1, 10, 20:40.

30 *Ibid.*, I, 3, 3, 2, 9:87-88.

31 *Ibid.*

32 The community of being Duns Scotus discusses within the quaestion of simplicity of God, *Ox.* I, 8, 1, 3, 9:580-636.

33 *Ox.*, I, 3, 2, 9:18.

34 Some scholars think that the doctrine of a real distinction of essence and existence can be found in Neoplatonism, *cf.* P. Geny, "Du progrès en Metaphysique," *AISP* 5 (1924): 410: "Il est, à vrai dire, assez difficile de préciser le lieu et l'époque de cette origine (scilicet the real distinction of essence and existence). Peut-être peut-on la trouver ... dans la thèse fondamentale de Plotin, qui place l'un, le premier, au-dessus même de l'être: un être, c'est une existence déterminée et donc, conclut Plotin, possédant un principe de limitation, de mesure, en d'autre terms, une existence recue dans une essence, or l'existence du Premier, ou mieux son esse, ne saurait être limitée; il n'est donc pas une être, ens, il est au-dessus, il est l'esse irreceptum: corrigez l'erreur qui fait de toute détermination une termination, une limitation, et vous aurez l'esse irreceptum de S.Thomas." *Cf.* also Louis de Raeymaeker, *Metaphysica Generalis* (Louvain:E. Warny,1935), 2:324; Marie D. Roland-Gosselin, *Le "De ente etessentia"*, 146-149; Schendele, "Aseität Gottes, Essentia und Existentia im Neoplatonismus," *PJ* 22 (1909): 166. For recent study on the origin of Aquinas's doctrine of the real distinction of essence and existence, see Kevin Corrigan, "A Philosophical Precursor to the Theory of Essence and Existence in Thomas Aquinas," *T* 48 (1984): 219-240; Scott MacDonald,"The Esse/Existentia Argument in Aquinas's *De ente et essentia*," *JHP* 22 (1984): 157-172.

35 *De ente et essentia* V, 3.

36   Cf. Etienne Gilson, *Being and Some Philosophers*, 203-204: "Abstraction and judgement are never separated in the mind, because essence and existence are never separated in reality."
37   Joseph Owens, *St.Thomas and the Future of Metaphysics*, 43-44.
38   Jacques Maritain, *Court traité de l'existence*, 36.
39   *I Sent* . 23, 1, 1.
40   *De Potentia* VII, 2 ad 5.
41   *CG* II, 54.
42   *Ox*. IV, 11, 3, 17:429. *Cf.* Germain Kopaczynski, "Some Franciscans on St.Thomas' Essence-Existence Doctrine," *FS* 38 (1978): 283-298.
43   *Ox*. I, 1, 2, 7, 11:63.
44   *Met*. IX, 2, 7, 7:535.
45   *Ibid.,* VII, 13, 16, 7:416.
46   *Ox*. II, 3, 1, 10, 12:55.
47   *Met*. VII, 13, 2, 7:404.
48   *Ibid.,* 17, 7:417f .
49   *Ibid,* 21, 7:422.
50   On the relationship between St.Thomas's and Duns Sotus's teaching on common nature, see Joseph Owens, "Common Nature: A Point of Comparison between Thomistic and Scotistic Metaphysics," *MSt* 19 (1957): 1-14.
51   *CG* I, 18; *ST* 1a. 3, 7.
52   *De Trinitate* VI, 3c.
53   *ST* 1a2ae. 27, 3c.
54   *CG* I, 22.
55   *ST* 1a2ae. 55, 1c.
56   *Ibid.,* 3, 2c. *Cf.CG* I, 73; II, 47; 52; 81; III, 97.
57   *ST Suppl.* , 82, 2.
58   *CG* I, 43.
59   *I Sent* . Prol., 2 ad 2.
60   *Cf.* Léon Robin, *Aristote,* 90-98.
61   *Met*. IX, 2, 7, 7:535.
62   *Ibid.,* 7:536.
63   *Ibid*.
64   *Ibid*.
65   Quoted after Diomede Scaramuzzi, *Il pensiero di G. Duns Scoto* (Rome: Antonianum, 1927), 5.

II. Usiadistic Order of Being

1   Metaphysics IV, 1. 1003a21-22.
2   Ibid., VI, 1. 1026a32.
3   Ibid., VII, 1. 1028a29.
4   Ibid., 1028b3.
5   Cf. Mieczyslaw Krapiec and Tadeusz Zeleznik, *Arystotelesa koncepcja substancji* (Lublin: Towarzystwo Naukowe KUL, 1966), 41-42.
6   De interpretatione 7. 17a39.
7   Posterior Analytics I, 29-30. 87b-88a.
8   Categoriae 5. 3b33.
9   Metaphysics VII, 10. 1035b28-29.
10   Categoriae 5. 3b10-17.
11   *Enneades* VI, 3, 3-5, in *Ennéades*, vol. 6 (1936), 127-131.
12   *Expositio in librum praedicamentorum Aristotelis*, 8, 1, in *Opera philosophica*, vol. 2 (1978), 164.
13   On Ockham's teaching on substance, see Meyrick Carre, *Realists and Nominalists* (London: Oxford University Press, 1961), 119; Ernest Moody, *The Logic of William Ockham* (New York: Sheed and Ward Inc., 1935),136-142. On Ockham's insufficient explanation of universal predication of being, see Carlos P. Norena, "Ockham and Suarez on the Ontological Status of Universal Concepts," NS 55 (1981): 348-362.
14   Metaphysics VII, 1. 1028a30.
15   Ibid., XI, 3. 1060b31-35.
16   *In primum sententiarium (Ordinatio)*, Prologus, 9, in *Opera theologica*, vol. 1 (1967), 258-259.
17   Ibid., 259.
18   Ibid., 3, 1, vol. 2 (1970), 392.
19   Ibid., vol. 1, 258.
20   Cf. Philotheus Boehner, *Collected Articles of Ockham* (St.Bonaventure, N.Y.: The Franciscan Institute, 1958), 380. On the attitude of Ockham to Duns Scotus in this respect, see Douglas C.Langston, "Scotus and Ockham on the Univocal Concept of Being," FS 39 (1979):105-129.
21   *Summa logicae*, 1, 38, in *Opera philosophica* (1974), 1:106-107.
22   Ibid., 3-2, 27, 554-555. For Ockham's teaching on essence and existence, see: Damascene Webering, *Theory of Demonstration According to William Ockham* (St.Bonaventure, N.Y.: The Franciscan Institute, 1953), 85-106.

23   *In librum primum sententiarium (Ordinatio)*, 2, 9, vol. 2, 322-323.
24   *Ibid.*, 323.

25   On analogical predication, see Matthew Menges, *The Concept of Univocity Regarding the Predication of God and Creature According to William Ockham* (St.Bonaventure, N.Y.: The Franciscan Institute, 1952),122-136. On evaluation of Ockham's teaching on relation, *cf.* Andre Goddu, *The Physics of William of Ockham* (Leiden: E. J. Brill, 1984), 92-95; Herman Shapiro, *Motion, Time and Place According to William Ockham* (St.Bonaventure, N.Y.: 1957), 138-141.

26   However, the real distinction between substance and quality Ockham does not understand in a metaphysical sense, *cf.* Gordon Leff, *William of Ockham* (Manchester:, Manchester University Press, 1975), 198; idem, *The Dissolution of the Medieval Outlook* (New York: Harper and Row, 1976), 67.

27   Gordon Leff, *William of Ockham,* 149.

28   *Cf. De posteritate Caini*, 48; *Legum allegoriarum*, 2, 1, 2; *De mutatione nominum*, 4, 27; in *Philonis Alexandrini opera*, vols. 1-3.

29   *De opificio mundi*, 2, 7-9, in *Philonis Alexandrini opera*, vol. 1.

30   *S.P.N. Gregorii Episcopi Nysseni opera omnia quae reperiri potuerunt omnis, PG* 45, 184.

31   *Theodoreti Cyrensis episcopi opera omnia, PG* 83, 33.

32   *Quomodo substantiae in eo quod sint, PL* 64, 1311. For the influence of Boethius on St.Thomas, see Ralph McInerny, "Boethius and Saint Thomas Aquinas," *RFNS* 66 (1974): 219-245.

33   *Cf.* Mieczyslaw Gogacz, "O koniecznosci studiowania metafizyki Awicenny," in *Avicenna, Metafizyka* (Warsaw: Akademia Teologii Katolickiej, 1973), 29-33.

34   *Berengarii Turonensis de sacra coena adversus Lafrancum liber posterior* (Berlin: Haude et Spener, 1834).

35   *ST* 1a. 13, 11c; ad 1. The notion of 'tetragrammaton' St.Thomas uses as the basis for analogy of being, *cf.* Robert A. Herrera, "Saint Thomas and Maimonides on the Tetragrammaton: The 'Exodus' of Philosophy," *MS* 59 (1982): 179-193. On the radical change of Aristotelian notion of substance, see Anibal Colon Rosado, "Filosofia de la substancia: Aristóteles y Santo Tomás de Aquino," *D* 18 (1983): 95-116.

36   *Cf. Posterior Analytics* I, 4. 73a34; *In Perihermeneias* I, lect. 10; *ST* 1a. 76, 3c.

37   *De ente et essentia* IV, 1.

38 *Metaphysics* V, 7. 1017a8-22; *In Meta*, V, lect. 9.
39 *Ibid.*
40 The relation of essence to *esse* in view of the judgement is discussed by Robert J. Henle, "Existentialism and the Judgement," *PACPA* 21 (1946): 44-46. *Cf.* also Owen Bennett, "Existence and the first Principles According to St.Thomas Aquinas," in *Philosophical Studies in Honor of I. Smith, O.P.*, ed. by John K. Ryan (Westminster: Newman Press, 1952),171-174.
41 *De ente et essentia* IV, 2.
42 Jordanus Wébert, *Essai de métaphysique thomiste* (Paris: Editions de la Revue des jeunes, 1927), 176-177. *Cf.* also Peter Hoenen, *Reality and Judgement According to St.Thomas* (Chicago: H. Regnery Co.,1952), 36-46.
43 *De ente et essentia* III, 1.
44 *In Meta*, X, lect. 3.
45 *In Perihermeneias* I, lect. 5.
46 St.Thomas following Avicenna joins the notion of essence to that notion of being, and considers them as they express both the subject and the composition of thing. *Cf.* Marie D. Roland-Gosselin, "De distinctione inter essentiam et esse apud Avicennam et D. Thomam," *Xenia Thomistica*, ed. Sadoc Szabó, vol. 1 (Romae: typis Polyglottis Vaticanis,1925), 281-288.
47 *I Sent* ., 19, 5, 1 ad 1.
48 *Ibid.*, IV, 1, 1, 4, 2 ad 1 : "Ens incompletum quod est in anima, dividitur contra ens distinctum per decem genera;" *De Potentia* VII, 7c:"Ens rationis dividitur contra ens divisum per decem praedicamenta."
49 *Ibid.*, 9c. *Cf.* Guido Mattiussi, "De principiis entis utrum legitime entis nomine donentur," *Xenia Thomistica*, ed. Sadoc SzabK, vol. 1 (Romae: ex typis Polyglottis Vaticanis, 1925), 338-339; Louis de Raeymaeker, *Philosophie de l'être* (Louvain: Institut supérieur de philosophie,1946), 210-213.
50 *II Sent* ., 3, 1, 5.
51 *Ibid.*, I, 17 1, 1, 8. *Cf. De Veritate* XXVII, 1, 8: "Omne creatum est in aliquo genere; " *In Meta*, XII, lect. 4: "Necesse est omne quod est, esse in aliquo genere."
52 *I Sent* ., 19, 5, 1 ad 1.
53 *In Meta*, X, lect. 3.
54 André Marc, *Dialectique de l'Affirmation* (Paris: 1952), 137-139.
55 Joseph Owens, "The Accidental and Essential Character of Being in the Doctrine of St.Thomas Aquinas," *MSt* 20 (1958): 1-40.
56 *De Potentia* VII, 3.

57   *Quodl.* II, 3c. The Angelic Doctor uses the term 'praedicamenta' and 'genera' convertibly, *cf. In Meta* V, lect. 9: "ens secundum se dividit in decem praedicamenta, quorum novem sunt de genere accidentis."
58   *I Sent.*, 8, 4, 2, 1; ad 1.
59   *In Meta*, XI, lect. 12.
60   *De spiritualibus creaturis*, 11.
61   *De ente et essentia* I, 1.
62   *II Sent.*, 37, 1, 2 ad 3.
63   A literal translation of Aristotle's: TO TI HN EINAI; *Posterior Analytics* I, 22. 82b38; *De Anima* III, 6. 430b28; *Metaphysics* VII, 3.1028b34. For example, see W. D. Ross, *Aristotle's Metaphysics*, vol.1 (Oxford: The Clarendon Press, 1948), 127; *cf.* also Désiré Mercier, *Métaphysique générale* (Louvain: Institute supérieur de philosophie, 1923), vol. 1, n. 19, 30: "L'étymologie de l'expression TO TI HN EINAI n'est pas facile expliquer. L'expression TO EINAI suppose un datif sous-entendu, p. ex.: TO ANTROPO EINAI, l'être propre à l'homme. - A la question: TO ESTI TO ANTROPO EINAI; quel est l'être propre à l'homme? On repond: TO ANTROPO EINAI, l'être propre à l'homme; le voici: c'est celui que fait connaître la definition de l'homme. Faut-il voir dans l'imparfait TI EN; quid erat, une forme archäique de l'expression TI ESTI; quid est? Ou est-il permis de voir dans cet imparfait TI EN; une idée profonde, celle de l'antériorité l'essence ideale, tant qu'elle est dans le monde des possibles, sur la réalisation physique dans la monde des existences?" *cf.* also Cornelio Fabro, "Le retour au fondement de l'être," *Saint Thomas d'Aquin Aujourd'hui, Recherches de Philosophie* 6 (1963): 177-196.
64   *De ente et essentia* I, 2. The word 'essentia' has in 13th century also the juristical meaning, e.g., property, possession, usufruct. *Cf.* Joseph de Ghellinck, "L'entrée d'essentia, substantia et d'autre mots apparentés dans le latin médiéval," *ALMA* 16 (1941): 77-112; "Essentia et substantia. Note complémentaire," *Ibid.* 17 (1942): 129-133.
65   *De ente et essentia* I, 2.
66   The latin word 'essentia' is an abstractive form derived from the same root as the words 'esse' and 'ens.' Quintilian in his *Institutio oratoria* II, 14, 2; III, 6, 23, says that the latin word ' essentia' corresponds to the Greek philosophical term 'ousia,' and as such it expresses the subject. St.Augustine, however, reserved the meaning of the word 'essentia' for being which has no subject; *cf. De Trinitate* VII, 5,10, *PL* 42, 942. For the historical development of the meaning of the word 'essentia,' see Etienne Gilson, "Notes sur le vocabulaire de l'être," 152-155.

67   Cf. Marie D. Roland-Gosselin, *Essai d'une étude critique de la connaissance* (Paris: J. Vrin, 1932), 64-67.

68   *De ente et essentia* III, 1.

69   *Quodl.* VIII, 1, 1c: "Secundum Avicennam in sua Metaphysica,triplex est alicuius naturae consideratio. Una, prout consideratur secundum esse quod habet in singularibus; sicut natura lapidis in hoc lapide et in illo lapide. Alia vero est consideratio alicuius naturae secundum esse suum intelligibile, sicut natura lapidis consideratur prout est in intellectu. Tertia vero est consideratio naturae absoluta prout abstrahit ab utrique esse; secundum quam considerationem consideratur natura lapidis, vel cuiuscumque alterius, quantum ad ea tantum quae per se competunt tali naturae."

70   Mary Dominica Mullen, *Essence and Operation in the Teaching of St.Thomas and in Some Modern Philosophies* (Washington: The Catholic University of America, 1941), 1-2: "Considered in itself the essence is neither universal nor individual. It abstracts from every condition and mode of existence, being purely and simply what the object is primarily as intelligible and what the definition expresses. It is indifferent to existence. It is equally present in the actual thing, individuated, in order to exist, and, in the mind, universalized in order to be known, To know the essence of any thing, it is not necessary to know the principle which constitute its individuality, since the essence considered in itself, is nothing individual."

71   Louis de Raeymaeker, *Metaphysica generalis*, 1:179: "Essentia est quidditas (quidditas vero est denominatio potius logica), modus essendi, et dicitur per ordinem ad esse."

72   *De ente et essentia* IV, 1.

73   St.Thomas's doctrine of genus, species and difference, is discussed by Gilbert B. Arbuckle, "St.Thomas Aquinas and the Doctrine of Essence," *Studies in Philosophy and the History of Philosophy*, ed. by John K. Ryan,2 (1963): 104-109.

74   *De ente et essentia* IV, 1.

75   Herman Shapiro, *Motion, Time and Place According to William Ockham*, 6.

76   *Einführung in die Metaphysik* (Tübingen: Max Niemeyer, 1966), 47, 87, 110.

77   *Die Philosophie in Tragischen Zeitalter der Griechen*, 5, in *Werke*, vol. 3 (München: Carl Hauser Verlag, 1956), 371-372.

78   Cf. Ryszard Palacz, *Ockham* (Warsaw: Wiedza Powszechna, 1982), 120; Oscar Rotella, "Santo Tomas y Wittgenstein," *Sap* 30 (1975): 261-272.

79   Jacques Derrida, *Margins of Philosophy* (Chicago: The University of Chicago Press, 1982), 187.
80   Léon Brunschvicg, *Les ages de l'intelligence* (Paris: Alcan, 1934), 65.

III. Predicational Order of Natural Things

1   *In Meta* , , Prooemium.
2   *Descartes* (Poznan: Poznanskie Towarzystwo Przyjaciol Nauk, 1937),60.
3   *Meditationes de prima philosophia*, 6, in *Oeuvres des Descartes*, publieés par Charles Adam et Paul Tannery, vol. 7 (Paris: Le Cerf,1904), 80.
4   *Ibid.*, R.O., 217, p. 158.
5   *Principia philosophiae*, I, c. 51, vol. 8 (1905), 24.
6   *Cf.* Robin G. Collingwood, *The Idea of Nature* (Oxford: Clarendon Press, 1945), 103-104.
7   *Principia philosophiae*, I, c. 52, pp. 24-25.
8   *Ibid.*, c. 53.
9   *Ibid.*
10   *Meditationes*, R.O., 4, 2, p. 246.
11   *Ibid.*, 6, p. 80.
12   *Ibid.*, p. 81.
13   *Ibid.*
14   *Ibid.*
15   *Ibid.*, p.82.
16   *Principia philosophiae*, II, c. 4, p. 42.
17   *Ibid.*, IV, c. 188, p. 315.
18   *Ibid.*, I, c.28, pp. 15-16.
19   *Meditationes*, Obj. 4, p.203. *Cf.* Jerry L. Jennings, "The Fallacious Origin of the Mind-Body Problem: A Reconsideration of Descartes' Method and Results," *JMB* 6 (1985): 357-372.
20   *Meditationes*, P.O., 4, 1, p. 222. On the unity between two substances in man, see Paul Hoffman, "The Unity of Descartes's Man," *PR* 95 (1986): 339-370.
21   *Meditationes, ibid.*

22 For a comprehensive study on the contemporary discussion of the mind-body relationship with an extensive bibliography, see Keith Campbell, *Body and Mind* (Notre Dame: University of Notre Dame Press,1980).

23 *De Veritate* I, 1c.

24 *Ibid.*, XXI, 1, 1. *Cf. iiid.*, 1c:"...nulla enim res naturae est quaesit extra essentiam entis universalis."

25 *Cf.*Antonin D. Sertillanges, *S.Thomas d'Aquin* (Paris: F. Alcan,1910), 1:67-68.

26 St.Thomas's theory of predication of predicaments we can find in his two classical texts: *In Phys*. III, lect. 5 and *In Meta*, V, lect. 9. Quoting the last text, Carl Feckes, *Die Harmonie des Seins* (Paderborn:Ferdinand Schöningh, 1937), 31-32, writes: "Das Mittel, Einteilungen zu gewinnen, ist also ein reich logisches; denn es liegt die Frage zugrunde: Wievielfach kann ein Prädikat einem Subjekt zugeschrieben werden ? Ich kann z.B. fragen: Was ist der Mensch ? Wie gross, wie dick usw ist er ? Wie steht er zum Raume, zur Zeit ? Was tut er ? usw. Darauf antwortet jedesmal eine andere Aussage, in der die Verknüpfungen zwischen Prädikat und Subjekt wesentlich verschieden sind. Zunächst entspringen diesem Verfahren nur logische Prädikamente oder Kategorien. Thomas aber, von der erkenntnistheoretischen Überzeugung geleitet, dass unsere Grammatik der Logik, die Logik der Ontologie folgt, dass alle Formen unserer Aussagen durch das in ihnen immer wiederkehrende Wörtchen 'Ist' auf die reale Welt hinstreben und in ihr Fundament haben, hält sichfür berechtigt, in diesen Kategorien auch verwirklichte Seinsweisen und damit ontologische Seinskreise zu sehen."

27 *In Meta*, V, lect. 13.

28 *Ibid.*

29 *Ibid.*

30 *Ibid.*

31 For the historical development of the concept of substance, see Regis Jolivet, *La notion de substance: Essai historique et critique sur le développement des doctrines d'Aristote à nos jours* (Paris:G.Beauchesne, 1929).

32 *In Meta*, VII, lect. 1.

33 *Ibid.*

34 *Ibid.*, V, lect. 10.

35 *Ibid.*, VII, lect. 1.

36 *Ibid.*

37 *Ibid.*, lect. 2.

38 *Ibid.*, lect. 1.
39 *Ibid.*
40 *Ibid.*, lect. 2.
41 *CG* IV, 14.
42 *In Meta*, VII, 3.
43 The meaning of substance is discussed by Joseph de Vries, "Die Substanz im Bereich des geistigen Seins." *Sch* 27 (1952): 38ff.
44 *CG* I, 25.
45 *ST* 1a. 3, 5 ad 1.
46 *Ibid.*, 3a. 77, 1 ad 2.
47 For a comparative study of the category between Aristotle and St.Thomas, see Marina Scheu, *The Categories of Being in Aristotle and St.Thomas* (Washington: Catholic University of America Press, 1944).
48 *CG* IV, 14.
49 *Meta.* VII, 1. 1028a15-20.
50 *In Meta*, VII, lect. 1.
51 The discussion about the being of accident, see Barry Fr. Brown, *Accidental Being: A Study in the Metaphysics of St. Thomas Aquinas* (Washington: University Press of America, 1985).
52 *I Sent* . 37, 2, 1.
53 *Cf.* J. Quentin Laurer, "The Determination of Substance by Accidents in the Philosophy of St.Thomas," *MS* 18 (1941):31-35.
54 *CG* IV, 66.
55 *Ibid.*, I, 23.
56 *Ibid.*
57 *Ibid.*
58 *In Meta*, VII, lect. 4.
59 *ST* 1a. 76, 4c.
60 *Ibid.*, 77, 6c.
61 *II Sent* . 17, 3, 1.
62 *CG* III, 54.
63 *Ibid.*, 64.
64 *ST* 1a. 29, 2 ad 3.
65 The metaphysical structure of the definition of a natural thing is discussed by Mortimer J. Adler, "The Hierarchy of Essences," *RM* 6 (1952):19-20.
66 For the Aristotelian background of St.Thomas's doctrine of composite substance, see Joseph de Vries, "Zur Aristotelisch-scholastischen Problematik von Materie und Form," *Sch* 32 (1957): 161-185.

67   *De ente et essentia* II, 3.
68   *In Meta* , VII, lect.9.
69   *ST* 1a. 75, 4c.
70   To be more specific, St.Thomas explains the difference between the definition of material and mathematical entities in terms of his doctrine of abstraction; *cf. ST* 1a. 85, 1 ad 2.
71   *De ente et essentia* II, 3.
72   *ST* 1a. 50, 5c.
73   *Ibid.*, 3, 8c.
74   *Ibid.*, 2c.
75   *Ibid.*, 75, 2c.
76   *Ibid.*, 7, 1c.
77   *In Post. Anal.* II, lect. 8; *In Phys* . I, lect.1.
78   *ST* 1a. 47, 1c; 2c.
79   *Ibid.*, 29, 2 ad 5.
80   *Ibid.*, 119, 1c; 1 ad 5.
81   *Ibid.*, 76, 7c.
82   *Ibid*, 50, 2 ad 2.
83   *CG* II, 30.
84   *Ibid.*, III, 78.
85   *Ibid*, II, 68.
86   *De ente et essentia* V, 1.
87   *CG* II, 50.
88   *De ente et essentia* V, 5.
89   *CG* III, 97.
90   *Ibid* II, 92.
91   *Ibid*.
92   *ST* 1a. 76, 3c.
93   *Ibid.*, 78, 1c.
94   *CG* IV, 58.
95   *ST* 1a. 76, 1c.
96   *Ibid.*, 1a2ae. 57, 2 ad 2.
97   *CG* IV, 81. *Cf. ST* 1a. 76, 4c.
98   *CG* II, 58.
99   *ST* 1a. 77, 4c; 85, 3 ad 1.
100 *Ibid.*, 77, 3 ad 4.
101 *Ibid.*, 78, 1c.
102 *CG* II, 72.

103 *Ibid*, I, 86.
104 *Ibid*, III, 81.
105 Cf. *Sancti Thomae Aquinatis Tractatus De Substantiis Separatis*, ed.by Francis J. Lescoe (West Hartford: Saint Joseph College, 1962).
106 *CG* II, 98.
107 *De ente et essentia* VI; *De Sub. Sep.* 16; *ST* 1a. 61, 1c. The bible calls the angels the principles of the universe; *cf.* Col., 1:16; 2:10; 15; I P., 3:22; Eph., 12:22; 3:10; 6:12; Jud., 6:1; Cor., 8:5; II P. 2:10; Gal., 4:3; 9; Col. 2:8; 20; Apoc., 14:10.
108 *CG* II, 46.
109 *Ibid.*, 46-101.
110 *Ibid.*, 91.
111 This conclusion is opposed to that of Aristotle. The separate substances according to Aristotle are of the same number as the movements observed in the heaven, *cf. Metaphysics* XII, 8. 1073a37. For St.Thomas's answer, see *CG* II, 92.
112 *Ibid.*, 50.
113 *Ibid.*, 55.
114 *Ibid.*
115 *Ibid.* 93.
116 *Ibid.*
117 *ST* 1a2ae. 50, 6c; *Quodl.* III, 7c.
118 *CG* II, 95.
119 *De ente et essentia* VII, 3.
120 *CG* IV, 63.
121 *ST* 1a. 14, 12 ad 1.
122 However, 'dispositio' here does not mean the first species of quality but is taken in a general sense of order of that which has parts; *cf. In Meta.* V, lect. 20.
123 *Metaphysics* VII, 1. 1028b10-14.
124 *ST* 3a. 76, 3 ad 2.
125 *Ibid.*, 1 ad 3.
126 The real distinction between substance and quantity is according to St. Thomas required by the sacrament of eucharist: "Necesse est dicere accidentia alia, quae remanent in hoc sacramento, esse sicut in subiecto in quantitate dimensiva panis et vini remanente: primo quidem per hoc quod ad sensum apparet aliquid quantum esse ibi coloratum, et aliis accidentibus affectum, nec in talibus sensus decipitur," *ST* 3a, 17, 2c.

127 CG IV, 65. *Cf. IV Sent* . 44, 2, 2: "quantitas dimensiva est quantitas habens situm."

128 Tilmann Pesch in his *Institutiones philosophiae naturalis secundum principia S.Thomae Aquinatis* (Friburgi Br.: Herder, 1880), 2:24, discussing various theories of quantity, says: "Est ergo optimos quosque auctores controversia, utrum formalis ratio quantitatis sit primario aptitudo ad impenetrabilitatem (ut volunt scholastici multi recentiores) an ad ipsam extensionem localem (ut affirmat Suares), an sit primario et per se ipsa extensio interna, i.e., extensio partium in ordine ad totum (id quod S.Thomas videtur docuisse). Hanc sententiam Suares communem apertis verbis dicit atque protestatur se non impugnare eam, sed explicare velle (In Sum. theol., 3, d. 48, s. 1, n.21). In qua controversia maior est verborum quam rerum discrepantia, et nobis quidem persuasum est sententias illas non difficulter inter se posse consiliari." Sebastian Reinstadler, *Elementa* philosophiae scholasticae (Friburgi Br.: Herder, 1937), 1:400, states: "Sexta denique sententia docet essentiam quantitatis in extensione esse extra partes in ordine ad se. Quae sententia tribuitur Suaresio neque a mente Aquinatis videtur esse aliena."

129 *Disputaciones metafisicas*, 40, 4, 7, ed. Sergio Rábade Romeo, Salvador Caballero Sánchez et Antonio Puigcerver Zanón (Madrid: Gredos,1960-1966), 6:49: "Existimo enim duplicem distinctionem inter partes materiae quae quantitati subsunt considerandum esse: unam entitativam, alteram situalem. Materia enim quae est in capite sub quantitate capitis, et est res partialis distincta a materia quae est in pede, et situ distat ab illa. De situali ergo distinctione dubium non est quin a quantitate radicaliter proveniat; de entitativa verso id censeo falsum et impossibile."

130 *Ibid.*, 15, 6:54.

131 *Ibid.*

132 *Ibid.*, 5, 6:48.

133 *Cursus Philosophicus* , Logica, II, 16, 1, 543.

134 *Disp. meta.*, 40, 2, 8, 6:25: "Neque sufficere potuisset distinctio modalis, quia substantia non potest esse modus quantitatis, ut per se notum est. Deberet ergo quantitas esse modus substantiae; at vero modus non est ita separabilis ab illa re cuius est modus, ut sine illa esse possit, ut in ea superioribus ostensum est; ergo quantitas non est tantum modus, sed res distincta a substantia."

135 Désiré Nys, *Cosmologie* (Louvain: E. Warny, 1928), 2:87-88: "Aristote, Saint Thomas et bon nombre de scolastiques anciens et modernes placent l'essence de la quantité dans la composition entitative du corps. Expliquons-

nous: D'elle-même, c'est-à-dire, abstraction faite de toute ajoute accidentelle, la substance corporelle ne comprend que deux réalités distinctes, la matière et la forme. Il existe donc en elle une composition qui la rend susceptible de division. Mais la division ne peut séparer ici que les deux éléments hétérogènes et consubstantiels dont l'être est constitué. On donne à ce genre de composition le nom de *composition substantielle*. Il n'en est pas question à l'heure présente. Outre cette dualité de principes essentiels,, nous concevons dans les corps une multiplicité beaucoup plus grande et d'une toute nature. Tout corps en effet se laisse fractionner en parties nombreuses homogènes, dont chacune contient une portion de matière et de forme. Les deux constitutifs unis d'une manière indivise sont ici le sujet de la division, de sorte que les parties obtenues s'appellent à bon droit'parties intégrantes' de l'être corporel. Elles ne concourent point, on le voit, à la constitution première de l'être substantiel, mais à l'intégrité de sa masse. Pour distinguer ce nouveau mode de composition on le désigne par le terme de composition entitative. D'après l'opinion thomiste, la substance matérielle n'a d'elle-même que le premier mode de composition; les parties intégrantes lui font totalement défaut.Aussi se montrerait-elle réfractaire à la division, si la quantité n'introduisait en elle la multiplicité potentielle. Essentiellement composée de parties, la quantité, en s'unissant à la substance, lui communique la composition qu'elle porte en son sein, et en fait un tout divisible."

136 *CG* I, 69.
137 *Ibid.,* IV, 65.
138 Désiré Nys, *Cosmologie*, 88: "Est-ce à dire qu'elle (la quantité) donne à son sujet la réalité des éléments intégrantes dont il est constitué ? Nullement; autant vaudrait affirmer que l'accident produit la substance qui lui sert de soutien. Mais la quantité est la raison pour laquelle la masse substantielle, d'elle-même indivisible, devient un tout potentiel, un multiple fractionnable en parties intégrantes."
139 *ST* 1a. 28, 2c.
140 *I Sent* . 8, 5, 2.
141 *Ibid.,* 19, 1, 1 ad 1.
142 *Ibid.,* ad 4.
143 *Ibid.,* 1.
144 *In Meta* , V, lect. 13.
145 *Ibid.*
146 *Ibid.*
147 *Ibid.*

148 *Ibid.*
149 *Ibid.*, lect.1
150 *Categoriae* 8. 8b25; *Cf. ibid.*, 10a27.
151 *Metaphysics* V, 14. 1020b14-25.
152 *De qualitate,* in *In Aristotelis Stagyrite praedicamenta luculentissima expositio* (Venetij, 1516).
153 *ST* 1a2ae. 49, 2c.
154 *Ibid.*
155 *ST* 1a. 45, 7c.
156 *Ibid.*
157 *Ibid.*, 1a2ae. 49, 2c.
158 *Disp. Meta.* 42, 1, 3, 6:200-201.
159 *Ibid.*, 5, 6:202.
160 *IV Sent* . 12,1, 1, 1, 3 ad 1: "Prima accidentia consequentia substantiam sunt quantitas et qualitas. Et haec duo proportionantur duobus principiis essentialibus substantiae, scilicet formae et materiae..., sed qualitas ex parte formae."
161 *Cf.* John of St.Thomas, *Cursus Philosophicus* , Logica, II, 18, 1,609ff.
162 Désiré Nys, *Cosmologie,* 2:86-87, discussing the Suarezian theory of extension, points out the following remarks: "Si, comme le soutient Suarez, l'essence corporelle possède, d'elle-même, des parties intégrantes, pourquoi ces parties n'auraient-elles pas aussi, d'elles-même, une aptitude naturelle à recevoir l'étendue ? Qu'y a-t-il de plus conforme à la nature d'un tout matériel que cette prise de possession d'un espace déterminé ? Il nous paraît donc inutile de greffer encore sur les éléments intégrantes de la substance, à l'effet de les prédisposer à l'actuation de l'étendue, les nouvelles parties intégrantes de la quantité suarézienne. A notre sens il y a là une superfétation manifeste, où vient s'evanouir l'être réel de la quantité." Cfr. also Guido Mattiusi, *Les points fondamentaux de la philosophie thomiste* (Turin: Marietti, 1926), 112-113.
163 II, 3c.
164 *Metaphysical Journal,* trans. by Bernard Wall (London: The Rockliff Publ. Corp. Ltd., 1952), 182, 288.
165 *Ibid.*, 99.
166 *Being and Having,* trans. by Katherine Farrer (New York: Harper and Row, 1965), 12, 27.
167 Immanuel Kant, *Critique of Pure Reason,* trans. by Norman Kemp Smith (New York: Random House Inc., 1958), 5f.

168 *Man Against Mass Society* trans. by G. S. Fraser (Chicago: Henry Regnery Comp., 1962), 120.
169 *Ibid.*, 118f.

IV. Teleological Order of Being and Becoming

1   Fr. 41; Diogenes Laertius IX, 1, cited after G. S. Kirk and J. E.Raven, *The Presocratic Philosophers* (Cambridge: The University Press,1962), 204.
2   Fr. 1, Sextus *adv. math.* VII, III, and Simplicius *De Coelo* 557, 25, *ibid.*, 267.
3   *Cf.* St.Thomas, *CG* II, 52: "Esse autem, inquantum est esse, non potest esse diversum: potest autem diversificari per aliquid quod est praeter esse; sicut esse lapidis est aliud ab esse hominis."
4   *Cf.* Alfred Worth Whitehead, *Process and Reality* (New York: The Social Science Bookstore, 1941), 71: "It belongs to the nature of every 'being' that it is a potential for every 'becoming'."
5   For Plato who was mainly concerned about *epistemene*, the question of genesis belongs only to *doxa*, *Cf. Timaeus* . 27d-28a.
6   *Creative Evolution* (New York: The Modern Library, 1944), 377.
7   *Ibid.*, 250.
8   *Process and Reality*, 45.
9   *Ibid.*, 239.
10 *Ibid*, 209.
11 "Introduction: The Development of Process Philosophy," in *Philosophers of Process*, ed. by Douglas Browning (New York: Random House,1965), XIX. For Whiteheadian notion of *esse*, see Larry Azar, "Esse in the Philosophy of Whitehead," *NS* 37 (1963): 462-471.
12 *The Concept of Nature* (Cambridge: The University Press, 1920), 28.
13 *Ibid.*, 3.
14 *Ibid.*
15 *Ibid.*, 5.
16 *Ibid.*, 4.
17 *Ibid.*, 3.
18 *Ibid.*, 4.
19 *Ibid.*, 4f.

20 *Ibid.,* 3.
21 *Ibid.,* 13.
22 *Ibid.,* 40, 46, 118.
23 *Enquiry Concerning the Principles of Natural Knowledge* (Cambridge:The University Press, 1925), 66.
24 *Ibid.,* 61.
25 *Ibid.,* 104. *Cf.* also *The Concept of Nature,* 76.
26 *Ibid.,* 75.
27 *Ibid.,* 167.
28 *Ibid* 143.
29 *Modes of Thought* (New York: The MacMillan Press, 1958).
30 *Ibid*
31 *Ibid.*
32 *Ibid.,* 205-206.
33 *Ibid.,* 206. *Cf.* David L. Schindler, "Creativity as Ultimate:Reflections on Actuality in Whitehead, Aristotle and Aquinas," *IPQ* 13 (1973): 161-171.
34 *Modes of Thought,* 207-208.
35 *Process and Reality,* 71.
36 *Ibid.,* 35.
37 1014b6-1015a19.
38 192b8-193b21.
39 *Physics* II, 1. 192b33-38.
40 *Metaphysics* XII, 4. 1015a13-19.
41 *Physics* II, 1. 193b7.
42 *Ibid.,* b17. The meaning of 'nature' as 'genesis' we can find in the Presocratics, *cf.* Empedocles in *Vorsokratiker,* 31B8, 1; B63; Plutarch, *ibid.,* B11; Plato, *Laws,* X, 892c.
43 *Physics* II, 8. 198b10.
44 *Ibid.,* 7. 198b3.
45 *Ibid.,* 8. 199a30.
46 *Ibid.,* 3. 195a24. *Cf. Metaphysics* V, 2. 1013b25-27.
47 *Ibid.,* 16. 1021b24. The teleological structure of nature indicates that nature has also a definite direction of its own actions. As a matter of fact, nature has a definite direction for its own actions, because nature does nothing by chance; *cf. De Coelo* II, 8. 290a31. Aristotle says: "We must first presuppose that in nature nothing acts on or is acted upon at random, nor may anything be made from anything else at random," *Physics* I, 5. 188a31-34.
48 *De Incessu Animalium* 12. 711a17-19.

49 *Physics* III, 2. 202a6.
50 *Ibid.*, 3. 202a16-21.
51 *Ibid.*, VIII, 4. 254b12.
52 *Ibid.*, 6. 259b1-20.
53 *Ibid.*, VII, 1. 241b24; 4. 254b15.
54 *Ibid.*, VIII, 5. 256a3-258b9. The relation between nature and the prime unmoved mover is in the order of final causality, *cf.* A. M.Festugière, "Le sens des apories métaphysiques de Teophraste," *RNP* 33 (1931):44-45; Jean Paulus, "La théorie du Premier Moteur chez Aristote," *RP* 33 (1933):408.
55 *Cf. In Phys*. II, lect.1. On St.Thomas's understanding of the concept of nature in Aristotle, see Alessandro Ghisalberti, "La concezione della natura nel commento di Tommaso d'Aquino alla 'Metafisica' di Aristotele," *RFNS* 66 (1974): 533-540.
56 *In Phys*. II, lect. 1.
57 *In Meta*, VII, lect. 8. However, St.Thomas identifies sometimes the form with a passive principle, especially when he speaks of the intrinsic principle of the falling bodies, *cf. In Phys*. II, lect. 1. But in other places, the principle of falling bodies is again recognized as an active principle, *cf. CG* IV, 97. This difficulty we can resolve by saying that St.Thomas describes the form of the falling bodies as a passive principle when he is distinguishing the heavy body from the living body; *cf. In Phys*. VIII, lect. 8.
58 *Ibid.*, II, lect. 1. The natural aptitude for the form can be also considered in regard to secondary and accidental principles of natural potentiality, as it is in the case of water becoming warm by fire. The potentiality of secondary and accidental principles appears as a characteristic from the substantial form, *cf.* Sheilah O'Flynn Brennan, "Meaning of Nature," *The Dignity of Science*, ed. by James A. Weisheipl (Washington: The Thomist Press, 1961), 247-265.
59 Leo R. Ward, *God and World Order* (St.Louis-London: Herder, 1961), 43. The author enumerates four reasons in which Aquinas goes beyond Aristotle, namely: 1. that nature is fundamentally unimpeded in its activity; 2. that no event ever exhibits Aristotle's spontaneity and chance; 3. that nature has a divine direction of its activity; 4. that God is a transcendent end of nature.
60 *Introduction à la Physique Aristotélicienne* (Louvain-Paris:Institut supérieur de philosophie, 1946), 258.
61 *CG* III, 2.
62 *Ibid*.
63 *Ibid*.

64   *Posterior Analytics* I, 22. 82b38-39; *In Post Anal.* I, lect. 33. Cf. *Metaphysics* II, 2. 994a5-b31; *In Meta* , II, lect. 2-4.
65   *CG* III, 2.
66   *Ibid.*, 3.
67   *Ibid.*
68   *Ibid.*, 16.
69   *In Meta* , V, lect. 1.
70   *De Veritate* XXII, 2c.
71   *CG* I, 23. *Cf. ST* 1a. 115, 1c.
72   *CG* I, 26.
73   *Ibid.*, II, 53.
74   *Ibid.*, III, 102.
75   *Ibid*, 22.
76   *De Veritate* XXII, 2c.
77   2. 185a20.
78   *Ibid.*, 5. 188b22-26.
79   *Ibid.*, 6. 189a21-34.
80   *Ibid.*, 7. 190b9.
81   *Ibid.*, b5-8.
82   *Ibid.*, b11-12.
83   *Ibid.*, 9. 192a4.
84   Cf. Auguste Mansion, *Introduction à la Physique Aristotélicienne* (Louvain: Institut supérieur de philosophie, 1913), 68-79.
85   *Physics* I, 3. 186b2ff; b14f.
86   *Ibid.*, 5. 188b10-22. *Cf. ibid.*, 7. 190b28ff.
87   *ST* 1a. 45, 1c.; *Cf. ibid.*, 2 ad 1; 44, 2 ad 1; *CG* IV, 1; 11. For a typical definition of *creatio* as *productio rei*, see *ST* 1a, 65, 3c.
88   *CG* II, 21.
89   *Ibid.*, 18.
90   *Ibid.*, 16.
91   *Ibid.*, 17.
92   *Ibid.*, 19.
93   *Ibid.*, 21.
94   *Ibid.*, 35.
95   *Ibid.*, 36.
96   *Ibid.*, 37.
97   *Ibid.*, 38.
98   *Ibid.*

99   *III Sent*. 25, 1, 2 ad 2; II, 1, 1, 2; 1, 5 ad 2. Examining Aristotle's doctrine of the eternity of the universe, St.Thomas says that his position is not effective, and his arguments are not apodectic; *cf In Phys*. VIII, lect. 2; *ST* 1a. 46, 1c.

100 *I Sent*. 44, 1, 2.
101 *CG* II, 44.
102 *De Spiritualibus Creaturis* I.
103 *CG* III, 97.
104 *Ibid*
105 *Ibid*., 20.
106 *Ibid*.
107 *Ibid*., 112.
108 *Ibid*.
109 *Ibid*, II, 46.
110 *Ibid*
111 *Ibid*., III, 112.
112 *ST* 1a. 60, 1c.
113 *CG* III, 64.
114 *Ibid*., 19.
115 *Ibid*., 20.
116 *Ibid*., 21.
117 *Ibid*.
118 *Ibid*., 97.
119 *Ibid*., 25.
120 *Ibid*.
121 *Process and Reality*, 319.
122 *Ibid*
123 *Ibid*., 147.
124 *Ibid*., 128f.
125 For Plato's *eide* as existing *a parte rei*. see *Timaeus* 52a-c. *Cf*. *Metaphysics* XIII, 9. 1086a-1087a.
126 *De Anima* II, 1. 412a6-9.
127 *Metaphysics* VII, 4.1029a27.
128 *Ibid*
129 *Ibid*., 17. 1041a9.
130 *Physics* II, 2. 194b.
131 *Ibid*, I, 7. 190b.
132 *Metaphysics* V, 1. 1013a; *On Generation and Corruption* II, 335b.
133 *Physics* I, 7. 190a-b.

134 *Metaphysics* IX, 8. 1050b; *De Anima* II, 1. 412a.
135 (Boston: Twayne Publ., 1984), 65.
136 *Ibid.*, 97ff.
137 *Ibid*, 106. *Cf.* 107.

ABBREVATIONS

A   *Aquinas*
AHDL   *Archives d'Histoire Doctrinale et Litteraire du Moyen ge*
AISP   *Annales de l'Institut Superieur de Philosophie*
ALMA   *Archivum Latinitatis Medii Aevi*
AP   *Ancient Philosophy*
D   *Dialogos*
Dia   *Dialoque*
DC   *Doctor Communis*
DTP   *Divus Thomas (Piacenza)*
DVLG   *Deutsche Vierteljahrschrift für Literaturwissenschaft und Geistesgeschichte*
E   *Espiritu*
FS   *Franciscan Studies*
FZPT   *Freiburger Zeitschrift für Philosophie und Theologie*
Greg   *Gregorianum*
GM   *Giornale di Metafisica*
H   *Hochland*
JHP   *Journal of the History of Philosophy*
JMB   *The Journal of Mind and Behavior*
JPQ   *International Philosophical Quarterly*
L   *Listening*
LTP   *Laval Theologique et Philosophique*
M   *Monist*
MS   *The Modern Schoolman*
MSt   *Mediaeval Studies*
NS   *The New Scholasticism*
PACPA   *Proceedings of the American Catholic Philosophical Association*

PJ   *Philosophisches Jahrbuch der Görresgeselschaft*
PR   *The Philosophical Review*
PT   *Philosophy Today*
RFNS *Rivista di Filosofia Neo-Scolastica*
RM   *Review of Metaphysics*
RNP *Revue Neoscolastique de Philosophie*
RP   *Revue de Philosophie*
RPF *Revista Portuguesa de Filosofia*
RPFE *Revue Philosophique de la France et de l'Étranger*
RPL *Revue Philosophique de Louvain*
RSF *Rassegna di Scienze Filosofiche*
RTP *Revue de Theologique et de Philosophie*
Sap *Sapientia*
Sapz *Sapienza*
Sch *Scholastik*
SJP *Salzburger Jahrbuch für Philosophie*
T   *The Thomist*
TF   *Tijdschrift voor Filosofie*
TP   *Teaching Pilosophy*
ZK   *Zeitung der Kirchegeschichte*

INDEX

A

abstraction 68, 75, 145f, 164, 207
accident 1, 12, 25, 30, 35, 44, 81, 83, 86, 99, 160, 162f, 167, 171, 180-185, 196ff, 202f, 205, 233f
- and substance 87, 168
act 1, 6, 24f, 27, 29, 31, 33ff, 44ff, 50-53, 61, 83, 87, 129f, 144, 150f, 165, 194, 206, 215, 218, 234f
- and potency 51ff, 87, 130, 146, 150f, 185
- of form 5
- of predication 163
action and activity 4, 6,13, 19f, 31f, 60, 63f, 82, 128, 163, 168, 191, 212, 218
actuality 24, 29, 45f, 50-53, 74, 98-101, 121, 144, 147, 150f, 180f, 185, 187, 203f, 214, 216f, 219, 235
- and potentiality 50-53, 150f, 167
Albert the Great, St. 80, 120
Alexander of Hales 24
aliquid 114
analogy 11, 76, 79ff, 84, 87, 159
appetency 34
apprehension 16, 47, 62f, 67, 69f, 75, 99, 103, 122, 132, 163
Aquinas *passim*
Aristotle 2, 11ff, 23ff, 28, 32, 42-47, 51f, 54, 59f, 67-69, 72-75, 80f, 124, 131, 137, 153-157, 160, 162, 173, 181, 183, 187, 196, 200f, 209, 214-217, 219f, 226ff
Arnauld 175, 177
assimilation 129
astronomy 4
attribute 175f, 179, 206
Augustine, St. 3, 28, 151, 201
Avencebrol 24f, 189
Averroes 188
Avicenna 109, 122, 161

B

Bacon, Francis 67
Bacon, Roger 24
beauty 32f, 40f
becoming 17, 37f, 41, 153, 156, 160f, 172, 209f, 213f, 220f, 225, 227
being, *passim*
- act of 5, 98, 101, 114
- act of existing 6, 24, 47ff, 67, 97, 99f, 103, 105, 108, 144, 162, 164, 166ff, 170f, 179, 186, 189f, 205f, 234
- *qua* being 1, 22, 46, 72, 75, 79f, 103, 105ff, 121, 145f, 148, 153ff, 157, 160f, 172,233f
- and *ens* 1, 114, 123, 144, 173, 184, 205, 235
- and *esse* 34, 46-50, 54, 75, 81, 86, 100-103, 105f, 115f, 119, 122-126, 130, 143-146, 148, 162f, 165,

167f, 171, 173, 180, 184ff, 201-205, 228, 233ff
- predication of 44, 54, 99, 103, 146, 161f, 167, 171
Bergson, Henri 120, 209
Berengarius of Tours 161
biblical tetragramaton 161f
body 2, 5, 34, 59, 175-178, 192, 206
Boethius 6, 26, 159, 161
Bonaventure, St. 24

C

Cajetan 81, 202
categories 12f, 44, 46, 8ff, 85, 112, 158, 167f, 179ff, 195f, 209, 227, 234
causality 13, 34, 41, 54, 63, 73, 76, 82, 135, 217f. 221f
- cause 3, 6,11, 15f, 18, 32, 34f, 40-45, 53f, 59, 61f, 69, 73f, 79, 82f, 124, 128 133, 176, 179, 201, 204, 214f, 218, 221, 225, 227f
- effect 86f
change 34, 44, 52, 209, 220, 227
chaos 1,17
Cicero 3
cognition 12, 15f, 47, 68, 72, 99, 126-129, 131, 146, 163f, 170, 191
community 97-102, 105f, 108, 116,121, 149, 157, 164, 173, 180

- and diversity 97f, 100-103, 108, 116, 235
- and unity 164
composition 5, 14, 21, 23-27, 35, 49ff, 53, 80, 85, 101f, 105, 143, 147-151, 165f, 178, 184, 186, 188, 190, 197f, 205
comprehension 67, 69, 83, 128
concord 4
connotation 119ff
Conrad, Joseph vii
constitution 132f
convenientia 18
cooperatio 18
cosmos 3
Cratylus 37
creation 4, 24, 30, 81, 193, 221f, 224f
creativity 210, 213, 219, 226
Czeżowski, Tadeusz 67

D

Dasein 119, 123, 125, 131-137
deduction 67, 69, 72ff
definition 155, 168, 181ff, 187f, 190, 202
degree 3, 6, 18, 81, 129, 150,194
demonstration 67, 71, 73ff
- deductive 67, 69
- inductive 67, 69, 71
dependency 26f 53, 159, 181, 185,
Descartes, René 173-178, 205ff
designation 170f

dialectics 38f
diathesis 11
difference 171
dignity 14, 27, 29, 83
distinction 5f,14, 17ff, 21, 24ff, 32, 34, 40, 49f, 83, 85f, 97, 125ff, 129,143-146, 148, 151, 158, 161, 163, 177f, 180, 182-185, 196ff, 201, 204, 206, 233f
disposition 1, 3, 6, 11, 27, 33, 50f, 53, 103, 108, 129ff, 150f,174, 184, 195f, 198, 201-204, 207, 233f
diversity 6, 17, 19, 25, 29f, 35,37, 65, 84, 97f, 101f, 105, 108, 121, 153, 160, 189, 198, 209, 220, 223f, 226
- and community 97f, 100-103, 108, 116, 235
dualism 206
Duns Scotus 143, 145f, 148f, 151f
duration 120, 221f

E

element 4f, 15, 19f, 26, 29, 40f, 122, 126
emanation 3f, 41, 221
end 6, 25, 31, 34f, 52f, 59, 64, 76, 82, 151, 215, 217ff, 223-226, 229
entity 44
epistemology 207
equivocity 157ff, 171

essence 1f, 12, 28, 34f, 42ff, 46-51, 71, 85, 97f, 102ff, 114, 123f, 128, 132, 134, 136, 144-152, 156, 159, 161, 164-171, 175, 179f, 182-190, 194, 214f, 221, 227, 233ff
- and existence 6, 49, 86f,101, 105f, 143, 146ff, 150, 153, 158f, 161, 235
event 212
evil 60
existence 1, 3, 13, 15, 18, 23f, 35, 42, 46-50, 54, 68ff, 72, 74f, 84, 98, 100, 106, 110, 122ff, 128, 131,134, 137, 144-148, 150-153,156, 159, 161, 165f, 169, 173-176, 182f, 185f, 190, 193f, 197f, 203, 205f, 213, 220ff, 224f, 227, 233ff
- and essence 6, 49, 86f, 101, 105f, 143, 146ff, 150, 153, 158f, 161, 235
extension 100, 115,196ff, 204, 206, 212

F

factuality 121ff
finality 11, 18, 33, 115, 176f, 210, 213, 217, 226
flux 172
form 3, 5, 18f, 24f, 28, 30-35, 39f, 42, 44ff, 53, 148, 179f, 186-191, 195, 201f, 204, 214ff, 219f, 223, 226f

foundation 19f, 27, 59, 82, 85
freedom 135ff, 177

G

generation 15f, 30ff, 40f
genesis 173, 215, 220f
genus 5, 18f, 21, 25, 30, 32, 39, 44, 46, 61, 67, 69, 81, 97f, 100, 102, 131, 159f, 164, 168,171, 189, 193, 195, 205, 233
Gilson, Etienne VIII, 48
God VIIf, 1, 4, 6, 24f, 32, 35, 50, 59, 62-67, 79, 83, 129, 138, 159, 161f, 173-176, 190, 193, 221-226, 229
good 3ff, 19, 27, 30, 34, 39, 54, 60f, 64, 107, 110ff, 115, 120, 215, 217ff, 222ff
Goudin, Antoine 86
gradation 6, 29ff, 61, 63, 128f, 143, 219, 224
grade 3f, 25, 28ff, 64,194, 222, 233
Gregory, St. 161
Grosseteste 159
Grycz, Czesław Jan ix
Grycz, Władysława IX
Grycz-Hernandez, Wanda IX

H

habit 81
harmony 2-5, 23, 35, 76, 149, 152,187, 221

Hartshorne, Charles 210
Hegel 120
Heidegger, Martin VIIf, 119, 121-125, 131-138, 172
Heraclitus 37, 121, 153, 160, 172, 209
hermeneutics 134
hierarchy 2ff, 6, 35, 145, 149f, 152, 217
Hume 209
hylomorphism 23ff, 178
hyperousia 161
hypostasis 161

I

identity 17, 37, 136, 154
inclinations 25, 31, 33f, 207, 217, 219
independence 175
individuality 67, 173
individuation 130
induction 67-73
integrity 155
intellect 16, 21, 39, 46ff, 51, 59-66, 82, 85, 99, 102ff, 106f, 110, 122, 126, 129ff, 133, 137f, 144-147, 155, 163ff, 167ff, 171, 179, 187, 189, 205f, 224, 226
intellectuality 126, 129
intelligibility 3, 46, 51f, 62, 67, 69, 100f, 114, 126f, 136, 144f, 147, 155, 168f, 187, 207, 225
intentions 21, 85, 163f, 159, 163ff, 200

intuition 37, 71f, 120

J

Jerome, St. 161
John of St. Thomas 197
judgment 48, 61ff, 71f, 131

K

Kant 206f
knowledge 4, 6, 12, 21, 38ff, 45ff, 60-74, 76, 81, 85, 120, 124, 129f, 145f, 164, 173, 176, 181f, 192, 206f, 211
kosmos 2
Kotarbinski, Tadeusz 172
Krąpiec, Mieczysław IX, 68f, 71, 73ff
Kuntz, Marion & Paul ix
Kuntz, Paul 228

L

Leibniz 206
Lescoe, Francis & Marie ix
Locke 209
love 34

M

man 177, 192
Manicheism 207

Mansion, Augustin 217
many 51, 103f
Marcel, Gabriel 206f
matter 3, 5, 18, 23ff, 30f, 34f, 42, 45f, 53, 177, 179, 180, 186, 187, 188, 189, 190, 191, 195, 202, 204, 206, 214-217, 221, 223
meaning 119, 121f, 126, 137, 146, 161
measure 12f, 25, 28f, 32, 35, 82, 179, 198, 201, 202
metabole 220
metaphysics VIII,1, 47f, 59, 64, 71ff, 75, 81, 119-125, 138, 148,153-162, 172f, 207
Mill, John Stuart 67
mind VII, 21, 38, 40, 45, 60, 65, 68, 70, 76, 85, 121, 136, 148, 163f, 169, 175-178, 206, 207
mode 6, 11, 13, 25, 28f, 33, 49, 201-204, 233ff
monad 3
monadology 206
Mońko, Leon 72
motion 4, 16, 29, 31, 34, 39, 41, 199f, 214ff, 219f
multiplicity 17, 24f, 30, 37, 54, 100, 120, 154, 157, 194, 222
music 4

N

nature 3, 5f, 11, 18f, 23, 25ff, 29, 31, 33, 40, 42, 50, 62, 76, 98, 101, 155, 157, 164, 168, 174-177, 179f, 189, 191ff, 200, 202, 209-220, 233, 235
negation 17, 132f
neognosticism 207
neoplatonism 3f
Nietzsche, Friedrich 125, 172
nothingness 122
number 2, 4f, 18, 25f, 28, 32, 35, 193f

O

object 206, 212, 228
occasionalism 178
Ockham 153, 155-160, 172
one 3, 51, 103ff, 107-110, 114f, 120f, 209
operation 11, 30f, 33, 47, 184, 188, 191, 203, 228
order *passim*
   - essence of 82
   - and relation 82ff
   - of being 1, 3f, 6, 11, 46, 51, 53, 76, 79f, 87, 99, 103, 113, 116, 119, 126, 143, 145ff, 148, 150, 154, 159, 167, 174, 179-187, 195, 205, 227, 233ff
   - of distinction 148
   - of nature 76
   - of perfection 149
   - of predication 79, 162f, 165, 169, 171
   - of priority and posteriority 110
   - of reason 76
   - of unity and plurality 104f, 146
ordo 1, 33, 80, 201
origin 14f, 20, 40f, 53, 63, 65, 87, 121, 133, 135
origo 20
Owens, Joseph IX

P

panhylomorphism 23f, 189
Parmenides 37, 121, 153, 209
participation 40ff, 50, 54, 171, 223
particularity 37, 67, 73
passion 13, 20, 82
perception 12, 81
perfection 1, 3f, 13, 25, 29f, 32, 52f, 59f, 62, 76, 80, 84, 87, 112, 144, 149f, 165, 191-194, 215, 219
phenomenology 119, 134f
Philo of Alexandria 161
place 3, 11, 14, 34, 60, 83, 199f, 202, 204
Plato 2, 46, 36-42, 46, 54, 67ff, 98, 226ff
Plotinus 3, 155, 161
plurality 1ff, 13, 17ff, 23, 25ff, 32, 35, 37, 41f, 49, 80, 83f, 98, 103, 105, 121, 130, 153,

INDEX 307

159f, 165, 171, 194, 198, 209, 217, 220, 223
pondus 33
position 29, 81, 196, 198f, 221
possession 81
posteriority 17, 27, 52
- and priority 14-17, 20f, 26, 28f, 52, 83, 87, 110, 127f, 143, 150, 159, 174, 180ff, 195, 200
potency 1, 24f, 27, 35, 44f, 50-53, 129, 150f, 165, 188f, 201f, 215, 219, 221, 235
- and act 51ff, 87, 130, 146, 150f, 185
potentiality 5, 23f, 29, 32, 50-53, 144, 150f, 166, 180, 187, 194, 203f, 213f, 216, 219, 226f, 235
- and actuality 146, 151
power 11, 59, 63
pre-Socratics 209
predicaments 87, 167, 179, 187
predication 44, 49f, 63, 66, 79f, 98f, 108, 116, 157-160, 162f, 165f, 169, 179, 189, 233
principle 3f,11, 13-33, 39, 41ff, 46, 48-51, 54, 61-65, 67, 70, 80, 83-87, 97ff, 101, 106, 108, 110, 115f, 126-129, 131, 136, 143f, 146f 150, 180ff, 184f, 187, 189, 199f, 202, 204, 213-220, 223f, 226ff, 233

priority 14-17, 39, 52, 68f, 119, 122, 144, 146, 158, 181, 209, 222
- and posteriority 14-17, 20f, 26, 28f, 52, 83, 87, 110, 127f 143, 150, 159, 174, 180ff, 195, 200
privation 220, 227
process 210, 213f, 219ff, 226f
Proclus 3
proportion 2-6, 32, 51, 59, 65, 76, 86f, 105, 146, 150, 159, 186f, 189, 198
proportionality 76
Pseudo-Dionysius 4, 6
pulchritudo 32
purpose 53, 59, 86
Pythagoreans 2, 4

Q

quality 13, 34, 43f, 47, 82, 134, 160, 179, 184, 195ff, 200-205, 216
quantity 16f, 20, 28, 32, 82, 84, 176, 179 184, 195-204
quiddity 47, 97f, 144, 158, 183, 198

R

ratio 6, 11, 14, 19f, 26, 29, 51,100, 115f, 133, 143, 145, 150f, 179f, 234
- *entis* 101, 123

- *ordinis* 14, 19, 26, 233
- *prioris et posterioris* 14, 19, 233
reason 40, 65f, 72f, 75, 207
reasoning 62, 66-69, 72f, 75
relation 1, 12-15, 17, 20f, 27ff, 32f, 46, 59f, 69, 79-86, 97, 129, 164, 179, 181, 185
res 114, 205
Russell, Bertrand 172

S

Sartre, Jean Paul vii
science 23, 44, 47, 59-63, 66, 67f, 72f, 75f, 120, 124f, 155, 158ff, 173, 193, 209f

separation 17, 41, 133, 177f, 206f
signification 19f, 108, 113f, 149, 160,
Simplicius 201f
singularity 37-40, 42-46, 54, 68, 70, 127, 129
- and universality 44, 54, 127
size 29
Socrates 43f, 67, 98, 127, 169f, 205
soul 2f, 31, 59f, 76, 128f, 137, 166, 177f, 191f
species 5, 11, 13f, 18f, 21, 25, 28, 30, 32, 43-46, 63, 67, 69, 84, 97, 102, 106, 129ff, 149, 159f, 164, 168, 171, 189f, 193ff, 201f, 217, 223

Spinoza 206
spirit 3
Stoics 3
structure 80, 101
Suarez 196f, 202-205
subject 182-185, 206, 209
subsistence 50, 148
substance 1, 5, 12, 24, 28, 31, 35, 38, 43f, 51, 64, 69, 75, 82, 99, 112, 124, 148, 153-160, 162f, 167f, 171, 173-178, 180-191, 193-198, 201-206, 209, 214, 220, 222, 226ff, 234
- and accidents 87, 168
substrate 44, 48, 148, 220f, 227
superiority 154
- and inferiority 29
Swieżawski, Stefan ix, 66
syllogism 67, 73
symmetry 2f, 33

T

taxis 3f
teleology 177
Teodoretus of Cypres 161
thing 174f, 177ff, 182
time 14, 29, 52, 83, 165f, 181f, 192, 199f, 222
totality 124f, 154
transcendality 87, 102f, 106ff, 113-115, 119, 126, 128, 134f, 137, 157

truth 44, 54, 60f, 65, 77, 107, 110ff, 115, 119f, 125f, 131ff, 136ff, 165, 174

U

understanding 60ff, 64, 66f, 75, 79, 85, 153, 155, 157, 160, 164f, 169, 186, 189
unity 2ff, 13, 17, 25ff, 32f, 35, 37, 41f, 49, 67, 80, 84, 103, 105f, 110, 114, 120, 130, 138, 149, 153, 157-160, 162, 175, 177f, 187, 189, 198, 207, 209, 213, 219f, 223
- and plurality 1, 6, 22, 26f, 49, 103, 105f, 108, 129, 148f, 153, 164, 209, 235
- and community 164
- of being 153, 172
universality 37f, 40, 42-46, 54, 67-70, 73, 75, 98f,, 101ff, 120,127, 154, 164f, 169ff, 233
- and singularity 44, 54, 127
universe 1f, 5, 23, 29f, 32f, 35, 65, 192ff, 218f, 222-226
univocity 146, 157ff, 171, 180
unum 114

V

verum 114
virtue 60-63, 76

W

weight 25, 28, 33ff
Whitehead, Alfred 23, 209-213, 226ff
wisdom 12, 59-63, 66f, 75ff

Z

Żółtowski, Adam 174